The Chicago Pragmatists
and American Progressivism

The Chicago Pragmatists and American Progressivism

ANDREW FEFFER

Cornell University Press

ITHACA AND LONDON

First published 1993 by Cornell University Press.

International Standard Book Number 0-8014-2502-6
Library of Congress Catalog Card Number 92-54974
Printed in the United States of America
*Librarians: Library of Congress cataloging information
appears on the last page of the book.*

⊗ The paper in this book meets the minimum requirements
of the American National Standard for Information Sciences—
Permanence of Paper for Printed Library Materials, ANSI Z39.48-1984.

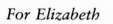

For Elizabeth

Contents

Acknowledgments

Many people left their special marks on this project, though they may no longer recognize those marks as their own. My interest in Chicago pragmatism began in Richard Schuldenfrei's introductory philosophy course at Swarthmore College. I am indebted to him for the questions he raised and the vitality he brought to the study of the history of ideas. The present study began under the direction of Bruce Kuklick, whose guidance and exemplary scholarship were indispensable to my understanding of American intellectual history in general and Dewey in particular. I am also thankful to other University of Pennsylvania faculty who helped strengthen my grasp of the American past, especially Henrika Kuklick, Walter Licht, Murray Murphey, Stan Vittoz, and above all Michael Zuckerman, who showed me as well how much I could learn from my own students.

I am indebted additionally to the many libraries and institutions that aided me in my research, including granting permission to quote from their manuscript collections: Chicago Historical Society; Special Collections, Morris Library, Southern Illinois University at Carbondale; Center for Dewey Studies; Swarthmore College Peace Collection; Sophia Smith Manuscript Collection, Smith College; Amherst College Archives; Department of Special Collections, University of Chicago Library; Newberry Library, Chicago; Manuscript Division, University of Illinois at Chicago. The Newberry Library also greatly aided my research with a timely grant.

Portions of Chapters 12 and 13 are drawn from my article "Sociability and Social Conflict in George Herbert Mead's Interactionism, 1900–1919," *Journal of the History of Ideas* 51 (1990): 233–54. I thank the journal for permission to reprint.

People who read and commented on this manuscript and the research that went into it include Dee Andrews, Maureen Corrigan, Erika Doss, John Feffer, Melvin Feffer, Angelika Fuerich, Robert Gregg, Elizabeth Griffin, David Gross, Camille Guerin-Gonzalez, Nancy Hewitt, Tom Knoche, Bruce Kuklick, Sybil Lipschultz, Karen Mittleman, Robert Pois, Naomi Rogers, Steven Sapolski, Michael Slott, Norbert Wiley, Richard Yeselson, and Al Zielenski. I am especially grateful for the guidance and encouragement of Peter Agree at Cornell University Press and the insightful criticism and good advice of Casey Blake and Leon Fink. Carol Betsch, Risa Mednick, and John Thomas helped make the final editing an unexpectedly painless experience.

There have been many witnesses to the writing of this book, no chapter of which could have been completed without patience, moral support, and wisdom from many quarters. At Union College my colleagues have suffered my absentminded preoccupation gracefully and supportively. So too have my students, whose classroom inquiries at Union, in Boulder, and at Penn have shaped this text in far subtler ways than they would have imagined. Without Mike Slott's friendship and generosity the project would have died an early death. He and countless other friends outside the academy helped place this book in a broad social and political context that most scholars lose the ability to perceive clearly. Jed, John, and Joan Feffer provided brotherly and sisterly encouragement, as well as the special sense of perspective siblings give to overly absorbed academics. My parents, Edith and Melvin Feffer, offered the depth and generosity of support one receives only from people of their wisdom and experience. Finally, Elizabeth Griffin, whose commitment to the study of history is even stronger than my own, shared in all that was difficult and rewarding in this project. Without her it would have been impossible.

ANDREW FEFFER

Schenectady, New York

Abbreviations

Addams Papers   Jane Addams Papers, Swarthmore College Peace Collection, Swarthmore, Pennsylvania.

Castle Papers   Henry N. Castle Papers, Special Collections, Regenstein Library, University of Chicago

City Club Papers   City Club Papers, Manuscript Collections, Chicago Historical Society

Dewey Papers   John Dewey Papers, Special Collections, Morris Library, Southern Illinois University, Carbondale

Early Works   The Early Works of John Dewey, 1882–1898. 5 vols. Jo Ann Boydston, ed. Carbondale: Southern Illinois University Press, 1967–1972.

Mead Papers   George Herbert Mead Papers, Special Collections, Regenstein Library, University of Chicago.

Middle Works   The Middle Works of John Dewey, 1899–1924. 15 vols. Jo Ann Boydston, ed. Carbondale: Southern Illinois University Press, 1976–1983.

Tufts Papers, Amherst   James Hayden Tufts Papers, Amherst College Archives, Amherst, Massachusetts.

Tufts Papers, Chicago   James Hayden Tufts Papers, Special Collections, Regenstein Library, University of Chicago.

The Chicago Pragmatists
and American Progressivism

The Two Souls of
Chicago Pragmatism

"[It is] a great thing and the beginning of greater," John Dewey declared of the Pullman strike. The 1894 uprising of American workers against corporate power pushed Dewey to a state of near euphoria: to him it signaled a moment in which philosophy could and would finally reenter the self-transforming struggles of the "social organism." Philosophers such as he could participate in the intelligent reconstruction of society and in so doing reconstruct their discipline as well.[1]

One-quarter of a century later, Dewey's closest colleague at the University of Chicago, George Herbert Mead, reacted quite differently to the class and racial conflicts of 1919. From the distance of a long, recuperative vacation in northern New Mexico, Mead surveyed the "bankrupt end" of reform efforts in Chicago. Disillusioned over the breakdown of social cooperation, Mead had grown pessimistic about the reconstructive potential of applying "intelligence" to politics. Viewing the cataclysms of that postwar year, which included massive strikes and race riots in his home city, Mead confessed a "bitter dissatisfied frame of mind that comes with never ending condemnation."[2]

Between 1894 and 1919 much had changed, in philosophy and in political outlook, for these men, the founders of the Chicago school

[1] John Dewey to Alice Dewey, July 2, 1894, Dewey Papers.
[2] George H. Mead to Irene Tufts Mead, August 30, 1919, Mead Papers.

I

of American pragmatism. What may appear to have been a familiar transit from youthful idealism to mature realism was in fact something much deeper, with greater significance for the history of American ideas and politics. Arriving in Chicago in the early 1890s, Dewey, Mead, and their colleagues addressed the emerging problems of cultural and industrial modernity, with its new relations of power and production. As participants in Chicago's diverse community of reform activists, they saw themselves as agents of historical change who would guide a popular social reconstruction with an enduring and vital intelligence toward a fuller democracy. By the time the Great War had devastated Europe and divided the United States, however, the Chicago philosophers' seemingly unmovable faith in human agency and democratic self-activity drifted—to a more programmatic politics of reasonable negotiation led by the educated and enlightened.

This book is a study of that transition, of the emergence of a political tradition we variously refer to as progressive, corporate, or twentieth-century liberalism, and of how the politically engaged philosophy these men and their colleagues established was unable to transcend its historical and conceptual limits. It is a study of ideas in context, of the place of pragmatist philosophy in the history of Chicago at the turn of the century.

There are many reasons for reviewing the history of Chicago pragmatism against the historical context. Although we look to intellectual traditions for inspiration and guidance, we also need constant reminders that sifting the past for useful theories can be as dangerous as it is rewarding. In this particular case, Chicago pragmatism seems to provide an alternative to a discredited Vietnam era corporatism, to the beleaguered Marxist orthodoxy, and to that peculiar mix of rapacious market individualism and pragmatic authoritarianism called neoconservativism. Across the span of the century the Chicago pragmatists may offer, some philosophers and political theorists have argued, a democratic option at once humanistic and hopeful, a theoretical guide for the achievement of communicative rationality and political decency.[3]

---

[3] For different versions of this hopeful appropriation of the Chicago Pragmatist tradition, see Richard Rorty, *Contingency, Irony, and Solidarity* (Cambridge, 1989); James T. Kloppenberg, *Uncertain Victory: Social Democracy and Progressivism in European and American Thought, 1870–1920* (New York, 1986); Robert B. Westbrook, *John Dewey and American Democracy* (Ithaca, 1991); Cornel West, *The American Evasion of Philosophy:*

There is much to recommend this latest reenlistment of Dewey and his colleagues in defense of humanistic communal democracy. Despite its many detractors, Deweyan theory was an important contribution to the history of philosophy. The pragmatist theory of truth, that knowledge is relative to social and behavioral "situations," that it is provisional, and that it evolves as an instrument in the ongoing process of problem solving, provided one cornerstone of twentieth-century philosophy. Additionally, Deweyan instrumentalism, as the Chicago philosophy was often called, philosophically justified the social scientific revolution, helping to replace the study of ideas and values that anchored nineteenth-century arts and letters with the purportedly scientific study of human behavior, social groups, and social institutions. And as a philosophy of rational democratic agency, Chicago pragmatism may offer the beginning of an alternative to deterministic theories (structural Marxism and reductionist psychology) and to neo-orthodox (and thereby neoconservative) pessimism. It is anything but "pragmatic" in the contemporary, cynically Machiavellian sense of the term.

But history and context limit our ability to apply Deweyan theory to the present. Dewey and his colleagues proposed their theory of action in political and philosophical contexts on which the Deweyan faith in human agency and rationality depended for coherence and meaning. Like all theories, this one carried additional discursive baggage: a nineteenth-century theological discourse largely abandoned or ignored by secular intellectuals and a political discourse from the same era that fits only uncomfortably in the twentieth century. Acknowledging the baggage does not necessarily mean abandoning pragmatism to the past. Rather, we have to do some heavier lifting to get the theory clearly into the present. By decontextualizing Chicago pragmatism, however, we risk not only leaving much of its meaning and substance behind but also misunderstanding those lessons about the role of human agency in political change which we hope to learn from the study of Dewey's or his colleagues' work.

Before we even reach Chicago pragmatism in its proper historical setting, we must first wade through the subsequent history of com-

---

A Geneology of Pragmatism (Madison, 1989); Richard J. Bernstein, "John Dewey on Democracy: The Task before Us," in *Philophical Profiles: Essays in a Pragmatic Mode* (Cambridge, 1986), 260–72.

mentary and criticism. This is another context we cannot abandon. Reappropriating Dewey and his colleagues involves resurrecting a tradition that has endured extensive, profound, and often damaging criticism, much of it directed at the work of Dewey, Mead, and their political associates in Progressive Era reform movements. It takes much effort to put such scathing critiques as Reinhold Niebuhr's far enough behind to permit us to embrace the pragmatist political theology without irony or chagrin. From the left and from the right, by the many descendants of Niebuhr and others we have been chastened in our uncritical acceptance of instrumental reason and progressive optimism.

The close association between Deweyan pragmatism and liberalism is but one legacy of that literature, about which this contextual study raises some questions. That link has hinged largely on the career of John Dewey, the University of Chicago philosophy department's first chairman and, until his departure in 1904, its most productive and prominent member. A brief look at the history of Dewey studies reveals how thoroughly subsequent commentators detached pragmatist theory from its historical context and underscores the general dangers of decontextualization.

Dewey and Liberalism

Dewey was always more than just a philosopher. For Henry Steele Commager he was "the guide, the mentor, and the conscience of the American people."[4] The reputation of Chicago pragmatism and its founder has been closely linked to the rising and falling fortunes of liberal politics in the United States, what Commager and others characterize as a modern, democratic humanism. Several generations of American writers, in the years overlapping the two world wars, found in Dewey's philosophy and psychology a warrant for both liberal political policy and social and educational reforms. Pragmatism and American culture mirrored their hopes for the continued dominance of liberal political values (as these critics defined them) in the twentieth century, and they defended their position by invoking and dressing up liberal icons like Dewey.

[4] Henry Steele Commager, *The American Mind: An Interpretation of American Thought and Character since the 1880s* (New Haven, 1950), 100.

Most of these early reflections on Chicago pragmatism's political and social significance, while lauding and justifying Dewey and pro-gressivism, disclosed little about the intellectual and social roots of the twentieth-century liberalism Dewey reportedly championed. Thus, according to the literature, pragmatism not only reflected the triumph of social science but expressed the will of an insurgent democratic majority which, during the Progressive Era and the New Deal, asserted the inchoate spirit of American liberalism and carried the nation to its modern, democratic political destiny. This literature offered few critical insights into the nature of American political or scientific values, institutions, and practices. As for the instrumentalist views of democracy and science, they were, in these accounts, obscured rather than elucidated.[5]

The celebration of Dewey's contribution to liberal political culture followed several interweaving strands of historical development. Even at its inception, Dewey's supporters viewed Chicago pragmatism as historically unprecedented. Thus, with great fanfare William James greeted the 1903 publication of the *Studies in Logical Theory,* au-thored by Dewey and his colleagues, as a new achievement for the University of Chicago and for American philosophy. It was, for James, "a new system of philosophy."[6]

Those who have chronicled the history of pragmatism have agreed with James: Dewey's philosophy not only was a new school of thought, but its appearance marked a new era in American culture. This was so for several reasons. Stressing novelty and thereby slighting Dewey's nineteenth-century past helped the heralds of a new era jus-tify his twentieth-century philosophy. To survive at a time when in-tellectual prestige was equated with scientific rigor, the second and third generations of American pragmatists tried to demonstrate in their own histories of the tradition that pragmatism, in a dramatic "revolt against formalism," had rejected the non-science of nine-teenth-century religious idealism. Similarly, the association between

---

[5] See, for example, Lewis Feuer, "John Dewey and the Back to the People Movement in American Thought," *Journal of the History of Ideas* 20 (1959): 545–68; also Arthur E. Murphy, "John Dewey and American Liberalism," and John A. Irving, "Comments," *Journal of Philosophy* 57 (1960): 420–26, 442–50. An excellent review of the literature and discussion of these issues is David Hollinger, "The Problem of Pragmatism in American History," *Journal of American History* 67 (June 1980), 88–107.

[6] William James, *The Letters of William James,* 2 vols. (Boston, 1920), 2:201–2.

pragmatism and evolutionary biology demonstrated, according to many twentieth-century Deweyans, the philosophy's rigor and scientific validity. Once again following Dewey's own lead, his disciples gave birth to a vast literature on the relation between the Darwinian revolution, as they misconstrued the evolution controversy of the late nineteenth century, and America's most celebrated contribution to the history of philosophy. Like Dewey, they perceived Darwinism aligned against "the powerful force of theological orthodoxy" which "impede[d] the progress of scientific culture." The historical importance of the founders of pragmatism, claimed historian Philip Wiener, was that they did not tolerate the intrusion of natural theology into the study of nature or permit the "theological fusion of scientific and ethical considerations." Thus, through historical justification the children of pragmatism rendered it the metatheory of hard science: empirical, experimental, nonideological, and nonmetaphysical.[7]

By passing down the pragmatist tradition in this manner, Dewey's disciples meant to transmit a particular liberal heritage as well. These latter-day "Darwinians" embraced evolutionary science and the homegrown philosophy it supposedly spawned as "democratic" forces in American history. This point is crucial for an understanding of how and why they rationalized pragmatism and liberalism in positivist terms. The impact of Darwin (and by implication its pragmatist offspring), wrote Deweyan Sidney Ratner, was the triumph of scientific method over irrationality and force. *The Origin of Species* led us to "throw overboard the sanctions of authority, ancient prejudices, and the hallowed rationalizations of a priori philosophy, and to embrace the method of science." Thus, the linking of Darwinism to pragmatism constituted an important chapter in the search for the American character by several generations of historians, who were convinced that both theories expressed the deep-seated values, the

---

[7] Dewey, "From Absolutism to Experimentalism," in *Contemporary American Philosophy: Personal Statements*, vol. 2, ed. George Plimpton Adams and William Pepperell Montague (New York, 1930), 13–27; idem, *Theory of Valuation*, International Encyclopedia of Unified Science, vol. 2, no. 4 (Chicago, 1939); Morton White, *The Origins of Dewey's Instrumentalism* (New York, 1943); Gail Kennedy, "The Pragmatic Naturalism of Chauncey Wright," in *Studies in the History of Ideas*, 3 vols., ed. Columbia University Philosophy Department (New York, 1935), 3:503; Bert James Loewenberg, "Darwinism Comes to America, 1859–1900," *Mississippi Valley Historical Review* 28 (1941): 346; Philip Wiener, *Evolution and the Founders of Pragmatism* (1949; rpt., Philadelphia, 1972), 17.

liberal democratic spirit, and the egalitarian scientific ethos of their society.[8]

Changing interpretations of Dewey generally paralleled changing assessments of the progressive reform movement to which historians linked Deweyan pragmatism. The celebration of pragmatism and the American spirit peaked in the 1930s and 1940s. Many writers of the 1950s and 1960s, by contrast, ascribed to Dewey and his philosophy a darker role in American history, corresponding to the intellectual and political countercurrents of the right and left against liberalism, Progressive Era reform, and the New Deal. Ironically, many who disputed pragmatist philosophy shared the Deweyans' own assumption that pragmatism's most important feature was its novelty, its revolt against the past. They differed only in considering this novelty undesirable. Building on earlier conservative criticism of the "idea of progress," those conservatives who disapproved of modernism found in Dewey the modernist, the utilitarian, scientist, and the liberal a useful foil. Conservative educationalists targeted Deweyan relativism and permissiveness during the attacks on progressive education in the 1950s, invoking neo-orthodox skepticism and transcendent moral values. During the 1960s the direction of attack changed and Deweyan pragmatism suffered by its, and Dewey's, association with the corporate liberalism of leading progressives such as Herbert Croly. Writers on the left described Deweyan pragmatism, and particularly Dewey's educational theory, as a thin intellectual veneer over the brute exercise of technocratic corporate power in modern America, reflecting the political and economic authoritarianism ingrained in liberal political culture.[9]

One shortcoming in this literature is its tendency to identify Dewey and pragmatism in general—including the very different pragmatisms of James and Charles S. Peirce—with a monolithic and poorly defined liberalism or "progressivism." Liberalism in the most laudatory of

[8] Sidney Ratner, "Evolution and the Rise of the Scientific Spirit in America," *Philosophy of Science* 3 (1936): 105.

[9] Lyle H. Lanier, "A Critique of the Philosophy of Progress," in *I'll Take My Stand* (1930; rpt. Baton Rouge, 1962), 122–54; Reinhold Niebuhr, *Moral Man and Immoral Society* (New York, 1932), xi–xxv; Arthur M. Schlesinger, Jr., *The Vital Center* (New York, 1949), chap. 3; Lawrence A. Cremin, *The Transformation of the School: Progressivism in American Education, 1876–1957* (New York, 1961), chap. 9; Clarence J. Karier, "Liberalism and the Quest for Orderly Social Change," *History of Education Quarterly* 12 (1972): 57–80.

these accounts boils down to the almost ineffable: a democratic American ethos, a scientific egalitarian spirit, a commitment (sometimes) to individual liberty. Left and right critical literature tended to reduce liberalism and progressivism to technocratic corporatism, when writers did not identify it with market individualism. Many of these accounts are based on substantive and well-argued historical studies. In many instances, progressive reforms served the cause of social engineering rather than the redistribution of power and wealth, as indicated by the class and occupational background of supporters of key legislation.[10] At the same time, structural forces often determined the effects of reform, regardless of the best intentions of middle-class and working-class activists. The market revolution, the growth of mass production, the formation of new class relations and identities often decided the course of social reconstruction far more than did the efforts of reformers.[11]

Yet we also know of a more complex and less self-serving progressive tradition, comprising definite policies and arguments affecting the tangible experience of Americans with the problems of poverty, inequality, race, gender, and national power. This liberal tradition, the historical one, the one we study in detail, contained many currents and countercurrents the knowledge of which both complicates and is essential to our understanding of what was meant (and what we mean)

[10] The most troubling examples of this argument search for ulterior motives, often reducing the intentions of writers and reformers (regardless of outcome) to social status. The most convincing arguments concern the alignment of industrialists and their allies behind business regulation. See Samuel Hays, "The Politics of Reform in Municipal Government in the Progressive Era," *Pacific Northwest Quarterly* 55 (October 1964): 157–69; James Weinstein, *The Corporate Ideal and the Liberal State, 1900–1918* (Boston, 1969); Robert Wiebe, *The Search for Order, 1877–1920* (New York, 1967); Steven Diner, *A City and Its Universities: Public Policy in Chicago, 1892–1919* (Chapel Hill, 1980). In this book I largely skirt the question of professionalization, mainly because it diverts attention from the open arenas of political conflict. The best theoretical statement is Magali Sarfatti Larson, *The Rise of Professionalism: A Sociological Analysis* (Berkeley, 1977); for excellent critical studies of the literature on professionalization, see Henrika Kuklick, "Boundary Maintenance in American Sociology: Limitations to Academic 'Professionalization'," *Journal of the History of the Behavioral Sciences* 16 (1980): 201–19; and "Restructuring the Past: Toward an Appreciation of the Social Context of Social Science," *Sociological Quarterly* 21 (1980): 5–21.

[11] Or, as David Hogan argues, through the efforts of well-intentioned reformers; David Hogan, *Class and Reform: School and Society in Chicago, 1880–1930* (Philadelphia, 1985), chap. 2. The effects of structural change on reform are discussed in Gabriel Kolko, *The Triumph of Conservatism: A Reinterpretation of American History, 1900–1916* (Chicago, 1963); Alfred D. Chandler, *The Visible Hand: The Managerial Revolution in American Business* (Cambridge, Mass., 1977).

by the terms "liberalism" and "progressivism." The history of Chicago pragmatism reveals above all the extent to which Dewey and his colleagues diverged from a politics we could comfortably (or smugly) call liberal. That history further documents how Dewey, his colleagues, and their activist associates struggled with conflicting liberal stances, some of which straddled the divides between liberalism and other political discourses of the left and of the right.

In this confusing historiography one finds as well a tendency to systematically disconnect the Deweyan tradition from its past. Whether to shore up liberalism or to attack it, many writers removed Dewey and his philosophy from the historical context in which he wrote, spoke, and published, including the traditional discourses from which he made his contributions. As in the original thesis of a revolt against formalism, on which much of the laudatory histories were based, most of the accounts before the 1970s emphatically detached Dewey from his own history, except for those features of that past which were useful in the development of latter-day polemics. Relatively uninterested in the roots of a philosophy that reportedly cut itself off at the stem, most chroniclers, not surprisingly, ignored two important traditions on which Dewey and Mead built their philosophical synthesis: liberal Protestant theology and late nineteenth-century producer republicanism. One of my purposes in this volume is to help restore that connection, for the pragmatists as well as for political traditions they helped create.[12]

[12] There are important exceptions to this generalization. The conservatives, who placed little stock in claims to de novo birth, often attacked Dewey as a continuation of nineteenth-century historicism and theological liberalism. This was also true of Niebuhr's critique. Among historians, see Daniel Day Williams, *The Andover Liberals* (New York, 1941), 53–58; for an account of theology's influence on Dewey's generation of social activists see Richard Hofstadter, *Social Darwinism in American Thought* (Boston, 1955), chap. 6, and Robert Crunden, *Ministers of Reform: The Progressives' Achievement in American Civilization, 1889–1920* (Urbana, 1984); among philosophers, a notable exception to the discontinuity argument is Richard J. Bernstein, *Praxis and Action: Contemporary Philosophies of Human Activity* (Philadelphia, 1971). Among Dewey studies, Neil Coughlan's intellectual biography of Dewey's youth and early career at the University of Michigan provides an excellent account of his involvement in the neo-Hegelian movement of the 1880s; *Young John Dewey: An Essay in American Intellectual History* (Chicago, 1973). Bruce Kuklick's study of the New England Theology, culminating in Dewey's work as philosophical apologist for Andover's Progressive Orthodoxy, reestablishes pragmatism's debt to theology; *Churchmen and Philosophers: From Jonathan Edwards to John Dewey* (New Haven, 1985). The most recent and perhaps best contribution to this growing literature are Westbrook, *John Dewey*, and Stephen C. Rockefeller, *John Dewey: Religious Faith and Democratic Humanism* (New York, 1991).

Context and Contextualism

Readers familiar with current disputes concerning the methods of intellectual history will recognize in this volume the kind of "radical contextualist" account that one historian recently called "the new orthodoxy." To the extent that it fits that characterization, this book deciphers what the Chicago pragmatists meant at the time by the terms in which they wrote and spoke. The need for such a historical translation is more readily apparent in the case of Plato or Confucius than in the case of a recent philosophical writer who speaks our own language. But we are distant enough from the years in which Dewey and his colleagues devised their theories to need to recognize the historical idiosyncrasies of their words and ideas. This process includes identifying the social and historical contexts in which Dewey's generation spoke and wrote and the inherited tradition of questions, dilemmas, and conflicts they tried to resolve.[13]

Because the context of tradition and conflict is historically and intellectually complex, we cannot simply translate from past terms to their equivalents in the present. Dewey's generation used expressions such as "industrial democracy" and "self-activity" as rhetorical tools in contentious political environments; such words signified neither personal nor consensual meanings but what Daniel Rodgers and others call "contested truths." Those fighting over territory and power in such cities as Chicago, in the academy and in the emerging institutions of reform, also fought over the meaning of words, over their use, over their reference, even over their rightful ownership. For the struggle over the discourses of political order and social transformation, Dewey and his colleagues appropriated politically loaded terms such as "cooperation," "democracy," "reconstruction," and "intelligence." Less clearly political terms such as "coordination," "self-activity," and "social control" figured into the contest as well. And because control of words and the discourses of political power were so important in determining the outcome of more tangible con-

---

[13] David Harlan, "Intellectual History and the Return of Literature," *American Historical Review* 94 (June 1989): 585; see also David A. Hollinger, "The Return of the Prodigal: The Persistence of Historical Knowing," ibid., 610–21. The relation between context and intention is discussed in Quentin Skinner, "Meaning and Understanding in the History of Ideas," *History and Theory* 8 (1969): 3–53.

flicts, political language was crucial in mapping out the political terrain of American history.[14]

Such a contextual history of pragmatism, a description of specific social and political involvements of the Deweyans and the conflicting dimensions of their inherited and created discourses, has not yet been done, or at least not yet been completed. Recontextualizing pragmatism in this manner adds new dimensions to the philosophy. It also may help us redraw the outlines of the progressive reform movement with which that philosophy was born. A more complex picture of the Progressive Era is still in the making, one that shows the ways language and ideology, the intentions of intellectuals and activists, and the confrontation of politically mobilized social groups—what Edward Said called the "heterogeneity of human involvement"—were all significant in the outcome of historical events.[15]

Two Contexts, Two Souls

Dewey's encounter with the Pullman strike in 1894 is an important reference point for the intersection of pragmatist philosophy and social context in what late nineteenth-century writers called "the labor problem."[16] In the aftermath of that strike the Chicago philosophers, following many of the leaders and members of the American labor movement, became increasingly outspoken in their criticism of the factory system that emerged after the Civil War and the new forms of mass production introduced at the end of the century. As an alternative to the degraded forms of industrial life they saw about them,

---

[14] Daniel Rodgers, *Contested Truths: Keywords in American Politics since Independence* (New York, 1987), 3–16; see also Rodgers, "Keywords: A Reply," *Journal of the History of Ideas* 49 (1988): 669–77; the latter response is to Mark Olsen and Louis-Georges Harvey, "Contested Methods: Daniel T. Rodgers's *Contested Truths*," ibid., 653–68.

[15] Edward W. Said, "Opponents, Audiences, Constituencies, and Community," in *The Anti-Aesthetic*, ed. Hal Foster (Port Townsend, Wash., 1983), 144–45.

[16] The title of this section and the introduction as a whole is drawn in part from Hal Draper's classic analysis of the socialist tradition, *The Two Souls of Socialism* (Berkeley, 1966). Draper's interests and subject matter are considerably different from mine, yet the inner conflicts of Deweyan pragmatism resemble the divided consciousness of the socialist tradition enough to warrant using the expression "two souls." An application to the American social democratic tradition more consistent with Draper's original meaning (though very different in interpretation from mine) can be found in Arthur Lipow, *Authoritarian Socialism in America: Edward Bellamy and the Nationalist Movement* (Berkeley, 1982), 1–15.

Dewey and his colleagues embraced a version of what historians now call "producerism"—an artisanal ethic celebrating the dignity of productive labor—as the source of civic virtue and the foundation of just government. As social activists who became increasingly involved in labor's struggle for economic justice, the Chicago philosophers defended the democratic rights of the laboring classes in the workplace, in the schools, and at the polls. As philosophers and publicists, Dewey and his colleagues defended what they believed were democratic foundations of the republic in productive work and worthy occupations.

Dewey and his colleagues helped formulate a social psychological version of the producer ethic, which would protect and enhance the autonomous "self-activity" of productive citizens. The individual independence, control of work processes, close integration of home life and work life, and strong sense of self-worth offered by older craft and agricultural occupations were necessary, they argued, for the development of human character. Like the craftworkers of the 1880s who led the Knights of Labor and other working-class movements, the pragmatists wanted to restore the psychological integrity of factory work by reasserting the autonomy workers supposedly enjoyed as artisans and farmers, thereby building an "industrial democracy" on the ruins of the preindustrial republic.

Discussions of the degradation and injustices of the factory system and mass production took place in Chicago's union halls and workplaces, where the "nobility of toil" served as the ethical and political touchstone for a generation. Recognizing that Dewey and his colleagues shared this concern and discourse with Chicago's laboring classes and social democrats might help us dispel some of the facile derogations of pragmatism as authoritarian or corporatist. For many progressives, moderate and radical alike, the call for industrial democracy meant liberating the laboring poor from the rapacious forces of the marketplace, authoritarian systems of management, and corrupt institutions of political control. At the very least, by stressing the importance of self-realization and self-fulfillment in the labor process, the Chicago philosophers aided efforts to end the stifling drudgery of factory work. And by championing the right to form trade unions for collective bargaining, they joined labor in efforts to limit the growing power of monopolistic corporations. It is only against this context, I would argue, that we can clearly understand what the

Chicago philosophers meant by key terms such as "self-activity," "industrial democracy," "intelligence," and "cooperation."

As we see in Chapter 1, the Chicago pragmatists first addressed these issues in the discourses of religion and theology; and, though adopting more secular language as they moved out of the church community, their approaches to labor and politics remained psychological and in some sense metaphysical. Their unique political and sociological contribution emerged out of their collective role in efforts to reconstruct liberal Protestant theology, to adapt it to changing social conditions and to save it from eroding empiricist and reductionist philosophies on the one hand and Calvinist orthodoxy on the other. The result of this effort was the pragmatist theory of action, a social and psychological coordination between head and hand, or mind and body, rooted in the Christian metaphysics of immanent redemption. Through the synthesis of head and hand the Chicago philosophers sustained a humanistic philosophy that implicitly and explicitly countered orthodox Calvinist and Darwinian rationalizations of industrial capitalism. It also reconciled, in principle, the social classes, whose divergent manual and intellectual ways of life were being further split by the alienating forces of modern industrialism.

Yet the pragmatists' call for reuniting manual and mental social functions resonated with conservative as well as radically democratic messages. While industrial democracy called for the self-activity and self-realization of industrial employees degraded by the factory system, it also called for the mediation of industrial disputes "intelligently," on terms essentially set by corporate employers. Thus we should not champion Dewey and his friends as radical democratic socialists any more than we should condemn them as corporatists. They tried to adjust the ethic of productive labor to the new world of mass production and mass consumption, to reconstruct it as they reconstructed the categories of philosophy and the relations of citizens in modern society. In doing so, they struggled to avoid the "class view," the intellectual allegiance with one or another class interest, and the utopian visions of a "producers' republic" or "cooperative commonwealth" that defined democracy for Chicago's working-class leaders such as Eugene Debs and Margaret Haley or radical anarchosocialist movements such as the Industrial Workers of the World.

The Chicago philosophers straddled several discourses, some of them conflicting, some only temporarily convergent. And they tried to bring those splitting and diverging discourses together, to resolve the dilemmas, not just between forms of expression but between the groups of people that used and listened to political speech. They hoped to reconstruct and combine the conflicting audiences into a more inclusive audience that shared a belief in a democratic discourse geared toward intelligent social reconstruction. They sustained this hope on the conviction that reason inhered in the productive agency of industrial growth and would provide the basis for a democratic reconstruction of society. Through class "cooperation," "social control," and "reconstruction," social reformers could reinfuse intelligence into working-class social movements.

But the Chicago philosophers did not succeed, as Mead's lament from the arid landscape of northern New Mexico indicated. They encountered new limits to the reconstructed producer ethic and to the discourse of industrial democracy they applied to Chicago. Even working-class producerism exhibited "sincere ideological ambivalence," giving a mixed political and ethical message. It glorified the role of productive labor in creating good citizens, but it also assumed common interests and common values among all "productive" members of society—values and interests that any "intelligent" person should recognize transcend the class differences of the moment. As mass production industry dominated, changing the composition of the workforce while disengaging it from the vestiges of community life, the class view that the Chicago pragmatists so abhorred prevailed.[17]

What was true of mass production was true of mass consumption, with troubling implications for the Deweyan ethic of responsible, informed conduct. Thus, as a self-realization theory the Chicago philosophy was similarly ambivalent. The pragmatist emphasis on personal growth was at first liberating. As new social institutions developed, however, the call for self-realization attached itself to new forms of power and new kinds of hierarchical social order, such as advertising, the entertainment industry, and social management

---

[17] For discussions of the ambiguities of Gilded Age producerism, see Leon Fink, *Workingmen's Democracy: The Knights of Labor and American Politics* (Urbana, 1983), chap. 1, especially pp. 6–9; Nick Salvatore, *Eugene V. Debs: Citizen and Socialist* (Urbana, 1982), chaps. 3, 5–6.

guided by social science.[18] Indeed, like later apostles of advertising and consumption, Dewey and his colleagues missed many of the contradictions between the drive for industrial democracy, the quest for self-realization, and corporate growth. They were not academic counterparts of Bruce Barton or Henry Ford, but their philosophy would be unintentionally congenial to the new order of things.

As the decades passed, and industrial growth and social reform transformed the urban context, the political emphasis of pragmatist philosophy changed. The fluid and dynamic context of the 1890s permitted Dewey and his colleagues to devise a critical philosophy that balanced social order and industrial development against a democratic humanism without sacrificing one to the other. Within a few years, as dramas of industrial transformation and reform played across Chicago's historical stage, the limits of progressive and pragmatist democracy became increasingly evident. The early pragmatist language of autonomous working-class self-activity sounded weakly against demands for citizenship and responsibility. The dream of industrial democracy, in which the pragmatist coordination of head and hand would help humanize productive enterprise, increasingly tied the labor movement, through new forms of arbitration and collective bargaining instituted in the 1910s, to the needs of a society run by business. This conservative drift culminated in the support, in the name of democracy, by many Chicago philosophy department members (and former members like Dewey) for the Allied war effort, considered by radicals such as Randolph Bourne to be the progressive liberals' ultimate folly and the undoing of a democratic tradition.

I began this work in the hope of constructively adding to new scholarship on Chicago pragmatism. Until recently, Dewey's intellectual biography was incomplete, especially the period of his career in which he and his colleagues developed the functionalist social psychology that became the centerpiece of instrumentalism. Robert Westbrook's excellent biography of Dewey has filled much of that gap, though with a broader scope appropriate to Dewey's extraordinary

---

[18] T. J. Jackson Lears, "From Salvation to Self-Realization: Advertising and the Therapeutic Roots of the Consumer Culture, 1880–1930," in *The Culture of Consumption: Critical Essays in American History, 1880–1980,* ed. Richard Wrightman Fox and T. J. Jackson Lears (New York, 1983), 3–38; Warren Susman, *Culture as History* (New York, 1984), chaps. 7–8.

longevity. Much less has been written on the career of George Herbert Mead, Dewey's closest collaborator at Michigan and Chicago, or that of James Hayden Tufts, the Chicago philosophy department's first member, with whom Dewey wrote a major book on naturalist ethics in 1908.[19]

This book divides into three parts. Chapters 1–4 cover the period up to the formation of the Chicago philosophy department under Dewey in 1894; in them I explore early involvement on the part of the department's three central members in late nineteenth-century liberal Protestantism. In Chapters 5–8 I review the years of Dewey's chairmanship, up to 1904, the year he broke with the University of Chicago. Chapters 5 and 6 show the involvement of Dewey and Mead in local activism: in Chapter 5 I recount the department's (primarily Dewey's) growing involvement in the reform movement centered in the city's settlement houses; in Chapter 6 I explore the manner in which the Chicago pragmatists formed their theory of action to address the problems of schooling in the industrial city. In Chapters 7 and 8 I argue that the new functionalist synthesis in psychology and ethics directly addressed the concerns of Chicago's reform community during this period.

The third group of chapters, 9–13, mainly covers the period after 1904, in which Mead and Tufts led the department. Chapters 9 and 10 pick up the account of the department's involvement in educational politics, overlapping Dewey's departure from Chicago in 1904. Department members applied and revised their theory of action in the context of Chicago's class-based conflict over school centralization and reform. In Chapter 11 I explore the direct involvement of Mead and Tufts in local labor reform, through the City Club, the 1910 garment workers strike, and local labor arbitration. In Chapter 12 I return to the department's psychology and philosophy, with a brief geneology of Mead's theory of social interactionism. Mead formulated his theory of the social self while he and Tufts played leading roles

---

[19] Westbrook, *John Dewey*. On early functionalism, see Coughlan, *Young Dewey*, chap. 8; see also Edna Heidbreder, *Seven Psychologies* (New York, 1933), chap. 6; a study of Mead that focuses on explication of his published work is Hans Joas, *G. H. Mead: A Contemporary Reexamination of His Thought* (Cambridge, Mass., 1985); see also David Miller, *George Herbert Mead: Self, Language, and the World* (Austin, 1973), and Dmitri Shalin, "G. H. Mead, Socialism and the Progressive Agenda," *American Journal of Sociology* 93 (1988): 913–51.

in municipal reform and the mediation of labor disputes. The book concludes in Chapter 13 with a discussion of the Chicago philosophers' response to World War I and the limits of their democratic theory.

My conclusions are, of course, provisional. Any reader who has waded through the extraordinary extent of Dewey's collected works or into the tangled complexity of Mead's few articles and lectures knows that there is plenty of room for reinterpretation. More important, as a contextual study that relies heavily on the work of others, this book must be contingent on the incremental and methodical work of social, cultural, and political historians piecing together pictures of the past in which these philosophers lived.

CHAPTER ONE

God in Christ

In 1892, William Rainey Harper called on James H. Tufts to help him recruit academic talent for the recently founded University of Chicago. After several false starts with prominent candidates from eastern colleges, Tufts suggested John Dewey, his former colleague from the University of Michigan, to head the university's philosophy department. Knowing that Harper took clerical matters seriously, Tufts recommended Dewey as "a man of religious nature,...a church-member and [one who] believes in working with the churches."[1] Dewey would not fully live up to his reputation, cutting formal ties with Congregationalism on reaching Chicago in 1894. Despite his departure from the church, however, Dewey came to Chicago with much of his theological baggage intact and in many ways he remained a religious man throughout his stay at Harper's university.

The religious upbringing of Dewey and his new colleagues at the University of Chicago in many respects typified their generation of American intellectuals. The faculty recruited by Harper came of age at a time when American religious culture was fluid, highly political, and increasingly focused on the problems of emerging industrial dis-

---

[1] James Tufts to William Rainey Harper (n.d.), reprinted in Robert L. McCaul, "A Preliminary Listing of Dewey Letters, 1894–1904," *School and Society* 87 (1959): 399; Darnell Rucker, *The Chicago Pragmatists* (Minneapolis, 1969), 10.

order in the United States. It was this shifting of interest from strictly theological questions of faith to more worldly issues that once led historians to view the 1890s as a watershed in the history of ideas, in which figures such as Dewey led their Darwinian revolt against the religious and philosophical formalism of the nineteenth century.

Since then, historians have better recognized that nineteenth-century theological controversies did not simply boil down to narrow-minded reaction against Darwinism and other evolutionary theories held to represent scientific progress. Many American ministers and theologians eventually accommodated the new biology introduced in 1859 by British naturalist Charles Darwin even if at first they had trouble doing so. They argued that accepting evolutionism did not always controvert religious faith, and some, such as Yale's George Park Fisher, did not mind when it did. Some of the most orthodox of American Calvinists, who had long accepted the principles of Newtonian physics, found Darwin's pessimistic atomism congenial to their notions of individuality and inherent human depravity. Those who embraced a more liberal, optimistic theology readily adopted, as did most American scientists and scholars, the less harsh evolutionism of Jean Baptiste Lamarck, the French naturalist whose theories attributed species adaptability to the inheritance of acquired characteristics rather than to natural selection by survival of the fittest.[2]

Although it grew out of the philosophical controversies spawned in part by the new biology, Deweyan pragmatism did not represent the triumph of science over religious dogmatism any more than Darwinism did. Instead, Dewey and his colleagues were part of a movement within, not away from, American Protestantism. In his youth Dewey was one of a large group of philosophers and theologians trying to reconstruct American theology along lines suggested by German religious scholarship, idealist philosophy, and evolutionary theory. In an effort to resolve problems created in American Protestantism by the legacy of Calvinist supernaturalism and to adjust church doctrine to the demands of a changing social environment,

[2] James R. Moore, *The Post-Darwinian Controversies: A Study of the Protestant Struggle to Come to Terms with Darwin in Great Britain and America* (Cambridge, 1979); Edward J. Pfeifer, "The Genesis of American Neo-Lamarckism," *ISIS* 56 (1965): 156–67. On the reception of evolutionism at Yale, see Louise L. Stevenson, *Scholarly Means to Evangelical Ends: The New Haven Scholars and the Transformation of Higher Learning in America, 1830–1890* (Baltimore, 1986), 77–79.

liberal theologians and their philosophical fellow travelers developed a theology based on the principle that God is immanent in the world. Dewey elaborated this new faith in articles written during the late 1880s and early 1890s, eventually constructing his social psychology as a philosophical demonstration of spirit's immanence in human experience.[3]

Although Dewey later abandoned explicit theological language in favor of exclusively social and psychological discourse, it would be a mistake to consider this transition a complete repudiation of the idealist theology in which he was versed as a young man. As I argue in the following chapters, the mature work of Dewey and his colleagues at Chicago followed patterns set in earlier attempts to shore up religious faith with philosophical idealism. Idealist notions of self, self-realization, the immanence of the spiritual in the real and the mental in the physical are particularly evident in Dewey's and George H. Mead's novel work in social psychology, with important consequences for the new politics they helped create. And from the received notions of spiritual and rational immanence, the Chicago pragmatists derived their central faith in historical agency of an informed citizenry led by engaged, civic-minded intellectuals.

Dewey's theological liberalism descended from early nineteenth-century revisions in the Calvinist tradition by students and followers of Jonathan Edwards, the founder of the New England Theology. The liberals challenged relatively orthodox Calvinists on a series of church doctrines, and their specific positions on these matters helped define them as liberal. But what most clearly marked the transition from the New England Theology to late nineteenth-century liberalism was an abandonment of the questions and paradoxes that had occupied New England divines for the previous hundred and fifty years.

The New England Theology began with doctrinal disputes that may seem obscure to us but were nevertheless of genuine importance to early American religious leaders and their congregations. Calvinist

---

[3] For a more traditional view, see Morton White, *The Origins of Dewey's Instrumentalism* (New York, 1943), and *Social Thought in America: The Revolt against Formalism* (Boston, 1957); Philip Wiener, "Chauncey Wright's Defense of Darwin and the Neutrality of Science," *Journal of the History of Ideas* 6 (1945): 27; Eric Goldman, *Rendezvous with Destiny* (New York, 1952). For a revised view of the relations between pragmatism and nineteenth-century religious idealism, see Bruce Kuklick, *The Rise of American Philosophy: Cambridge, Massachusetts, 1860–1930* (New Haven, 1977), and *Churchmen and Philosophers* (New Haven, 1985).

Protestantism began in sixteenth-century Europe as a movement to purify the Reformed churches of any vestiges of Catholic clerical and religious practice. The doctrines associated with the belief in human depravity (original sin, the covenant of works, the covenant of grace) challenged the corrupt worldliness of the impure churches (the Vatican and the Church of England); human depravity also made sense of a world decimated by war, disease, and famine by sustaining an absolute separation between the realms of heaven and earth. For the Calvinists, believers must necessarily struggle with their sinful natures on earth and, as God's agents, help cleanse the world of filth and degradation. Yet, compared with Catholicism, Calvinists' worldly attainments had little bearing on what they believed they would face after death, in hell or in heaven, where only the saved, or "saints," resided. The belief in predestination, in which only God determines who is saved (and admitted to heaven), presumably limited the role of social distinctions and of institutional mediation (by the church and the priesthood) in the individual's attainment of salvation.

The paradoxical relation between the divine and the worldly contributed to the well-known internal tensions that characterize the history of American Calvinism. By the late seventeenth century, American Calvinist (that is, Puritan) leadership had compromised the severe restrictions the church had once placed on membership and blurred the sharp distinctions it had drawn between worldly accomplishments and the otherworldly attainment of spiritual grace. The erosion of doctrinal purity involved fundamental theological questions addressed by Edwards and other divines who led subsequent revivals of religious enthusiasm throughout the English colonies.

The characteristic questions raised in eighteenth-century disputes addressed the paradox of divine sovereignty: why would a righteous God allow humans to be blighted by original sin? They also addressed the problem of reconciling God's supremacy in heaven with human moral and religious responsibilities on earth: If by his supreme will God caused Adam to fall from grace and then condemned his descendents to perpetuate original sin, how could the Puritans hold each other responsible, as they did, for acts of worldly depravity?

Most important were those questions concerning the election of community members to sainthood: how could a human who was innately depraved and sinful be absolved of original sin to become a member of the elect? It was particularly important to answer this question because, in seeming contradiction of the doctrine of predestination, the Calvinist orthodoxy also held that receiving grace must be a voluntary act, an act in which the will is controlled by a supreme authority, but an act of will nonetheless. One must accept Christ, yet how did a sinner become able to do this? According to more evangelical adherents of the faith, this act would occur in a moment of revivalistic epiphany in which one would experience God and accept salvation. But how could one know who was saved and who was not? The experience of God's grace was personal and direct, without the mediation of the clergy, and God arbitrarily conferred grace on the elect regardless of their worldly achievements or their knowledge. But even more technical questions that seem even more scholastic and obscure to us perplexed New England divines: could an individual prepare for salvation, or would grace be given regardless of what one did in this earthly life? Answering such questions seemed vital to the Protestant communities. If one could do nothing, what good was a church, or religious worship, or even reading the Bible? What good was a minister if the only agent in granting salvation was God himself?

In general, earlier Calvinists had answered these questions by referring to God's mystery and absolute sovereignty. They fared best on questions concerning God's motives: depraved humans could neither know God's intentions nor question them. Early theologians fared less well on questions of human responsibility and free will: the absolute predestination of human sin and atonement did not fit with their sense that individuals are responsible for their actions inside and outside the church (including sinning and receiving grace) in ways that reflected on their inner characters and their status in the community. Nor did predestination fit with general expectations that membership in the church, the central institution of the Puritan community, would be hereditary and controlled, to some extent, by ministers and other church authorities. When, as the years passed, the children of the Puritan elect who originally settled the Massachusetts Bay Colony did not receive grace directly from God in a conversion experience, as was required for true church participation, some accommodation had to be made. Church elders allowed a relaxation of standards (as well as more earthly measures of grace) by the middle of the seventeenth century, just a few short years after the founding of the colony.[4]

[4] Although other variants of Calvinism crossed the Atlantic, English Puritanism was the

The decline in church membership, the loosening of standards, the waning of community piety, and the conundrum of theological questions all had parts in the main religious event of Protestant colonial American, the Great Awakening, an evangelical revival of religious sentiment and church participation that swept the British colonies between 1734 and 1752. With religious revival came theological revision. Edwards, the most prominent theologian produced by Britain's American colonies, joined other religious leaders in the mid-eighteenth century in an effort to revive religious enthusiasm, enhance genuine participation in the church, and resolve some of the dilemmas Calvinist doctrine imposed on the faithful. Though poorly appreciated by his contemporaries, Edwards surpassed many of his successors in providing sophisticated responses to such dilemmas, reconciling Calvinism's worldly and otherworldly concerns and God's authority with human agency. Edwards's teachings on the nature of the will at least provisionally enabled humans to bear responsibility for their fates, recognize their own salvation (though not facilitate it), and participate in an orderly church. Partly in response to and justification for the revival movement he helped create, Edwards himself argued for an evangelical religion of the heart, the will, and the revival meeting, not only of the head, biblical exegesis, and well-learned doctrine. But the problems of the atonement, of free will and predestination, continued to haunt succeeding generations of religious leaders and theologians, for Calvinism had still not eliminated the contradiction between divine authority and human responsibility.[5]

In the century after Edwards's death, Calvinist supernaturalism continued to founder on the conflict between the Calvinists' acceptance of absolute divine sovereignty and their belief in human accountability, between the strictly rationalized and learned doctrines of the church and the direct heartfelt experiences of the faithful. Theologians and philosophers of lesser intellectual stature than Edwards continued to juggle these issues, stimulated by the ebb and flow in church attendance, by sectarian conflicts, and by the threats to the

tradition's main American representative. Sidney Ahlstrom, *A Religious History of the American People* (Garden City, 1975), 174–78, 192–205, 208–16; Perry Miller, *Errand into the Wilderness* (Cambridge, Mass., 1956), chap. 1; Kuklick, *Churchmen and Philosophers*, chaps. 1–2; Daniel Day Williams, *The Andover Liberals: A Study in American Theology* (New York, 1941), 1–14.

   [5] Ahlstrom, *Religious History*, chaps. 18–19; Kuklick, *Churchmen and Philosophers*, chaps. 2–3.

conservative clergy and clerical order from the waves of revivalism that periodically swept the American landscape.[6]

By the early nineteenth century, these questions produced an array of answers and doctrines, at theological seminaries across the United States and in the pulpits of various denominations, some of them newly formed along the ever emerging lines of doctrinal disagreement. For our purposes the most important new trends occurred in the seminaries and colleges still associated with New England Congregationalism. At Yale College and Andover Theological Seminary the doctrinal descendants of Edwards continued to battle over questions of free will and atonement. Leading divines such as Nathaniel William Taylor of Yale increasingly began to promote doctrines that historians conventionally label liberal. Taylor's liberalism consisted of tendencies to downplay (though never deny) the doctrine of human depravity and to consider God benevolent and rational in his earthly manifestation rather than arbitrary. Liberalism crept in even at Andover, founded in 1808 to defend orthodox catechism by absolute authority (professors were required to sign a pledge every five years) after heretical Harvard went Unitarian. President Edwards Amasa Park began to stress the moral sentiments of the community as standards by which to judge church teachings. The religious experiences of the heart, such as conversion and revivalistic enthusiasm, were more important than doctrine. Humanity increasingly became a measure of religious truth, symbolized by Jesus, God's incarnation on earth as a man.[7]

Many liberals ministering from churches and teaching in seminaries after the Civil War challenged the harsh puritanism of the Calvinist orthodoxy even further on the questions of sovereignty and original sin as they portrayed God as benevolent and immanent in a humanely rational world. Many stressed the emotional side of Edwards's New England Theology at the expense of the rationalist apologetics and biblical literalism of the religious academics, continuing a tradition that included heterodox exponents of Edwardsianism as well as more dramatic departures from Trinitarian doctrine, such as Horace Bushnell's. An influential preacher and theologian in the 1840s and 1850s,

---

[6] Elizabeth Flower and Murray Murphey, *A History of Philosophy in America*, 2 vols. (New York, 1977), 1:142–67; see Kuklick, *Churchmen and Philosophers*, chap. 4, for a basic historical outline of New England Theology.
[7] Ahlstrom, *Religious History*, chap. 26; Kuklick, *Churchmen and Philosophers*, chaps. 6–7; Williams, *Andover Liberals*, 14–22.

Bushnell argued that redemption, if it could not be acquired as a reward for moral acts, as in Catholicism, nevertheless could be encouraged in an individual through education, nurture, and the effects of a changing social environment. A large segment of this new liberal movement espoused a religious modernism that expanded the belief in God's worldly immanence to relativize religious doctrine to cultural conditions and the "spirit of the age."[8]

Like Bushnell, the later liberals stressed the organic unity between God and humanity, symbolized by Christ's role as God's earthly incarnation. They diminished the significance of original sin in human and divine affairs and freed human will from divine authority to an extent inadmissable even by reconstructed Trinitarians such as Taylor or Park. Liberal theologians argued that natural and social events showed evidence of divine purpose in a coherent and nonarbitrary fashion. They rendered life intelligible in a way orthodox Calvinists could and would not: the divine inhered in the real, and mind was in the world. Rather than the product of incomprehensible and arbitrary intervention, historical events manifested a coherence that could be conferred only by an immanent and comprehensible spirit. Good and evil likewise ceased to be in strictly metaphysical conflict; instead, their relation became a matter of the temporal and progressive realization of divine will, culminating in a Kingdom of God on earth, rather than just in heaven. The liberal position gained prominence after 1870 in a series of heresy trials prosecuted by the orthodoxy against leading modernists such as David Swing, Egbert Smyth, and Charles A. Briggs. By the late 1880s, the liberal perspective, sometimes called the "Progressive Orthodoxy," reigned at Andover, eastern Congregationalism's leading seminary, after the infamous coup of 1883 in which Park and proponents of a more orthodox Edwardsianism were deposed.[9]

At this point, Dewey entered the history of religious disputation as an enthusiastic, young adherant of Andover liberalism. But before Dewey's role can be understood, one more point needs to be made

[8] William R. Hutchison, *The Modernist Impulse in American Protestantism* (Cambridge, Mass., 1976), Introduction and chap. 2; on modernism at Yale, see Stevenson, *Scholarly Means*, chap. 1.

[9] Barbara Cross, *Horace Bushnell: Minister to a Changing America* (Chicago, 1958), 28, 48, 61–64; Ahlstrom, *Religious History*, 610–13; Hutchison, *Modernist Impulse*, 48–77.

about the shifting and conflicting theological traditions. Through the nineteenth century, Calvinist religious disputes explicitly addressed questions about the relationship between God and the individual; about how that relationship could be defined without the evidence of worldly achievement (or failure) or the sanction of established clerical institutions. But these questions can also be seen as part of an extended, more implicit discourse, expressed in religious and theological terms, concerning the nature of the self and the extent or possibility of human agency. The Puritans saw themselves engaged as God's agents on an earthly errand. Yet according to Sacvan Bercovitch their literature discloses as well a concept of the self in which "selfhood appears as a state to be overcome, obliterated; and identity is asserted through an act of submission to a transcendent absolute." Among Puritan divines, the impulses of the individual worldly self, for gratification, earthly love, the fulfillment of desire, seemed antithetical to the main concern of Protestant faith, the salvation of the spiritual self and the abandonment of worldly desire. This divided notion of the self occupied Protestant leaders for the better part of two centuries as they questioned the nature of the will and human agency. Was the individual a significant being only in his or her relation to that ultimate significant being, God? Or did the individual's active relation to institutions and to other people have some bearing on that person's salvation and on those other ultimately significant events in all human existence, Adam and Eve's fall from grace and Christ's crucifixion? Were humans entirely determined by circumstances beyond their control, such as the original sin? Or, did they have some control, over themselves and over their destiny, in heaven, or on earth?[10]

With the rise of the Progressive Orthodoxy, mainstream Protestantism, descended from the original Puritan congregations through the Congregational and Presbyterian ministries, abandoned the discourse of the New England Theology. In doing so, they made the implicit discussion of the self explicit in their revised notions of selfhood and new concepts of self-realization and self-activity. At the same time, they came to a very different understanding, not only of God's relation to the finite, human world, but also of the human capacity for earthly redemption and true self-realization. Theologians

[10] Sacvan Bercovitch, *The Puritan Origins of the American Self* (New Haven, 1975), 8–17.

and ministers reconceived the conflict of salvation and sin as a matter of progressive self-realization in the historical world, an act or series of acts that helped achieve God's grander, spiritual design. Self was spirit and spirit self. The growth and realization of one was the growth and realization of the other. Concurrently, by abandoning strict Calvinist notions of original sin and inherent human depravity progressive theology opened up the possibility, which Dewey especially exploited, of arguing for an entirely new conception of the self—one in which the individual would no longer feel humiliation and contempt for earthly desire and, no longer seeking absolution only in heaven, would recognize earthly self-realization as part of God's design.

CHAPTER TWO

Early Years

In February 1885, George Herbert Mead wrote his friend Henry Castle a woeful note: "My life looks dreary and fruitless before me," he concluded, "as if it was going to run out like an Australian river." On the verge of his twenty-second birthday, Mead had found none of the fulfillment or clarity he expected from adult life. Stuck in an unrewarding teaching job, he had somehow, so he believed, moved off his proper life's track, which in an earlier age would have led him to a respectable (and powerful) ministry such as his father's. Reflective and intellectually active, Mead allowed his recent experiences to convince him that he had lost all control over his future and all social and intellectual agency. Mead's lament echoed the sense of dislocation expressed by some college-trained intellectuals, who twenty years earlier would have been ministry bound but who by the 1880s were confounded by the clerical and academic currents of their age. Some, like Mead, experienced actual social dislocation, becoming marginalized in a middle class that was shifting many of its institutional locations—from church and charity to university and social reform organization, from ministerial oration to political polemics.[1]

The future members of the University of Chicago philosophy de-

---

[1] George H. Mead to Henry N. Castle, February 8, 1885, Mead Papers; Robert Crunden, *Ministers of Reform* (Urbana, 1982), chaps. 1–2. Louise L. Stevenson pushes the transition back farther to the generation of Noah Porter and George Park Fisher; *Scholarly Means to Evangelical Ends* (Baltimore, 1986), chap. 2.

partment made the transition with varying degrees of success. Though the oldest, John Dewey moved from his role as traditional clerical intellectual to university-based professional with the greatest fluidity, ease, and mastery; James Tufts and Mead had more difficulty. Younger departmental members, with one exception, never trained for the evangelical life and so had relatively little problem finding their social location and historical purpose. Yet the fact that these men moved into new, secular institutional settings should not mislead us into assuming that they abandoned the religious preoccupations of their youth. As young men in the 1870s and 1880s, Dewey, Tufts, and Mead, the key department members until the twentieth century, studied the tradition of theological dispute that defined liberal Protestantism. In the familiar discursive context of their college years, orthodox proponents of original sin and absolute arbitrary divinity pitted themselves against the liberal heresies of immanent redemption and divine benevolence. Dewey fit prominently into this tradition as a philosophical apologist for the liberal camp, prepared for that role by teachers who addressed these controversies as problems in academic philosophy, in a manner characteristic of the liberal perspective. Tufts and Mead occupied more minor roles as students of the liberal heresy.

John Dewey

John Dewey was born the second of three sons of Archibald and Lucina Dewey in Burlington, Vermont, October 20, 1859, the year Charles Darwin published *The Origin of Species*. Archibald, the son of a farmer, ran a prosperous grocery business in Burlington at a time when the town was a rapidly expanding lumber center. Dewey's mother, the daughter of a wealthy and prominent farm family, was a major force in Dewey's upbringing, schooling her sons in the evangelical pietism she had embraced as a young woman. Dewey rankled under his mother's constant moral and religious surveillance. He entered the local First Congregationalist Church on her insistence. There the Reverend Lewis O. Brastow preached a "liberal evangelicalism" that was becoming popular in the New England churches and was less strict and more rationalistic than Lucina's puritanical Calvinism. Dewey's commitment to Congregationalism was sincere and serious.

In his twenties he had a religious mystic experience, and until he quit the church in 1894 he attended services regularly, taught Bible classes, and involved himself in other church-related work.[2]

After attending local high school, Dewey enrolled in the University of Vermont in 1875, where he first learned to apply the philosophical doctrines of the German romantics to defend religious faith. One of Jonathan Edwards's great contributions to the history of ideas was his synthesis of Westminister Calvinism with John Locke's Newtonian psychology, allowing natural theology to coexist with Newtonian science without succumbing to deistic heresies that characterized the universe as a self-regulating machine built by God. Far from opposing modern scientific theory, evangelical Protestantism since Edwards often adopted a natural theology based on mechanistic Newtonian science and Lockean epistemology.

But the course of empiricist philosophy at the end of the eighteenth century complicated this congenial relation between rationalist science and Calvinist theology. The distinction between primary and secondary qualities, on which Lockean epistemology was based, became increasingly problematic, challenged in turn by George Berkeley and David Hume. Berkeley argued that Locke had no basis for maintaining that the primary qualities of extension and substantial resistance were independently constituted. Primary qualities are no different in this respect, he argued, than secondary qualities such as color or taste; they are effects on the percipient, not "external" qualities. Instead Berkeley claimed that the "objectivity" of these perceptions is sustained by God along with the rest of human experience. Elements of Berkeley's objective idealism suited an Edwardsian understanding of divine sovereignty and intervention in the world, and Edwards incorporated his own version of it into his natural theology.[3] But Hume's systematic critique of induction, which argued that even the relations of cause and effect between discrete sensations cannot be known directly from experience, undermined the coherence and order of the phenomenal world as depicted by Locke and Berkeley. Moreover, Humean skepticism threatened not only the foundations of knowledge

---

[2] George Dykhuizen, *The Life and Mind of John Dewey* (Carbondale, 1973), 1–8; Bruce Kuklick, *Churchmen and Philosophers* (New Haven, 1985), 230–31.

[3] Edwards apparently arrived at a similar understanding of Locke without knowledge of Berkeley; Elizabeth Flower and Murray G. Murphey, *A History of Philosophy in America,* 2 vols. (New York, 1977), 1:142.

but also those of faith, which like science depended on a Lockean notion of causality and the testimony of experience.

The German idealists, led by Immanuel Kant, attempted to put knowledge and faith on new foundations. Accepting Hume's argument that relations between discrete sensations are not constituted independently of the perceiving subject, Kant placed all the necessary conditions of knowledge within the mind of the subject. There may be an objective reality out there, a "thing in itself," but we do not know it as it really is. Rather, we know the world as *we* construct it in our experience, using a priori categories of understanding such as space, time, and causality.

German philosophy entered American theological discourse from the margins, introduced to American readers in the 1830s and 1840s by "amateurs" such as Ralph W. Emerson and by philosophy instructors in small provincial colleges. In the nineteenth century, religious liberals within the Calvinist denominations began to turn to German philosophy as an alternative to British empiricism, to give a firmer epistemological basis for faith in spiritual as well as scientific truths. In this emerging philosophical and religious discourse, Kant's categories became extensions of the universal understanding and spirit that we know as God.[4]

The University of Vermont was one such provincial college through which German idealism entered the American academy. An early university president, James Marsh, was a well-known proponent of the "Burlington philosophy," an idiosyncratic mixture of Scottish realism and Kantian idealism. Other Vermont professors argued that the best philosophical defense of the Calvinist tradition against philosophical and religious skepticism came from the Kantian tradition.[5] On leaving the University of Vermont in 1879, Dewey took a job teaching school in Oil City, Pennsylvania, the major center of America's young oil extraction industry. He did not, however, neglect his interest in neo-Kantian apologetics. In addition to having his religious

---

[4] Kuklick, *Churchmen and Philosophers*, chaps. 8–9. The application of German idealism accompanied a long-term transition from professional theology to academic philosophy.

[5] Dykhuizen, *Life and Mind*, 9–18; Kuklick, *Churchmen and Philosophers*, 231. Marsh was also important in introducing Hegelian idealism to the United States through his edition of S. T. Coleridge's influential "Aids to Reflection." For the most complete recent discussion of Dewey's education in the Burlington philosophy, see Steven C. Rockefeller, *John Dewey: Religious Faith and Democratic Humanism* (New York, 1991), 51–65.

experience, during his two years in Oil City Dewey published his first
major philosophical articles in William Torrey Harris's *Journal of
Speculative Philosophy,* then the leading organ of American Hegelianism. Both essays addressed Dewey's and the liberals' preferences
for German idealism over empiricism and other mechanistic theories
of knowledge. Encouraged by his success, Dewey applied to graduate
school at the recently founded Johns Hopkins University, to which
he was admitted without a needed scholarship in 1882.[6]

At Johns Hopkins, Dewey came under the wing of George Sylvester
Morris, a leading American interpreter of idealist philosophy, well
known for his attacks on British empiricism in the 1880s. Morris
sponsored the younger scholar through his early academic career and
guided him through the neo-Hegelian movement in Anglo-American
philosophy and theology of the 1870s and 1880s. A theist, Morris
tried to reassert the essentially spiritual nature of the universe without
denying the findings of science or the testimony of experience (including mechanistically inclined experimental sciences). He also tried
to defend theism without resorting to dualistic or transcendental systems such as the neo-Kantians', which divided the universe between
the known, phenomenal realm of constructed experience and the un-
knowable, noumenal realm of the thing-in-itself. Like many liberal
Protestants in the 1870s, Morris moved steadily into the Hegelian
camp. Although Kantianism answered some of the epistemological
problems raised by Hume in a manner congenial to heterodox American Calvinists, it still tended to undermine religious faith by locking
all knowledge into phenomenal, or subjective, experience. Included
was knowledge of religious truths; although one could argue, as many
did, that the categories of knowledge represented in the individual
mind the presence of divine spirit, the absence of an independently
constituted object suggested religious as well as philosophical solips-
ism. The unknowability of the thing-in-itself made knowledge of God
seem even more distant than in empiricist natural theology, in which
God's presence could be read in natural events and the Bible as well
as in direct evangelical religious experiences.

The teachings of G. W. F. Hegel followed Kantian idealism to the

---

[6] Dykhuizen, *Life and Mind,* chap. 2; John Dewey, "The Metaphysical Assumptions of
Materialism" (April 1882), and "The Pantheism of Spinoza" (July 1882), *Early Works*
1:3–8, 9–18.

United States in the middle of the century. Hegel emphatically criticized the Kantian division of knowledge from object, of phenomena from noumena. Experience, Hegel argued, in a way that would provide the foundation of Dewey's later theory of action, does not need an independently constituted thing-in-itself to sustain a truth or reality independent of the perceiving subject. The truth of knowledge, for Hegel, is constituted in its genetic development from simplest to most complex form, in the individual and in the history of human understanding. Consequently, philosophers should study not the unchanging categories of knowing, as the Kantians maintained, but the historical unfolding of increasingly rational forms of sentient experience, the history of human culture. There are no timeless noumena either, only what is known and created in the course of collective human existence. Kant's categories, then, to the extent that we still accept them, are historical categories, intellectual artifacts of a time and place. Reason and spirit are immanent in history, since the record of human experience, according to the Hegelians, reflects the ascent of humanity to higher and higher levels of rationality and spiritual understanding.

Hegelianism allowed Morris and others to revitalize theism by restructuring the relation between God and the temporal world. Morris argued for a Hegelian organicism that allowed the perception of God in the world of true objects, though they were objects constituted outside the individual subject in the highly spiritualized realm of history. In addition, Morris's Hegelianism balanced God's immanence with the open-ended character of history and individual experience, stressing the role of human will in personal and historical redemption. God is in experience, Morris argued, but only through the unfinished action of intelligent beings in a social and institutional context (a principle Dewey would later purge of theistic reference). Thus, Morris identified revelation and redemption with individual self-realization, a position taken by many of the religious liberals at Andover and Yale: God reveals himself through human personality struggling for worldly redemption. Hegelian idealism allowed Morris to accommodate (to his own satisfaction) theism to experimental science, which as a systematic study of the phenomena of human consciousness constituted a higher, more spiritual form of experience. These notions of spiritual immanence also reconciled emotional experience of grace (the focus of evangelicalism) with worldly experience (the focus of science and politics). Finally, because the worldly revelation of spirit came about through the intentional efforts of individuals, the earlier Edwardsian problem of the freedom of the will and human accountability for sin disappeared, or at least took on new shapes. Human will no longer competed with divine will for the fate of the world— one was simply a part of the other.[7]

Dewey's writings from this period show that like Morris he sought philosophical justification for Andover Seminary's progressive orthodox theology of immanence. In "Knowledge and the Relativity of Feeling" (1883), Dewey tried to demonstrate internal inconsistencies in Lockean empiricist and other mechanistic theories of knowledge then popular in the United States and Britain. Sensationalists such as Hume or Herbert Spencer, then the most popular exponent of mechanistic empiricism in the United States, cannot, Dewey argued, maintain that all knowledge is relative to "feeling" (that is, discrete, unmediated sensations) without implying an objective standard ("objects which are not known through feeling") by which to determine that those experiences are in fact relative. According to Dewey, the contradictions of British empiricism thus showed that only idealism could provide the higher philosophical principles, demonstrating the objective basis by which to understand the relativity of knowledge to individual experience.[8]

But, following Morris, Dewey rejected the Kantian solution to Hume's skepticism. Over the next fifteen years this effort to show the superiority of Hegelian historicism occupied much of Dewey's philosophical labors. In "Kant and the Philosophic Method" (1884) he tried to show that Kantian philosopy is subsumed in Hegelian subjective idealism "dialectically," or by the resolution of Kantianism's internal contradictions. In Kant's system, Dewey argued, the transcendental categories, from which mind constructs experience, need the independently constituted noumena to become "real," that is, for the construction of experiential "objects." While explaining the coherence of our experience, however, Kant's method introduces a new problem, the contradictory relation between the categories and the noumenal realm, creating a new subject, the constructive mind, and

[7] Marc Edmund Jones, *George Sylvester Morris: His Philosophical Career and Theistic Idealism* (Philadelphia, 1948), chaps. 8, 11, 12.

[8] Dewey, "Knowledge and the Relativity of Feeling" (January 1883), *Early Works* 1:19–33.

a new, even more distant object, the thing-in-itself. Hegel, Dewey continued, resolves this contradiction by removing the independently constituted noumena: subject and object (in this case phenomenal objects of experience rather than noumena) are instead aspects of absolute self-consciousness acting in the finite world. Mind knows that its object is real because of the relations among the categories of knowledge, between the categories and their object, and between the individual subject, as a collection of ideas and constructed objects (experience), and absolute self-consciousness. "The only conception adequate to experience as a whole," wrote Dewey, is "organicism." Truth, thus, is conferred on experience by the coherence of these relations and, ultimately, by Reason, the absolute idea (or God).[9]

Both Dewey and Morris believed that psychology would provide the scientific basis for philosophical organicism, a position into which Dewey entrenched himself even more resolutely after Morris's death in 1889. Dewey further argued that, quite apart from their origins in evolutionary biology, the methods and findings of the New Psychology of the 1880s, which Dewey studied with G. Stanley Hall at Hopkins, confirmed Hegelian organicism. Such physiological psychology did not reduce mind to anatomy, Dewey maintained, in his next article, written for *Andover Review*. He was responding to influential British writers such as Spencer and Alexander Bain, who conceived of physiological psychology as a solely biological science and who tended to reduce human behavior to mechanical responses to environmental stimuli. They fit this conception to a more orthodox Darwinian evolutionism driven primarily by natural selection.

This reductionism, Dewey contended, follows from a popular misconception. As he saw it, experimental laboratory psychology demonstrates two nonreductionist psychological givens: the active role mind plays in constructing experience, and the organic relation between mind and its objective environment. The results confirm not only the links between mind and body but the institutional aspects of Hegelian historicism, since social institutions are part of the environment. What is more, since the New Psychology stresses the role in psychological processes of a goal-oriented will, it reaffirms the teleological and ethical character of experience and reality, treating "life as an organism in which immanent ideas or purposes are realizing

---

[9] Dewey, "Kant and the Philosophic Method" (April 1884), *Early Works* 1:34–47.

themselves through the development of experience." Within the new psychological methods and constructions Dewey found godliness as well: "As [the New Psychology] goes into the depths of man's nature it finds, as a stone of its foundation, blood of its life, the instinctive tendencies of devotion, sacrifice, faith and idealism which are the eternal substructure of all the struggles of the nations upon the altar stairs which slope up to God." Rational science, then, in the form apparently most threatening to idealism and religious belief, confirms rather than denies life's spiritual origins and essence: "It finds no insuperable problems in the relations of faith and reason, for it can discover in its investigations no reason which is not based upon faith, and no faith which is not rational in its origin and tendency."[10]

Few would mistake Dewey for a brilliant dialectician or even a reliable exponent of conventional Hegelian arguments. He did, however, effectively apply Hegelian idealism to clerical and collegiate polemics, with great professional success as well. Dewey acquired a post at the University of Michigan in 1884, a position made permanent as a condition of Morris's call to head the department in 1885. In March 1889, Morris died suddenly, leaving the chair of the Michigan department open. The Michigan trustees offered the job to Dewey, who the year before had hired on as a full professor at the University of Minnesota. Although taking over Morris's position meant a $200 drop in pay (to $2,200), Dewey accepted after much deliberation. W. S. Hough, who had replaced Dewey at Michigan the year before, filled the opening left by Dewey at Minnesota, vacating his junior position at Michigan. For that slot Dewey hired James H. Tufts, recently graduated from Amherst College and Yale Divinity School. Tufts's educational history differed from Dewey's, but his intellectual and spiritual interests fit well with Dewey's own philosophical agenda.[11]

James Hayden Tufts

Schooled like Dewey in the New England evangelical tradition, James Hayden Tufts was the only child of James Tufts, a seminary-trained Massachusetts academy teacher, and his wife Mary, descendent of

[10] Dewey, "The New Psychology" (September 1884), *Early Works* 1:60.
[11] Dykhuizen, *Life and Mind*, 64.

Bay Colony settlers. Tufts's paternal grandfather, who studied with Nathaniel Emmons, preached a somewhat emotional variant of Edwardsian Trinitarianism as Congregationalist minister in Wardsboro, Vermont, raising Tufts's father in an intensely pious home and community environment that was regularly convulsed by religious revivalism. James Tufts, destined for the ministry, entered Andover Seminary after graduating from Yale in 1838, but poor health forced him at age 40 to abandon his calling for a considerably less prestigious position as principal of a small boys' boarding school in the central Massachusetts town of Monson, where James Hayden was born on July 9, 1862. Even that employment overtaxed Tufts's father, forcing him to make a living boarding and teaching students in the Tufts family home, a working farm outside the village. Despite (or perhaps because of) his father's failure to enter the ministry, James Hayden aspired to a clerical career, which he never fully abandoned until his second year at Yale Divinity School.[12]

Late nineteenth-century theological controversy drew young Tufts into philosophy much as it had Dewey. After attending Monson Academy until the age of 16, Tufts taught in local public schools and occasionally preached in the town's Congregational church. Within a couple of years he had saved enough money to enter Amherst College, closer to home and cheaper than Yale. Tufts attended Amherst under president Julius Seelye, a devout, Union Theological Seminary-trained cleric and opponent of evolutionism who nevertheless was known for his religious tolerance. In education Seelye was a liberal and, like president Charles William Eliot of Harvard and other entrepreneurs of higher education in the 1880s, he was responsible for developing Amherst from a small seminary into a leading liberal arts college through expansion of curriculum and introduction of an elective system.[13]

Seelye also brought several unconventional professors onto campus, including philosophy professor Charles E. Garman, who would have a strong hand in Tufts's early philosophical development. A hypochondriacal and reclusive eccentric, Garman was far more tolerant than his superior of the new biology and anthropology and gave over

---

[12] James H. Tufts, "Autobiography" (n.d., n.p.), Tufts Papers, Chicago.
[13] Claude Moore Fuess, *Amherst: The Story of a New England College* (Boston, 1935), 208–27.

much class time to drawing out its implications for philosophy and theology. Using the conceptual tools and rhetoric of German idealism to defend theism, Garman insisted that mind could not be completely reduced to the naturalistic, reductionist explanations given by the physiological psychology of his day. Nevertheless, he found nothing about experimental psychology in general that made it incompatible with his theistic idealism; a close friend of William James, he was the one person most responsible for introducing laboratory psychology as a subject at Amherst.[14]

Garman's tutelage put Tufts on his way toward Dewey's synthesis of Hegelian idealism and laboratory psychology. Tufts's masters thesis, "The Growth of the Love of Nature in English Poetry," reflected his somewhat unorthodox philosophical training: strongly indebted to romantic idealism, the essay was an attempt to demonstrate the intrinsic connections between the poetry of Wordsworth and Shelley and the "divine poetry" immanent in history (in the Enlightenment and republicanism) and in nature. Nature, wrote Tufts, is "the visible manifestation of an informing Spirit which revealed itself under another aspect in the soul of man." English poetry, Tufts argued, was "broadened and deepened with life" by German idealism's replacement of Lockean empiricism in British arts and letters in the early nineteenth century. Ultimately, the right philosophical outlook, built on idealist foundations, would allow poetry and art a grander and deeper vision of spiritual immanence in which "every bush will burn with the divine presence, every cloud shine with the divine glory, and men will find the soil on which they tread is holy ground."[15]

After one postgraduate year as a high school principal in Connecticut and two years teaching mathematics at Amherst (filling a post once held by Garman), Tufts entered Yale Divinity School as a second-

[14] Thomas Le Duc, *Piety and Intellect at Amherst College, 1865–1912* (New York, 1946), 106, 112. Garman's following among students was unparalleled at Amherst at the end of the century, due as much to his extravagant pedagogical style as to growing student dissatisfaction with the orthodox teachings of the American academy, which culminated at Amherst in a student petition protesting obligatory recitations of the Westminister catechism (Tufts did not sign). Tufts's respect for his teacher bordered on veneration. The younger scholar edited a commemorative edition of Garman's letters and addresses as well as a volume of essays by former Garman students in honor of their mentor; Tufts, "Autobiography"; LeDuc, *Piety and Intellect*, 108, 110; James H. Tufts, ed., *Studies In Philosophy and Psychology* (Boston, 1906).

[15] Tufts, "The Growth of the Love of Nature in English Poetry," Amherst College masters thesis (1884), Tufts Papers, Amherst.

year student. There he absorbed firsthand the liberal theological teaching he previously had gotten only in derivative form. With William Rainey Harper he studied Hebrew and applied "higher" historical criticism to the Old Testament. Then Yale's leading advocate of an accommodation between evolutionary science and religious thought (he believed it brought no "loss of spiritually valuable truth"), Harper studied the Old Testament's tribal origins and traced the evolution of monotheism through biblical writings. Tufts studied theology with George Park Fisher, Samuel Harris, and John Russell, advocates of higher criticism. Tufts also worked with George Ladd in philosophy and William Graham Sumner, whom Tufts considered one of the three major influences on his thought, in anthropology. Little of Sumner's social philosophy reappears in Tufts's writings, but Sumner's application of evolutionary anthropology in the study of comparative religions had a strong impact on Tufts's work at Ann Arbor and Chicago.[16]

After his second year at Yale, Tufts traveled to Grand Forks City, North Dakota, for the Home Missions to take the place of the town's pastor, who had to leave his post when his wife and child were murdered by a hired hand. Through the summer Tufts gave three services a week in this ministerial apprenticeship, taught two Sunday schools, led the choir, and visited parishoners' homes—the full responsibilities of a small-town pastor. The experience must have been positive for Tufts (though he later recalled that he was most impressed by the hardships experienced by the local wheat farmers), for he strongly considered returning to Yale to continue reading in philosophy of religion. The offer that summer from president James Angell, Sr., of the University of Michigan (through Angell's old friend Seelye at Amherst) to fill Dewey's former instructorship ended Tufts' commitment to divinity studies.

Around Christmas 1890, Harper informed Tufts that a new university would be established in Chicago and in the spring he offered the young philosopher an assistant professorship at $2,000 a year (Tufts was receiving $1,500 from Michigan). The offer prompted Tufts to travel to Germany for his doctorate, before returning in 1892 to take on his new responsibilities at the University of Chicago.[17]

[16] Tufts, "Autobiography."
[17] Ibid.

George Herbert Mead

To replace Tufts at Michigan, Dewey brought in George H. Mead, who by 1891 had moved from the hinterlands to a center of higher learning, Berlin, where he was struggling to finish his advanced degree. Mead's schooling went considerably less smoothly than Dewey's or Tufts's. One reason for Mead's difficulty may have been that he was subjected to a much more conservative version of the New England Theology than either of his future colleagues. Until he reached Harvard, where he studied with Josiah Royce and became a protégé of William James, Mead's university education was fraught with confrontation and disillusionment.

Like Tufts and Dewey, Mead too was a New England Congregationalist by birth and heritage. Born in South Hadley, Massachusetts, on February 27, 1863, George Mead was one of two children of Elizabeth Storrs and Hiram Mead. The granddaughter and sister of two prominent New England ministers, Mead's mother taught at Oberlin College and eventually served as president of Mount Holyoke during the first formative decade of its existence as a college. His father, a minister, graduated from Andover Seminary in the late 1850s and received a doctorate of Divinity at Middlebury College. The family moved to Ohio when Hiram Mead obtained a position as professor of sacred rhetoric at Oberlin Seminary in 1869. He went on to become a chief defender of Oberlin's perfectionist evangelicalism during the 1870s and 1880s and provided the major theoretical statement of Oberlin's "new creed," a moderate liberalization of orthodox Calvinism that incorporated few of the innovations (for example, higher criticism or German idealism) being introduced in eastern seminaries like Andover and Yale. Mead's parents brought him and his sister up in relatively strict adherence to evangelical codes, forbidding him even the pleasures of the theater and instilling a formidable distaste for all social "vices" that lasted well into his adulthood.[18]

Mead attended Oberlin's preparatory school until entering Oberlin College in fall 1879. Perfectly geared to his upbringing, Oberlin

[18] Mary Sumner Benson, "Elizabeth Storrs Billings Mead," in *Notable American Women, 1607–1950*, ed. Edward T. James et al. (Harvard, 1971), 519–20; Albert Temple Swing, *James Harris Fairchild; or Sixty-Eight Years with a Christian College* (New York, 1907), 279–320; Henry N. Castle to parents, March 30, 1883, Castle Papers.

provided an intellectual and social environment that Mead would later recall was confining, narrow-minded and culturally impoverished. Oberlin in the late 1870s and early 1880s had changed little from the days of revivalist president Charles Grandison Finney. Students lived and studied under a set of strict social and doctrinal rules, including early hours, gender segregation, required Bible study, mandatory services, and prohibitions on tobacco, gambling, dancing, and alcohol. The college maintained the Finneyite tradition of holding revivals every three or four years and weekly prayer meetings (led by the college president) in which students frequently experienced conversions.[19]

In philosophy instruction Oberlin was conservative. The presidency (1866–89) of James H. Fairchild brought a generally stated philosophical open-mindedness and reasserted the radical perfectionist tradition that made Oberlin an abolitionist center under Finney's direction. Fairchild nevertheless stayed well within the Calvinist orthodoxy. In philosophy classes he and his senior philosophy professor, John Ellis, upheld Trinitarian doctrine, often dogmatically arguing that the literal interpretation of Scripture and a belief in miracles were necessary for faith in God.[20]

Mead's most formative intellectual experience at Oberlin came out of his battles with Fairchild and Ellis over Calvinist dogma and its philosophical justifications. It was in the course of this "border warfare," as he later described it, that young Mead befriended Henry Northrup Castle, fellow student and philosophical dissident, whose friendship would be inseparable from Mead's struggle for philosophical and personal direction over the next eight years. The youngest son of Hawaiian missionaries and prominent sugar barons, Castle was a child of privilege whose erudition and social graces instilled in Mead feelings of admiration and inferiority that would dog their relationship until Castle's death at sea in January 1895. Their correspondence richly documents Mead's intellectual growth in the years before his coming to Chicago, spanning his rejection of Scottish or-

[19] Mead, "Recollections of Henry in Oberlin, and after," Afterword to *Letters* of Henry N. Castle (London, 1902), 809–11; Mead to H. N. Castle, March 16, 1884, and July 18, 1884, Mead Papers; John Barnard, *From Evangelicalism to Progressivism at Oberlin College, 1866–1917* (Columbus, 1969), 16–25.

[20] Barnard, *Evangelicalism to Progressivism*, 10–13.

thodoxy, his introduction to German idealism, and his enthusiasm for Dewey's philosophy in the 1890s.[21]

In their last years at Oberlin, Mead and Castle found themselves together in the same philosophy classes with the same aversion to the Scottish philosophy then used by Oberlin faculty to defend the faith. The Scots, and particularly their American interpreters, dominated philosophy in the American academy well into the postbellum era. Scottish realism in America was largely derivative and molded to the purposes of clerical apologetics. In the eighteenth century, Thomas Reid, Dugald Stewart, and other Scottish originals developed, from a starting point in Berkeley's criticism of Locke's nominalism, a sophisticated philosophy that to varying degrees adhered to a constructivist epistemology (mind provides the categories of knowing) and a realism concerning universals. Some Scottish philosophers, notably Sir William Hamilton, whose books appeared on most American philosophy curricula, drifted toward more explicitly idealist theories of knowledge based partly on Kant's transcendental metaphysics (and even Hegel in Hamilton's case) and partly on Berkeley's objective idealism. The American realists, such as Noah Porter or James McCosh, were a different matter: they have won reputations, for Scottish philosophy in general as well as for themselves, as unimaginative, banal thinkers. Whether that assessment is deserved or not, the teaching of Scottish theory in orthodox American academies lacked the innovation and depth of the originals. In the interest of defending the faith, the Americans promoted only those doctrines that would serve in the battle against epistemological and moral skepticism. They tended to deny Humean skepticism by simply asserting that the categories of knowledge (space and extension, for instance) by which mind constitutes phenomenal experience reflect an object world as it really (that is, independently of the perceiver) is. Despite owing a great deal to the idealist tradition via Hamilton, many American followers of Scottish realism strongly resisted the introduction of German ideas in the academy. This seemed to be the case at Oberlin, even though the midwestern center of Congregationalist evangelicalism had a far more liberal reputation than conservative bastions such as Princeton.[22]

---

[21] Helen Castle Mead, "A Few Recollections of Henry's Childhood," Introduction to *Letters* of Henry N. Castle. Henry Castle's family published his letters after his death.

[22] Flower and Murphey, *History of Philosophy*, vol. 1, chap. 4.

Mead and Castle had little access to any philosophical alternatives, save the German ideas that filtered through the writings of Porter and Hamilton or could be absorbed from English and German romantic poetry. A direct systematic study of Kant was impossible at Oberlin, where, besides the Scots and their American derivatives, students were exposed only to British empiricist psychology, Hamilton, Mill, Spencer and Darwin. Mead regarded this instruction (especially in the writing of McCosh and Porter) as a form of dogmatic clerical indoctrination. He and Castle, however, "had no higher criticism to rationalize Christianity" outside the teachings of the Scots and "knew personally of no profound moral life outside the dogma of the Church," Mead wrote twenty years later. "We saw the systems of the German Idealists gleaming like the fortunate isles in the unmeasured distance."[23]

The philosophical problems of religious faith continued to trouble Mead after Oberlin. In 1883 he taught school in Berlin Heights, Ohio, a difficult personal and vocational experience. Perhaps as a result of his personal insecurities, Mead developed an almost fanatical concern for the salvation of the community in which he lived. Berlin Heights, he wrote Castle in fall 1883, was "wholly given up to idolatry," spiritually dead, a town in which the minister could not "awake an appetite for a spiritual regimen among his sheep" because he lacked "emotional power." "Three saloons are in full working order," Mead complained, and the town boys, many of whom were in Mead's class, were "going to the devil with a vengeance." So Mead took on the task of "waking up the community to some spiritual life," by working with his students and the local minister. Christianity was for Mead not only the path to individual salvation but, in a classic perfectionist identification of spiritual with social rebirth, also the only viable mechanism for moral reform in a depraved society such as he believed he saw around him. Mead felt compelled to work among the ordinary and unregenerate, "the common people," and, although he saw himself as only a reluctant and unworthy candidate for the ministry, he believed that "there is nothing capable of reaching humanity save Christianity."[24]

---

[23] Mead, "Recollections of Henry," 810–11; H. N. Castle to family, May 24, 1882, Castle Papers; H. N. Castle to Carrie (sister), March 15, 1882, Castle Papers.

[24] Mead to H. N. Castle, October 7, 1883, and March 16, 1884, Mead Papers.

The regeneration of Berlin Heights, however, or even a mild revival of spirit, slipped beyond poor Mead's grasp. In March 1884, uncontrollable disciplinary problems (a few of Mead's most "sinful" charges apparently "thrashed" him), together with a precipitous drop in attendence, led the Berlin Heights school board to disband Mead's school, putting him out of his job and essentially throwing him out of the community. Despondent, Mead attributed his failure as a teacher to a lack of character, which he in turn associated with his inability to find spiritual conviction. He could not succeed "in the world," he wrote Castle that spring, because he was too "lazy, shiftless, characterless, forceless." Mead would have liked to enter the ministry, a calling he felt would especially please his recently widowed mother (Hiram Mead died in 1881), if only he had "settled beliefs," but he felt he was "wallowing in the depths of agnosticism," unable to rectify his faith through will or intellect. At best he could achieve a "sentimental" commitment to "the most unreasonable faith"; "like a poor feminine devotee I follow my feelings and not my beliefs. I can't tell you my boy what temptations of the most insidious and perplexing kind I have had to resist to keep from becoming a Christian with no reference to my reason but out of deference to my sensibilities, which seem to be clamoring for Christianity."[25]

Mead found his most serious inadequacies in his inability to rationalize his faith according to philosophical doctrines of the church and Oberlin. He traced his spiritual doubt to philosophical skepticism about the orthodoxy, to his inability to accept President Fairchild's rationalizations of the faith using Scottish realist and Spencerian assertions that our immediate knowledge of extended resistance indicated spiritual and material being. He questioned why this perception was any less subjective than one's perception of secondary qualities. Still insecure about his own grasp of the philosophical issues, he continued to blame his doubts on his own intellectual shortcomings.[26]

Although Mead found some emotional solace in prayer and revivalism, he took a perverse intellectual support from his first systematic reading of Kant, whose transcendental metaphysics he applied to the problems of knowledge and faith raised by orthodox doctrine. Read-

---

[25] Mead to H. N. Castle, March 7, 1884, March 12, 1884, March 16, 1884, [spring] 1884, Mead Papers.
[26] Mead to H. N. Castle, May 3, 1884, Mead Papers.

ing Kant directly rather than through the Scottish interpretations did little to restore Mead's spiritual condition, but it confirmed his dissatisfaction with the Oberlin orthodoxy. His still immature exploration of transcendental idealism aggravated his doubts about God's existence as it removed the philosophical confirmations of Trinitarian faith: the immediate perception of divinely ordered reality with the aid of the mental faculties. Mead as yet did not draw optimism from the romantic stress on mind's active role in the construction of knowledge. Undiluted Kantianism instead gave him a sense of futility about the inaccessibility of the noumenal realm, a feeling of solipsistic isolation:[27]

> A more resolutely subjective system than Kant's cannot be conceived.
> . . . It is the most depressing philosophy that I have met with, rendered more so by the constant claims he makes to have bounded all thought and have completely clipped the wings of errant apriorism. . . . There is something supremely depressing in establishing apriori truth[s] by proving them forms of thought and hence with nothing beyond oneself. This is the opponent of Hume's agnosticism.[28]

At the same time, Mead's residual adherence to a deterministic social philosophy, probably absorbed from the Spencer and Mill he had read at Oberlin, reinforced his personal and philosophical confusion, his despair of spiritually uplifting the people around him, and his sense of futility over his personal fortunes. He felt entirely without agency, pushed and pulled by social forces that led him to a miserable and unfulfilling life of unrealized potential. Thus he saw his life disappearing beneath the sands of Australia, the most desolate continent he could imagine.[29]

In April 1884, Mead took a job surveying for the Wisconsin Central Railroad in eastern Minnesota. His spirits barely improved and, although the physical labor eventually may have helped him pull out of his deepest depression and self-doubt, he complained to Castle about living conditions in the surveying camps, his inability to study, and his fellow workers, who were given to all the social vices Mead had tried to purge from the Berlin Heights community. Mead surveyed

[27] Mead to H. N. Castle, April 23, 1884, and May 16, 1884, Mead Papers.
[28] Mead to H. N. Castle, August 16, 1884, see also September 14, 1884, Mead Papers.
[29] Mead to H. N. Castle, February 8, 1885, Mead Papers.

for the railroads through fall 1884, all the while corresponding with Castle about the sporadic reading of German philosophy he managed in the camps. That winter Mead moved to Minneapolis, where he supported himself by tutoring local students in preparation for Oberlin. During the next two years he dreamed of starting a Latin school in Minneapolis with Castle (to be underwritten by Castle's wealth) and of procuring a position for Castle teaching philosophy at the University of Minnesota.[30]

But Mead felt himself stagnating intellectually and he aspired to study in Germany, an unlikely prospect given his financial straits. His first definite plan for his own future, to study philosophy at Harvard, came under the encouragement of Castle, who had begun Harvard Law School in fall 1886. After visiting in Cambridge that winter, Mead struggled to collect enough money for tuition and living expenses. Castle suggested rooming together and offered to pay Mead's rent. That summer Mead frantically tried to catch up in philosophy and improve his command of German, hoping to register for Josiah Royce's course on Kant in the fall 1887 semester. By August he had obtained a loan from a family friend and the vague promise of tutorials in Cambridge. It was none too soon. As Castle wrote his sisters, Mead had gotten nowhere in his three years out of school: "My feeling has passed utterly away from objects which his still glorifies, and in philosophy he has had to stand still." "Ye Gods and little fishes," Mead wrote his friend, "what a dry sterile time I have had of it during this and last year."[31]

Mead could read German only well enough to audit Royce's seminar and, because Oberlin's curriculum was limited, he was forced to complete another year of undergraduate work at Harvard. Nevertheless, he spent an entirely successful year there, taking full advantage of Cambridge philosophy's "golden age." During his first semester, besides sitting in on Royce's seminar, Mead studied ethics with George Herbert Palmer and Spencer and Spinoza with Royce. Of Mead's

[30] Mead to H. N. Castle, April 23, 1884, May 3, 1884, December 14, 1884, January 31, 1885, February 8, 1885, October 29, 1885, November 30, 1885, February 28, 1886, and June 16, 1886, Mead Papers. At the time, the behavior of his fellow workers convinced Mead of humans' inability to rise above animal impulse. Their drinking, swearing, violence, and patronizing of prostitutes, he decided, contradicted the Tolstoyan faith in the common man; see Mead to H. N. Castle, April 23, May 3 and 16, and July 18, 1884, Mead Papers.
[31] H. N. Castle to sisters, January 9, 1887, Castle Papers; Mead to H. N. Castle, August 28 and 31, 1887, Mead Papers.

professors, Royce probably influenced the younger scholar the most. Two years earlier Royce had published *The Religious Aspect of Philosophy,* in which he presented a voluntaristic idealism indebted to Kant and Berkeley. In the book Royce wrestled with problems raised by his phenomenological version of the Kantian theory of apperception: there is no thing-in-itself, Royce argued, only what is given to consciousness in present experience and what the mind brings to the present as signs of past experience and future possibility. This was a thoroughgoing idealism in which ideas constituted the totality of experience. Royce's problem arose over the correspondence between ideas and some sort of "reality" that could provide the ground for objective truth and the basis for distinguishing truth from error. As a solution, Royce turned to absolute idealism: ideas are incomplete versions of a larger, timeless idea, an absolute that validates and verifies present conceptions, including perceptions of what is "out there." An individual, determined by what he knows, is, then, an incomplete part of the absolute self, or God. Science, in Royce's view, is our conception of the absolute as manifest in the finite world, in time.[32]

By his own account Mead was impressed with Royce's talent for philosophical argumentation and his command of logic. Aspects of Royce's idealism can also be seen in Mead's later work (particularly in his theory of the social self) and collaborations with Dewey at the University of Michigan. Mead, however, did not have much opportunity to absorb directly the wisdom of America's foremost absolute idealist, for he would spend only one year in Cambridge. In the spring, Mead's performance in his honors exams so impressed his professors that William James personally asked him to tutor the James children in New Hampshire that summer. Although the department offered him a scholarship for the following year, it was not as much as Mead expected. And although James offered to loan Mead money and arrange journal reviews, Mead decided that the fall would be a good time to travel to Germany. By October he was settled in Leipzig.[33]

Mead remained in Germany three years, while Castle shuttled back and forth between the family business and newspaper editing in Ha-

[32] Bruce Kuklick, *The Rise of American Philosophy: Cambridge, Massachusetts, 1860–1930* (New Haven, 1977), 150–58; Josiah Royce, *The Religious Aspect of Philosophy,* (Gloucester, Mass., 1965), chap. 11.

[33] Mead to H. N. Castle, July 18, 1888, Mead Papers.

waii, law school in Cambridge, and study in Berlin. Mead had not yet undertaken work on his dissertation when Dewey offered him Tufts's post in summer 1891. Mead planned to stay in Berlin to finish his thesis, "a criticism from a Kantian or a least metaphysical standpoint of the sensational doctrine of space," and return for his orals in the spring. The University of Michigan let him stay until November, though by that time he still had not finished his dissertation, which was never completed. Before leaving, he married Castle's older sister, Helen, who had been her brother's regular companion at Oberlin and in Berlin.[34]

[34] G. H. Mead to H. N. Castle, October 20, 1891, and July 22, 1891, Mead papers; Dewey to Alice C. Dewey, June 23, 1894, Dewey Papers.

CHAPTER THREE

The Psychological Standpoint

Ann Arbor was still a quiet midwestern town when Mead arrived for his new position at the University of Michigan in fall 1891. Visiting in spring 1893, his friend Henry Castle found it "one of the loveliest villages," with "all the streets pretty, up hill and down, fine lawns, old trees, and all about the undulating meadows and pasture, and forest."[1] Despite this bucolic setting, the University of Michigan was far from provincial, eschewing religious sectarianism and introducing coeducation at an early date. The largest midwestern university of its day, Michigan grew nearly twofold between 1885 and 1895. Under the presidency of James Angell, it reflected the most advanced trends in educational reform. Like the many university reformers of his generation, Angell aimed for a more democratic, open institution that diminished class differences among students, eliminated privileged social organizations, and responded to the broader public. Though seldom successful in achieving these goals, Angell made the university and the philosophy department extremely comfortable for Dewey and his new colleagues, encouraging cooperation between faculty members and fostering a democratic atmosphere in which dissent and unconventionality were possible. Angell yet more successfully re-

---

[1] Henry N. Castle to parents, June 10, 1893, *Letters of Henry N. Castle* (London, 1902), 730. The original Castle letters, including many not published in the 1902 volume, are available in the Henry N. Castle collection, Regenstein Library, University of Chicago.

structured teaching and the curriculum around the new utilitarian
ideal of public service that guided university reform in the 1870s and
1880s, responding to social and student demands for expertise, practical vocational training, and intellectual tools more appropriate to
modern industrial life than those provided by the dogmatic provin-
cialism of the old denominational college system. Following the lead
of Charles William Eliot of Harvard and Andrew Dickson White of
Cornell, Angell relaxed entrance requirements, introduced a modified
elective system, removed a required curriculum stressing the classics
and ancient languages, and encouraged professorial experimentation.[2]

The atmosphere at Michigan gave Dewey some latitude in broad-
ening and redirecting philosophical studies. Arriving in 1889, Tufts
found the Ann Arbor department—determined by a triangle of "theological interpretation," British empiricism, and German idealism—
congenial to his way of thinking. By then under Dewey's leadership,
Ann Arbor philosophy took a critical direction that incorporated
evolutionism and the new physiological psychology yet did not diverge
from the fundamental tenets of late nineteenth-century idealism. Without having studied any but "apologetic" psychology, Tufts himself
took on two sections in that subject in his first year, indicating the
extent to which experimental psychology coexisted with more ethereal
studies.[3] When Mead replaced Tufts in 1891, Dewey was still enthusiastically engrossed in the reconstruction and defense of philosophical
idealism. The intellectual atmosphere in philosophy under Dewey
resonated with Mead's own theoretical and political interests in weld-
ing idealist and theistic metaphysics to social reform and laboratory
study. There were "some surprising bits of American speculation
springing up about here," he wrote Castle that winter.[4]

Dewey's work during this period had two main objectives. He first
hoped to present a convincing critique of associationist epistemology
and psychology, with all its religious and ethical implications. He also
wanted to revise existing idealist theory to enable it to withstand the

---

[2] Thomas McIntyre Cooley, *Michigan: A History of Governments* (Boston, 1888), 310–
13, 325–26; Laurence Veysey, *The Emergence of the American University* (Chicago, 1970),
57–68, 291–92. On departmental lifestyle, see H. N. Castle to parents, June 10, 1893,
Castle Papers.

[3] George Dykhuizen, *The Life and Mind of John Dewey* (Carbondale, 1973), 45–46;
James H. Tufts, "Autobiography," in Tufts Papers, Chicago. Tufts used Dewey's recently
published text (he found it "fortunately" not so "modern").

[4] Mead to H. N. Castle, December 19, 1891, Mead Papers.

encroaching popularity of associationist psychology, Darwinian evolutionism, and utilitarian ethics. Despite the American sources of Dewey's theological concerns and the fact that both of these objectives served Dewey's role as an apologist for religious liberalism, much of his discussion echoed British debate, especially the work of British idealists Thomas Hill Green and F. H. Bradley.

By the late 1880s, idealism had triumphed in British academic philosophy, not to be dislodged until well into the twentieth century. According to the idealist version of this history, empiricism had dominated the philosophical discourse through the middle part of the century. It was not until the ascension of a new generation to posts in a reformed British academy that empiricist hegemony faltered. The leading figure in this triumph of idealism was Green, professor of moral philosophy at Oxford University. For Green the main shortcoming of British philosophy had been its reliance on a mechanistic individualism derived from the empirical sciences and the psychology of John Locke, at the unnecessary expense of absolute spirit and without adequate consideration of critical continental philosophy. Green's main targets in this reappraisal were associationist psychology and utilitarian ethics.[5]

Initially formulated by David Hume and David Hartley, associationism soon became a model of psychological simplicity (and simplification). As a refinement of Locke's Newtonian psychology, associationism inherited and intensified the individualistic tendency of British philosophy since Locke, which reduced philosophical and psychological issues to matters of individual experience. Hume and his followers were determined to eliminate from psychology all mental states that could not be confirmed directly in experience, by reducing them to sensory impressions. There exist no mind, no innate ideas, no independently constituted objects whose existence can only be intuited or deduced. Associationists argued that all complex ideas or concepts, all complex relations, including causality, are built out of simple sensory impressions through the laws of association, which do no more than describe consistent patterns by which sensory impressions tend to cluster together. For Hartley, the laws of association

[5] On Green, see Melvin Richter, *The Politics of Conscience: T. H. Green and His Age* (Cambridge, Mass., 1964), chap. 6. Green's critique of utilitarianism is found in Thomas Hill Green, *Prolegomena to Ethics* (1883; rpt. New York, 1969), pt. 3, chaps. 1–2.

boiled down to one, the law of contiguity in time. In the case of causal relations, we know that one event is the cause of another by the regularity with which the first event, for instance a lightning strike, is followed by the second event, thunder.

To idealists, associationism suffered many philosophical flaws, particularly an inability to explain human capacities necessary for the constitution of a coherent experience. Causality does not reduce completely to contiguity, idealists argued, for we understand implicitly that the relation between a cause and its effect is intrinsic, not simply a matter of coincidence. Distinctions between real and imagined objects, to use another important example, are hard to explain without reference to more complex relational concepts (for example, selfhood) that do not reduce to laws of association.

By the time of the triumph of Oxford idealism in the 1880s, however, the lines of dispute were not so clearly drawn. Britain's leading associationist, Alexander Bain, had conceded much to the idealists, allowing for a more consistent unity of consciousness, for the role of agency in the formation of experience, for mental anticipation of possible responses, and for belief as preparatory to action. This stance led later critics to declare Bain the immediate ancestor of American pragmatism. Bain, however, only qualified an associational framework in which individual consciousness was still constructed out of sensory elements. He continued to defend associationism, partly on philosophical grounds, partly by linking it to emerging neurophysiological studies that reduced human psychology to the interplay between sensory stimulus and behavioral response.[6]

For their part, few idealists abandoned associationist terms altogether in analyzing human perception. Britain's leading idealist psychologist, James Ward, championed physiological psychology almost as enthusiastically as Bain. Instead, Green, Ward, and Bradley argued that active phases of behavior such as attention and discrimination were far more significant in the formation of consciousness and experience, representing the presence of spiritual and mental elements the associationists disavowed. Full agreement on these issues was,

---

[6] On Bain and the rise of sensory-motor models, see Robert M. Young, *Mind, Brain, and Adaptation in Nineteenth Century: Cerebral Localization and Its Biological Context from Gall to Ferrier* (Oxford, 1970), chap. 3.

however, rare, even in the idealist camp. At best one can say that most idealists (following Green's lead) disputed associationism as part of a more comprehensive critique of materialist philosophies, especially the reductionist evolutionism of Herbert Spencer and the use of associationist principles by British radicals such as Jeremy Bentham and John Stuart Mill as the psychological foundation for utilitarian ethics.[7]

Dewey picked up the British idealist attack, with what he considered an important adjustment. For him, Bain's strength was the affinity he drew between associationist principles and the neurophysiological models of human behavior emerging in the new discourse of experimental psychology. Unlike his idealist counterparts, Bain (whom Dewey labeled a "subjective idealist") rested the conclusions of philosophy increasingly on experimental science. Despite the reductionist implications of much of the physiological literature, Dewey drifted toward this position during the 1880s. In many respects his work paralleled Ward's influential efforts to incorporate physiological psychology into the idealist framework. Both Ward and Dewey agreed that discoveries by anatomists, physiologists, and physiological psychologists, even if they implied that behavior corresponded to neurological function and structure, did not necessarily controvert idealist assumptions about the nature of man and spirit. But Ward, more cautious than Dewey, still separated philosophy and the conclusions of speculative and logical inquiry from psychology and the findings of laboratory science. Dewey argued that this division was unnecessary and dangerous: in an age of science and evolutionary paradigms, one could and must demonstrate idealist principles in the study of observable behavior. But this was not merely a matter of academic prudence. A true idealist psychology, Dewey argued, was additionally necessary to correct for the principle shortcoming of existing idealism,

[7] See, for example, F. H. Bradley, "Association and Thought," *Mind* 12 (1887): 354–56. Bradley and Ward expressed their differences in 1886 and 1887 issues of the British journal *Mind*. Despite the commitment of utilitarians to social reform, idealists connected associationist and utilitarian individualism to the erosion of communitarian values in modern society, the substitution of market relations for traditional customs, the intrusion of technological development into community life, and the replacement of traditional relations of economic production by the factory system. This kind of comprehensive critique was favored by Green, who viewed social ethics as a psychological issue and psychology as derived from metaphysics. See Richter, *Politics of Conscience*, chaps. 6–8.

the tendency to *assume* extra-experiential mental and spiritual entities without demonstrating their presence through the psychological study of experiential phenomena.[8]

Thus, British idealists and associationists alike failed to take the "psychological standpoint," which in Dewey's way of thinking was the true idealism and the best psychology. From the psychological standpoint, Dewey believed, the discipline of psychology served simultaneously as an empirical science, a study of verifiable phenomena, and a moral science, a method by which to analyze spiritual truths. This standpoint allowed an alternative, genetic explanation of the categories of understanding, which exploited the new psychology to produce a more thoroughgoing, according to Dewey *truly* Hegelian, case for spiritual immanence than the strictly "philosophical" idealists, the neo-Kantians and neo-Hegelians like Green.

The New Psychology

The "new psychology" adopted by Dewey and his contemporaries emerged during the 1870s in the medical and university laboratories of Europe. Drawing on advances in physical anthropology, evolutionary theory, brain physiology, and anatomy, pioneers such as Wilhelm Wundt in Germany began to study patterns of human reaction, perception, and cognition by means of laboratory experiments that divided human capacities into measurable events. Although Wundt and his followers did not abandon traditional philosophical conceptions of mind, they established scientific practices and discourses closely tied to an evolutionary perspective on brain functioning. When American students of the new physiological psychology such as G. Stanley Hall and William James opened similar laboratories in the United States, they stressed (though by no means exclusively) the role of cognition in biological adaptation.[9] An evolutionary understanding of mind, however, did not preclude philosophical idealism, as Dewey's work during the 1880s and 1890s made readily apparent: one might

---

[8] Dewey, "The Psychological Standpoint" (January 1886), *Early Works* 1:136–37.
[9] Edwin G. Boring, *A History of Experimental Psychology* (New York, 1950), chap. 21; Robert Brett, *History of Psychology*, ed. R. S. Peters (Cambridge, Mass., 1967), 504–14, 584–91; on the contribution of British physiology, see Young, *Mind, Brain*, chaps. 5–6.

situate mind in a biological framework and still regard measurable mental and behavioral events as manifestations of spiritual truths.

This integration of the new physiological psychology with neo-Hegelian theories of mind most impressed Mead when he arrived in Ann Arbor: "I have at last reached a position I used to dream of in Harvard—where it is possible at least to apply good straight phys. psy. to Hegel and I don't know what more a mortal can want on this earth." Dewey apparently had demonstrated, to Mead's satisfaction, that mind could be read into the total functioning of the body and into all aspects of human behavior. "You will see what a new thing Phys. Psy. becomes," Mead wrote Castle, "when one sees that thinking represents the activities of the organs of the body and not molecular processes of the brain except in so far as these are part of those."[10] Impressed as much by the religious implications of Dewey's theory as anything else, Mead considered Dewey's conception of immanent spirit no less than "a great universe-formula" that applied to music, psychology, and theology as well as it did to the acquisition of arithemetic concepts. The circle of consciousness "goes around again 3 times I believe," Mead wrote Castle, sweeping through higher levels of knowledge on each revolution, from "undetermined consciousness" through consciousness, until achieving "universe as subject-object."[11]

Physiological psychology in fact had, according to Dewey, "revealed no new truth concerning the relations of soul and body." First, physiological studies showed that mind resides not only in the central nervous system but in the periphery as well. Experiments in which decapitated frogs continued to respond to stimuli demonstrated that "the psychical is *homogenously* related to the physiological." We "think" with our entire body, claimed Dewey; "the soul is, through the nerves, present to all the body. This means the psychical is immanent in the physical." The same physiological experiments demonstrated Dewey's second point. Decapitated frogs responded to stimuli not with arbitrary movement but with purposive action, showing that behavior, even when not controlled by the central nervous system, is teleological. All nervous activity and therefore all behavior, Dewey contended, is a process of adjustment to conditions, a "recip-

---

[10] Mead to H. N. Castle, December 1, 1892, and June 10, 1892, Mead Papers.
[11] Mead to H. N. Castle, December 27, 1891, Mead Papers.

rocal function of stimuli, excitation, and inhibition, control through repression." Thus, soul is not just immanent in body. It is "teleologically immanent."[12]

Dewey did not mean that mind or soul is identical with body or experience. In 1886, while still George S. Morris's assistant, Dewey considered body merely the "organ" of the soul, its "outward form and living manifestation." The soul is immanent in body insofar as its purposes are realized in it, but, because the soul through its "informing, creating activity" controls body, it is greater than body and therefore transcends it.[13] Thus, from the psychological standpoint Dewey viewed a strictly theistic universe, in which the events of experience unfolded from the worldly manifestation of spirit. "The individual consciousness," he wrote in 1886, "is but the process of realization of the universal consciousness through itself." To be consistent, idealists must recognize that an absolute subject, spirit, creates individual self-consiousness and conscious experience, as well as the "material" world contained therein, as an act of self-expression.[14]

In principle, Dewey believed that spirit transcends experience as something more complete and harmonious. During the 1880s, however, he sought to mediate between existing forms of absolute idealism on the one hand and empiricism on the other. He argued that spirit can be known only through experience and only *as* it is manifested in experience, in time and space: "Is the absolute self-consciousness complete in itself, or does it involve this realization and manifestation in a being like man?... For man as object of his philosophy, this Absolute has existence only so far as it has manifested itself in his conscious experience."[15] This was still the idealism of Green, who found its defense difficult without a notion of a personalistic deity "out there."

Later, by 1890, Dewey's earlier qualms about British idealists expanded into a full-blown criticism of Green and a crusade against

---

[12] Dewey, "Soul and Body" (April 1886), *Early Works* 1:96, 98.

[13] Ibid., 112–13.

[14] Dewey, "Psychological Standpoint," 142. Mead described Dewey's hypothesis more boldly and in more extravagantly Hegelian terms than Dewey himself was willing to commit to paper. "All thinking," Mead wrote Castle in explaining the Deweyan theory, is "the process of thinking things as at the same time the same and the same time different—a process capable of unlimited complexity and systemization"; Mead to H. N. Castle, December 19 and 27, 1891, Mead Papers.

[15] Dewey, "Psychology as Philosophic Method" (April 1886), *Early Works* 1:157.

what Dewey considered the "false Hegelianism" of the British school. Green, Dewey maintained, held onto an illusory, extra-experiential, transcendent notion of the absolute, quite out of keeping with Hegel's real, experiential, and immanent spirit: "The movement from the world to mind, and from both to God," rather than being a "regress," a process of abstraction, "is a movement from the partial to the complete, from the abstract to the concrete, in which the lower becomes a factor in the spiritual process of the higher." This is, in fact, the process of knowledge and of philosophy. We can know the absolute, come to self-consciousness, only through this process, the most significant stage of which is the awareness, confirmed by evolutionary theory and by Hegelianism, that the process exists.[16] The absolute is manifested only in consciousness as the individual's self-conscious awareness of the absolute, through religion, through personal spiritual and practical self-development, and through the scientific confirmation of evolutionary progress.

Striving for consistency in his immanent metaphysics, Dewey dismissed many earlier idealist theories such as Green's as dualistic, dealing in separate realms of existence that had no clear relation to each other. Kantian dualism (and the dualism of all those who did not radically recast the relations among self-consciousness, the categories, and experience) led to skepticism, as Mead understood in a rudimentary way while reading Kant in the backwoods of Minnesota. Kantian metaphysics, with its abstract notion of understanding and unfathomable spirit, implied the separation of science, the study of experience, of events occurring in time and space, from religion and ethics, the studies of absolute truths, of the unchanging moral content of knowledge and of the spiritual in humanity. Kant subverted faith by isolating it from science, that is, from legitimate, verifiable knowledge. Dewey thus meant to save religion from being eroded by scientific materialism *and* from the misconceptions of idealist philosophy (such as Green's "Kanto-Fichteanism") which allowed the erosion to take place.[17]

For Dewey psychological method enabled philosophy to study mind and being properly, by examining the nature of experience, within

[16] Dewey, review of Edward Caird's *The Critical Philosophy of Immanuel Kant* (March 1890), *Early Works* 3:182.
[17] Ibid., 183.

which ideas, objects, subject, universals, and so on, the "things" philosophy studies, are found. From the psychological standpoint one sees that "nothing shall be admitted into philosophy which does not show itself in experience, and its nature, that is, its place in experience shall be fixed by an account of the process of knowledge—by Psychology." Psychology functioned in Dewey's thinking as the developmental analysis of experience and its phenomena, a methodological position taken on the assumption that experience comprised the sum total of all that is real and knowable. Since the content of experience was at the same time essentially spiritual, constructed by mind, psychology, even physiological psychology, was thus an idealist enterprise—in fact, the true Hegelianism and the true idealism.[18]

Idealist Psychology

To demonstrate the superiority of the psychological standpoint, Dewey wrote *Psychology,* published in 1886. This work is considered by some the first American textbook in the new psychology, preceding George Ladd's *Elements of Physiological Psychology* by a few months and William James's *Principles of Psychology* by four years. Although he devoted a large part of the book to experimental method, Dewey really conquered no new methodological territory. He introduced no new techniques, resolved none of the multitudinous technical disputes then raging in experimental circles, and, according to Hall, confused a good deal of the data and methods that Hall and others had discovered in the laboratory.[19]

Dewey's *Psychology* did, however, break some conceptual ground. Although Dewey used many terms from British empiricism, he nevertheless subordinated the laws of association to the idealist framework. The principles guiding Dewey's synthesis were the immanence of teleology in the central nervous system and the involvement of active, constructive mind in all facets of experience. As in earlier articles, he

[18] Dewey, "Psychological Standpoint," 124, 142.

[19] The date of publication is 1887, but the book appeared a year earlier; "A Note on the Text," *Early Works* 2:xlix–liv; J. C. Flugel, *A Hundred Years of Psychology, 1833–1963* (New York, 1964), 127. Characterizing the 1886 text as new psychology is not acceptable in all accounts of Dewey's intellectual development; see, for example, Herbert Schneider's "Introduction" in *Early Works* 2:viii; G. Stanley Hall, review of *Psychology,* in *American Journal of Psychology* 2 (1887): 157.

tried to unite physiology and psychology without simply drawing a parallel between the laws of association and neurological mechanisms. This effort, derivative in parts but unique in its synthesis, was considered bold and problematic in Great Britain and the United States.[20]

Dewey's immediate objective, parallel to his effort to link the speculative idealist's study to the physiological psychology laboratory, was to demonstrate the necessary connection between knowledge and feeling. The unifying principle, he argued, was the will, the essentially active and purposive quality of all knowing.

Dewey devoted a large part of the text to demonstrating the essential role at all levels of experience played by inner reflection, or "apperception," a concept that would be central, under various guises, in later Deweyan psychology. Idealists proposed apperception as an alternative to the laws of association and the skepticism of Hume. Kant responded to Hume by arguing that mind constructs perceived experience by applying categories of understanding to sense data. Kant's perceiving subject intuits those categories prior to experience by apperception, a form of inward reflection (rather than outward, on the senses) that includes an intuition of the self as perceiver. Post-Kantian idealist psychologists and philosophers (for example, Green) shared Kant's argument that the continuities of experience and of self depend on the continuity of consciousness provided by some sort of apperception. Subsequent debates within the idealist camp revolved around the inner source and nature of this cognitive continuity, that is, around the Kantian notion that the categories of apperception are transcendental, that they exist outside the individual's experience and may only be intuited a priori. Kant's conception of the self or subject also perplexed later critics, especially Dewey.[21]

Kant distinguished sharply between the intuited understanding of the transcendental categories and perceptual or experiential knowledge. Hegelians such as Dewey argued that the process of knowing itself constitutes the subject of knowledge (the self), its categories of understanding, and its objects. The philosopher is responsible for examining the history of that process, on what Dewey called a psychological level, but also on the level of the history of ideas and

---

[20] George Croom Robertson, review of *Psychology, Mind* 12 (1887): 439–43.
[21] Dewey dealt with the problem in "On Some Current Conceptions of the Term 'Self' " (January 1890), *Early Works* 3:56–74.

culture, the hallmark of Hegelian idealism and an important pursuit of the Chicago philosophers during the next century.

Although Dewey was a Hegelian, he also borrowed from other writers in the idealist tradition, particularly in psychology and pedagogy. In his psychological revisions of Kant, he owed much to Johann Friedrich Herbart, one of the many claimants to the mantle of neo-Kantianism, who eroded Kant's ontological distinction between experiential perception and intuitive apperception. Arguing that apperception must entail something more than intuitive knowledge of the transcendental categories, Herbart modified Kant in three ways. First, he temporalized apperception, making it the cumulative formation of a bulk of interrelated ideas and memories, similar to what later psychologists would call habits. Second, while still maintaining some distinction between apperception and perception, Herbart made the "apperceptive mass," as he called the individual's mental predisposition, a product of perception. New perceptions added to the apperceptive mass, depending on the affinity of those perceptions to given collections of ideas (which, as in Locke, included both perceptual presentations and the representations of earlier perceptions), in a manner similar to that described by associationists. But, third, unlike associationists, Herbart made ideas inherently active. Each idea had an intrinsic force through which it imposed itself on the apperceptive mass and, when accepted, contributed to the character of that inner disposition. The relations could be mathematically calculated, Herbart argued, submitting the idealist analysis of cognition (and ethics) to an unparalleled scientific rigor.[22]

Herbart's alternative version of apperception was challenged on several grounds by later idealists, notably Hermann Lotze in Germany and Green, Ward, and Bradley in Great Britain. Like Herbart, they considered mind a continuous totality. All objected, however, to Herbart's rigidly mathematical calculation of the apperceptive process. Lotze argued that mind actively responds to the qualities of perceptions; it is not the sum of a quantifiable perceptual force (Herbart's mass of ideas). For the British Hegelians as for Lotze, the continuity of consciousness is provided by the purpose guiding the individual's

---

[22] Brett, *History of Psychology*, 551–54, 558, 561; Flugel, *Hundred Years*, 16, 19; Johann Friedrich Herbart, *A Textbook in Psychology* (1891; rpt. Washington, D. C., 1977); Robert Ulich, "Apperception," in *Encyclopedia of Philosophy* (New York, 1967), 138–.40.

activity, not merely by the habits of mind governed by the apperceptive mass. They argued that each idea presented to mind, from the sensory manifold or by recollection, has a feeling attached, determined by the idea's value to the individual's well-being. The notion of well-being, however, presumes an entity that precedes conscious existence or is coterminous with it but somehow separate. Lotze thus argued that one must assume the existence of a soul to explain the mind's constructive powers and the phenomena of experience, a position shared by Green and initially adopted by Dewey. In England, both Bradley and Ward characterized thinking as an activity integrated into activity in general and stressed the role of attention in perception and cognition. Both positions became a fundamental part of Dewey's functionalism.[23]

Dewey hoped to insert an idealist notion of apperception into the framework of modern psychology. He believed that the New Psychology had not moved from the fundamental truth that telos guides all action and thought, even though psychologists claimed to be more scientific. Like most idealists since Kant, however, Dewey wanted to move away from transcendental idealism's heavy reliance on the logical categories Kant deduced as prerequisites of intelligible experience. Not only was intuitive knowledge of the categories mysterious and unexplained, but the outer, noumenal world was perpetually distanced from the mind. The objective ground of experience for Kant lay entirely beyond actual experience. Moreover, Kant's rationalism became less convincing as psychology demonstrated that irrational impulses, as much as logic or a priori synthetic categories, governed the constructive habits of mind.

Dewey defined apperception much as the Herbartians did, although he rejected Herbart's mathematical pretensions and dramatically simplified the concept's formulation. The phenomena of experience, ar-

---

[23] Hermann Lotze, *Outlines of Psychology* (1886; rpt. Washington, D. C., 1977), 34, 46, 106, 108, 118, 122–24, and *Microcosmus*, 2 vols. (1885; rpt. Freeport, N.Y., 1971), 1:293; Brett, *History of Psychology*, 595, 597, 600; James Ward, "Psychological Principles, I," *Mind* 7 (April 1883): 153–69, and "Psychological Principles, II," *Mind* 7 (October 1883): 465–86; F. H. Bradley, "Is There Any Special Activity of Attention?" *Mind* 9 (July 1886): 305–23. Bradley and Ward often disagreed, especially on the nature of the self and the relation of attention to other elements of consciousness; see Ward, "Mr. F. H. Bradley's Analysis of Mind," *Mind* 12 (1887): 565–75. On the mutual influence between Bradley and Dewey as "functional left wing Hegelian[s]," see John Hermann Randall, Jr., "F. H. Bradley and the Working-out of Absolute Idealism," *Journal of the History of Philosophy* 5 (1967): 245–54.

gued Dewey, are the product of "the reaction of mind by means of its organized structure upon the sensuous material presented to it." Apperception, together with its opposite, what Dewey called "retention" ("the reaction of the apperceived content upon the organized structure of the mind"), governs all the activities of mind. Within the apperceptive process, Dewey argued, association, dissociation, and attention occur, the primary constructive processes of the apperceiving consciousness.[24]

For Dewey this meant association originates in a "fusion" or "integration" of all presented sense data, against which all subsequent experience is compared. As in earlier idealisms, association "never leaves sensuous elements isolated but connects them into larger wholes," or "redintegrates" them. "Redintegration," a term borrowed from the Scottish idealist Sir William Hamilton, was for Dewey the comparison of new percepts with the already existing cognitive whole. This aspect of association brought a present element in relation to past elements, thereby calling up the total "act of cognition," as Hamilton put it, of which the present element was once a part (for example, the percept "red" recalls "red ball"). Association, therefore, in the form of redintegration, drastically differed from what one would find in the associationism of J. S. Mill or Bain. Redintegration was the connection of part to whole rather than element to element, and that whole was an act. Association does not create a "mechanical mosaic," argued Dewey. What it "gives us . . . is not a loosely connected aggregate of separable parts, but a new total experience."[25]

For sense "elements" to be added into the apperceptive whole, they must at the same time be differentiated from the chaotic multitude of sense stimuli. Like his fellow idealists Dewey emphasized the selective powers of mind. Integration, which could be confused with the passive aggregation of ideas, implied redintegration, which required active selectivity. Mind found not only similarities of present elements with the past but incongruities that had to be assimilated to the "apperceiving activity" of consciousness and to which mind must adjust.

It was in the process of dissociation, which Dewey would incor-

---

[24] Dewey, *Psychology, Early Works* 2:83, 78, and "Knowledge as Idealization" (July 1887), *Early Works* 1:190.

[25] Sir William Hamilton, *Lectures on Metaphysics and Logic*, 4 vols. (Edinburgh, 1861) 2:238; Dewey, *Psychology*, 85–88.

porate into his later functionalism in the concepts "interest" and "doubt," that the active powers of mind were most evident. Following Ward and Bradley, he considered dissociation "more complex and less passive than association." The mind, Dewey argued, finds certain percepts (like Bradley and Ward he called them "presentations") incongruous with the total cognitive activity. The incongruity reflects the value that particular presentation has for "mental life." This value constitutes the "interest" that sensory or perceptual events have for the "self," the individual's organically integrated activity. "To say that a present experience is connected with a past," wrote Dewey, "is to say that it is related to the *self* in a definite way, and this relation to self is what we mean by interest." Interest can be "natural" in origin, for example, concerning certain inherently agreeable "organic sensations" such as the satisfaction of hunger and thirst.[26] These natural values then form the basis for "acquired" interests, which are determined by the individual's past experience. In fact, interest in this biological sense governs all experience.

The concepts of apperception, attention, and interest that Dewey inherited from Herbart and the Oxford idealists became the basis for a revised notion of the self and self-realization strikingly similar to his later concepts (after 1894), despite persistent reliance (in 1886) on idealist notions of absolute spirit. Like Green, Dewey found it hard, at least until the early 1890s, to conceive of a goal-directed activity that did not imply the existence of a soul, but he had no trouble reconciling that belief with his own conviction that mind's origins are biological. The "self," as Dewey defined it, was a spiritual entity but also a biologically based, organically structured activity: "Through its activity the soul is." The telos or purposive activity Dewey discovered at even the most primitive levels of cognition involved a "selective activity of intelligence" which, when speaking of the self's goals, Dewey addressed as the activity of "attention." If dissociation and interest referred to past experience, attention, which "has always an end in view," referred to a future goal, "some end which the mind has in view, some difficulty to be cleared up, some problem to be solved, some idea to be gained, or plan to be formed." Mind selects only those elements that are significant, signs of some-

---

[26] Dewey, *Psychology*, 107–10.

thing beyond themselves, beyond the immediate present. Otherwise sensations do not enter into our knowledge.[27]

Signification involves representation not of objects in the Lockean sense or of noumena in the Kantian sense but of past and future experience through ideas provided by mind, which Dewey called "idealization." All knowledge, then, is self-knowledge, in the dual sense that the mind constructs its reality and that the ideas formed in cognition refer to some past or future condition of the self. The goals of knowledge, and of all "self-activity," are equally self-referential: first, self-realization, the self's "ultimate unity" which is both "perfectly harmonious" and internally complex; second, God, the self in its most universal form of "perfectly realized intelligence."[28]

Feeling and Will: A Model of Action

Embedded within the processes of apperception, Dewey insisted, lies the essence of human agency and constructive mind, an active, creative "will." No philosopher denied the existence of some sort of final motive antecedent to action, but each defined the will differently. Associationists tended to reduce it to the last impulse or reaction in a series, the product of earlier impressions. Even the Herbartians tended to describe the will mechanistically, as the final outcome of a quantifiable apperceptive deliberation. Philosophers whom Dewey would count as closest to his way of thinking conceived of the will in classic idealist terms, as a independent psychological faculty and philosophical category (the connative) that made mind's constructive activity exceed the sum of its determining antecedents (sensations, memories, constraints, and so on). But for Dewey the will overlapped the traditional boundaries of faculty psychology and idealist metaphysics, building itself up out of the complex aspects of experience. For the will to have any substantial meaning or relation to the world of experience, it must, Dewey argued, be rooted in a verifiable psychology of emotions and behavioral response. For this reason Dewey treated Bentham's and J. S. Mill's hedonism as an aspect of constructive idealism. By combining with hedonism, he believed transcendental idealist metaphysics acquired a substantial content and ceased being

---

[27] Ibid., 216, 120, 119; also Dewey, "Soul and Body," 93–115.
[28] Dewey, Psychology, 122, 212.

transcendental. Thus Dewey seemed to acede much to empiricist philosophy, leading later critics to consider him a type of hedonist and contributing to the impression that Dewey had led a revolt against idealist formalism. Dewey, however, still sought in the psychology of feeling and impulse a way to ground idealism in the phenomena of experience, to demonstrate a truth contrary to utilitarianism, that spirit (and a true ethics of duty, fealty, and brotherhood) is immanent in the world of tangible behavior.

Thus, volition for Dewey is simultaneously affective, purposive, and rational. Volition begins with the "sensuous impulses," the mind's immediate reaction to stimuli. Feeling reflects, he argued, through the experiences of pleasure and pain, the interest the self has in an act. Pleasure indicates that an act furthers self-development. It also follows on a stimulus to which the mind achieves "easy adjustment without excess of activity." Pain, on the other hand, indicates the hindrance of self-development and uneasy adjustment. Pleasure and pain, like all affects, are not sui generis or the simple product of sensory impressions but the accompaniments of an act. Affect provides the basis for interest and attention, which in turn directs the mind's activity, but affect itself is generated by the organism's practical and mental activity. Like all elements of experience, the impulse is an active response, "a reaction against the stimulus," the product of mind's inherent tendency to "make something outside of itself part of itself."[29]

The initial impulse is complicated by the fact that, not only does it spur the subject to a particular activity, but it interrupts the activity already engaged in, as a new, incongruous perception or as a feeling of disharmony, or as both. Partly because of the disharmony with the given in consciousness, the impulse must be "regulated" and "harmonized" to fit with the mind's predispositions. Above all the impulse must be adjusted to the existing goals that guide the subject's "self-activity" and "consciously directed towards the attainment of a recognized end which is felt as desirable."[30] Thus impulse is rationalized to fit the mind's predispositions and the needs of the organism through the process of apperception.

With the publication of his *Psychology*, Dewey represented mind

---

[29] Ibid., 216, 299, 302; see also Dewey, "The Theory of Emotions" (November 1894 and January 1895), *Early Works* 1:152–88.

[30] Dewey, *Psychology*, 309.

as one aspect in the activity of an organism that evolves through its relations to its environment. Humans, he maintained, are creatures with impulses that drive them, like other creatures, toward the satisfaction of need. But they also have a rational intelligence capable of assessing the means to satisfy impulsive need, of inhibiting insatiable impulses, and of delaying gratification for a more propitious set of future circumstances. In this last capacity the mind is able to (and must) project goals into the future. Those goals take the form of ideas, or "idealizations," as Dewey often called them, the building blocks of our rationality.

As in all his attacks on opponents, whether idealist or empiricist, Dewey hoped to subsume their arguments into a more inclusive, neo-Hegelian theory. But the philosophical argument addressed other concerns. By defining and defending the psychological standpoint, Dewey defended a theistic idealism that not only coexisted with experimental psychology but made better sense of it. Ethically, Dewey's apologetics partially resolved the persistent dilemma of the Calvinist and other theistic traditions which divided agency and responsibility between God and humanity. For Dewey this was a central concern, as we see in the next few chapters. Green's "false Hegelianism," his transcendental notion of spirit, undermined the ethical responsibility of humanity, severing spirit and rationality from the human (biological and social) forces that could achieve a Christianized, reasonable social order.

CHAPTER FOUR

From Socialized Church to Spiritualized Society

In Dewey's day, psychology and philosophy did not stand as they do now, detached from the social and ethical consequences of human behavior by professional boundaries. Dewey's mentors in the United States and Great Britain attacked associationism in part because of its apparent connection with ethical and political currents abhorrent to the defenders of a theistic and communitarian tradition. T. H. Green welcomed some of the philosophical insights of associationism, hedonism, and their ethical counterpart, utilitarianism. But Green and his students found the free-market mentality those theories rationalized unacceptable even if the Oxford idealists themselves continued to support English capitalism. The fact that Jeremy Bentham and J.S. Mill were radicals, advocating electoral and social reform, that Green's leading philosophical critic, the utilitarian Henry Sidgwick, agreed with much of Green's politics, or that Green's student F. H. Bradley, a Tory, shared many communitarian social values with his mentor only complicated the link between politics and philosophy; it did not bury or eradicate it. Then as now, political alignments did not always conform to current ready-made vocabularies of political disagreement.[1]

[1] On the ambiguous political alignments of Anglo-American philosophers, see James Kloppenberg, *Uncertain Victory* (New York, 1986), 30–35, 145–70. Melvin Richter ties Green's philosophical idealism much more directly to his political communitarianism; *The Politics of Conscience: T. H. Green and His Age* (Cambridge, Mass., 1964), chaps. 8–9.

Green's own history as a liberal reformer reflected a profound sense of philosophy's social responsibilities and a strong affinity between his idealist organicism, his theism, and the Christian collectivist adjustments he hoped to make to the British market economy. His advocacy of public education, social welfare legislation, protective labor laws, and other forms of state regulation conformed to his systematic philosophical argument that God was immanent in social and political institutions. For Green the goal of social reform was ultimate: the full self-realization of individual and society, in which the public interest and individual self-development were safeguarded by the Christian spiritual values embodied in the state and its laws.[2]

Dewey and his colleagues at Ann Arbor spoke a similarly metaphysical language of political and social "reconstruction" through the early 1890s. Although Dewey eventually criticized Green and his students for their adherence to a transcendental metaphysics, he used their arguments to condemn the mechanistic individualism at the core of associationism and utilitarianism. By implication, and sometimes more explicitly, members of the Ann Arbor department also criticized the unrestricted capitalism of the Gilded Age. Green's parliamentary and distinctly British political agenda, however, did not easily move across the Atlantic. Instead, the social reformist followers of the Progressive Orthodoxy and the early adherents of a "social" gospel provided the most viable counterpart to Green's reformism in post-Reconstruction United States. It was with these primarily religious movements that Dewey and his colleagues shared the language of communitarian social reform during their tenures at Michigan.

Social Christianity emerged out of the broader stream of religious modernism that included the Progressive Orthodoxy and other currents of evangelical and nonevangelical religious liberalism. Social Christians included Unitarians and Quakers, but by the 1880s the most prominent adherents followed some version of the new theology. Believers in the immanence of God in history and humanity, they promoted new doctrines and practices intended to force Protestant churches to confront the problems of modern culture in general and Gilded Age industrialism in particular. They directed the attention of

<hr />

[2] Richter, *Politics of Conscience*, 98–105; see Green's famous essay, "Liberal Legislation and Freedom of Contract," in *Works of Thomas Hill Green*, 3 vols., ed. R. L. Nettleship (London, 1911), 3:365–86.

the religious-minded away from questions concerning individual salvation and church attendance. It should be focused instead, they argued, on hitherto nonclerical issues: the plight of the poor,
unemployment, monopolistic business practices, and in some cases
trade unionism. These were matters of social redemption and required
viewing salvation as a matter of reforming a broader array of social
and political institutions to encourage the movement of history toward
a collective salvation, a Kingdom of God on earth, the product of
God's presence in nature (as indicated by a progressive and ultimately
humane evolution) and in human endeavor. Based on these principles,
social Christianity held that the church should no longer be confined
to saving individual souls through doctrinal purification, revivals, or
even limited church reforms. Instead, it should actively work to change
the social conditions of spiritual growth.[3]

Although the product of a complex theological and church history,
social Christianity in part represented a clerical response to what
seemed to be the unraveling of the social fabric during the Gilded
Age. American Protestants embraced it partly out of fear that declining
church membership after the Civil War would lead to loss of the
churches' social power and to the disintegration of a Christian social
order. These fears deepened in the mid–1880s as the practices and
priorities of industrial development tore at the seams of American

---

[3] C. Howard Hopkins, *The Rise of the Social Gospel in American Protestantism, 1865–
1915* (New Haven, 1940), 19, 60–61; Sydney Ahlstrom, *A Religious History of the American People* (New Haven, 1972), 772, 786–90. On Andover, see also Daniel Day Williams,
The Andover Liberals (New York, 1941). On religious modernism and the rise of evangelical
liberalism, see William R. Hutchison, *The Modernist Impulse in American Protestantism*
(Cambridge, Mass., 1976). Examples of social Christian writing during the 1880s and
1890s abound; some of the best known are Washington Gladden, *Applied Christianity*
(Boston, 1892), Lyman Abbott, *The Evolution of Christianity* (Boston, 1892), Richard Ely,
Social Aspects of Christianity (New York, 1889). The most popular reformist Christian
tract was Josiah Strong's *Our Country* (New York, 1885), though the position it presents
is less clearly social Christian than simply a call for the revival of Christian charity. I am
using the term "social Christianity" to refer to the religious doctrines and practices that
sought Christian redemption through social reform. Because of its close association with
the later teachings of Walter Rauschenbusch, I am avoiding the term "Social Gospel"
preferred by many historians. Christian socialism, roughly, is a more radical version of
what I am calling social Christianity. Social Christianity did not exclude revivalism, as
demonstrated in the evangelical character of much of its sermonizing. On the influence of
religious reformism on progressive activists, see Robert M. Crunden, *Ministers of Reform:
The Progressive Achievement in American Civilization, 1889–1920* (New York, 1982); for
the influence of Christian socialism, see Dorothy Ross, "Socialism and American Liberalism:
Academic Thought in the 1880s," *Perspectives in American History* 9 (1977–78): 5–79.

class and cultural unity. A new set of economic and social relations dominated American commerce, growing out of the Union triumph over the South in the Civil War and the development of industrial factory production based on wage labor. The symbolically pivotal year for this transition was 1877, when American railway workers struck the entire industry. That summer, riding a wave of discontent built up over four years of depression and joined by sympathizers in the major industrial cities of the Midwest, participants achieved the first general strike in United States history. When local police and militia, bolstered by federal troops withdrawn from military occupation in the South and from Indian wars in the West, fired on strikers, the movement turned toward insurrection. Angry demonstrators burned the Pennsylvania Railroad yards in Pittsburgh, and in St. Louis strikers took over the city. Minimally armed laborers could not prevail over the military, however, and the strike was crushed.[4]

In 1886, the year Dewey finished his psychology text, public attention was riveted once more on events unfolding in centers of American factory production. Emboldened by a successful strike against the Jay Gould railroad empire, their ranks swelled by new members, local chapters of the Knights of Labor initiated a movement to reduce the length of the workday to eight hours. In Chicago, the eight-hour movement quickly overflowed Knights locals into more radical sectors of the organized and unorganized working class, led by Marxist and Lassallean socialists, anarchists, and anarcho-socialists. Violence on the part of police and factory guards escalated into the notorious May 4 confrontation during a rally in Haymarket Square in which police fired on retreating demonstrators, killing four and injuring a score, after a bomb was thrown by an unidentified assailant (seven policemen died). Police subsequently arrested eight anarchists who had helped organize the event, holding them responsible for the violence. The trial of the "Haymarket martyrs" occupied the press for the next eighteen months. For many workers, the execution of four of the accused in November 1887 signaled the arrival of class warfare in America.[5]

---

[4] Strong, *Our Country*, 89. On the 1877 strike, see Philip S. Foner, *History of the Labor Movement in the United States* (New York, 1972), 464–74; Jeremy Brecher, *Strike!* (Boston, 1972), 1–24.
[5] Brecher, *Strike!*, 25–52; Bruce Nelson, *Beyond the Martyrs: A Social History of Chicago's Anarchists, 1870–1900* (New Brunswick, 1988), 177–200.

Partly in response to these events, religious liberals began to argue in the 1880s that the manner in which American churches preached the gospel had to change: preachers must adjust to changing social realities and make the gospel appealing to a growing industrial working class, by that time alienated from the Protestant establishment and attracted to anticlerical political ideologies. Popularizers such as Washington Gladden, Lyman Abbott, and Richard Ely provide the best-known examples of these class-based ministrations. Gladden plied a gospel of reconciliation between capital and labor from pulpits and rostrums across the country during the last three decades of the century. He and Abbott promoted the socialization of the church as well as the application of Christian principles to soften the effects of the disordered and excessively competitive marketplace, to move American economic life back to more cooperative and constructive forms of production. Ely even more emphatically tied social redemption to the fate of the nation's laboring poor and the need for official Protestantism to promote Chistian behavior in the business class.[6]

Similar arguments percolated up through the professional ministerial hierarchy into seminary-based theological discourse, where they found a receptive audience among the doctrinal descendants of Horace Bushnell. The immanent theology of evangelical liberalism already encouraged liberal critics to view the church as an organic part of the larger, changing culture. Religion adjusts, they argued, to the spirit of the age, expressing the presence of God to a progressively greater degree in human institutions. Social conflict, the emerging labor problem, the rise of national trade unions, and the intensification of industrial consolidation encouraged theologians to examine the Trinitarian controversies of the previous century in a new light. It became increasingly evident in the writings of church elders and publicists that the view of self and society inherited with the New England theological tradition did not suit the historical context unfolding about them.[7]

During the mid-1880s, good examples of these social Christian

---

[6] Washington Gladden, *Applied Christianity,* 102–45, and *The Ruling Ideas of the Present Age* (Boston, 1895), chap. 1; Lyman Abbott, *Christianity and Social Problems* (Boston, 1896), 268–96; Ely, *Social Aspects of Christianity,* 39–48, 65–67; Charles Augustus Briggs, *Whither? A Theological Question for the Times* (New York, 1889), chap. 1.

[7] Hutchison, *Modernist Impulse,* chap. 3; Williams, *Andover Liberals,* 114–15, 121.

arguments appeared regularly in the sermons and articles of Newman Smyth, whose New Haven pulpit was closely associated with Andover Seminary. Smyth was particularly concerned that declining influence in lower-class communities prevented the church from mediating conflicting political and economic forces. In the series "Sermons to Workingmen" published in *Andover Review* in 1885, Smyth called on Protestant leaders to revise their stance on working-class issues. If working people would not come to the church to hear the word of God, the church must bring to the worker the word translated into meaningful social terms. "Let the church go to the working man," wrote *Andover Review* editor William J. Tucker in his introduction to Smyth's sermons, "meet him on his own ground, listen, if need be, to his grievances and recognize his right to open discussion and his capacity for it." Moreover, to dispel lower-class enmity, the church must abandon its otherworldly focus. "I do not propose," resolved Smyth from his pulpit, "to meet men who tell me that this world is a purgatory to them by preaching merely a future heaven."[8]

As Tucker's words indicate, this version of social Christianity involved a humanitarian response by some liberal ministers to the social distress caused by postbellum industrial growth. Drawing on the romantic antirationalism of liberal theology with its emphasis on the more compassionate teachings of the early Christian church, ministers fashioned a moderate critique of the Gilded Age's ruthlessly competitive capitalism. Influenced by German criticism of classical economics, these preachers believed that unrestricted competition violated Christian ethics and must be modified to conform to enduring Christian humanist values of brotherhood and mutual aid. On the same grounds, social Christianity also attacked the social Darwinists and conservative Calvinists who justified a Hobbesian economic system by contemptuously holding the poor responsible for their own plight. In search of alternatives, social Christian ministers tentatively explored statist economics, although they did so only to the extent of advocating government intercession on behalf of society's helpless.[9]

But, if in these writings we can find sympathy for the plight of the laboring poor, we also find that Andover's social Christianity

[8] William J. Tucker, "Some Problems in the Pulpit," *Andover Review* 3 (April 1885): 300–301; Williams, *Andover Liberals*, 121–22; Newman Smyth, "The Claims of Labor," *Andover Review* 3 (April 1885): 300.

[9] Hopkins, *Social Gospel*, 26; Ahlstrom, *Religious History*, 789–90.

expressed conservative anxiety that the hardships caused by late nineteenth-century capitalism would lead to social disorder and the catastrophic destruction of Christian institutions, including those identified with capitalism itself: property and political authority. Symptoms of social disintegration were already widely evident by the 1880s. When Josiah Strong penned the popular tract *Our Country*, he grafted sympathy for the poor to a hyperbolic prophesy of national decline. For Strong, "Romanism," immigration, and intemperance, concentrated in "rabble-ruled cities" like Chicago, sapped American vitality, undermining the foundations of a Protestant republic by fostering authoritarianism, anarchism, and the single tax.

Although less belligerent and less sanctimonious than the rest of the middle class, social Christian ministers preached reconciliation between labor and capital in large part because they were terrified that social conflict would be resolved by the ideological triumph of revolutionary socialism. Strong devoted an entire chapter to the perils of socialism, which he blamed on immigration and industrialization, and finished with the declaration that "there is nothing beyond republicanism but anarchism." Gladden repeatedly raised the specter of an incipient communism as the price American churches would pay for not heeding the demands of an exploited working class. Even bona fide Christian socialists such as Ely and George Herron warned against the rise of an angry and irrational anarchism.[10]

As liberal ministers saw it, reconciliation could be accomplished in several ways, all meliorative and all committed to the preservation of Christian social harmony. For many liberal ministers, increasing church influence among the working class was a means to a greater end—restoring the church's ability to mediate currently pitched warfare between social classes. Workers and employers could be reconciled, argued Smyth, only through dialogue, discussion, scientific study, and meliorative social and industrial welfare programs, all of which the churches would facilitate by inviting contending parties into the House of God. There political and economic differences could be subordinated to a common Christian ideology. Thus Smyth's first goal was attracting workers to his solidly middle- and upper-class

[10] Strong, *Our Country*, chap. 8; Gladden, *Applied Christianity*, 125–28; Ely, *Social Aspects of Christianity*, chap. 5.; George Herron, *The Christian State* (New York, 1895), 138–46.

congregation, even if only for a short time, so that workers and capitalists would be in the same room together and be "a moral object lesson" to each other.[11]

Theirs was an ambivalent and often complicated stance. When forced during strikes to choose between the directors of giant industrial firms and their employees, Gladden, Abbott, Tucker, and others increasingly sided with the workers. In general, labor sympathies grew among liberal church reformers with the rising tide of industrial violence in the 1880s; for this the 1885 Gould strike provided an important turning point. Until that time, Protestant leaders (including liberals) condemned trade unionism together with communism, anarchism, and socialism. But the railroad workers' grievances and the violence with which the strike was repressed led many religious writers to revise optimistic theories about social harmony, to support labor unions, and even occasionally to advocate a Christianized socialism. The spokesmen for the Progressive Orthodoxy favored labor unions as the only representatives of workers which could effectively bargain with corporate management, an argument that would recur in secular discussions in Chicago in the 1890s. Few liberal ministers would accept the principle of striking for higher wages, preferring that labor disputes be resolved by arbitration through a neutral party. They felt that the principle of mediation should prevail over the tendency in American society for violent conflict. Ideally labor and capital would reach a harmonious coexistence, an "industrial democracy" in which employees would become junior partners through profit sharing.[12]

To give religious liberals credit, violence was not their only concern. They also reacted in principle to the new kind of capitalism represented by Gould's rail conglomerate. In May 1886 (the month the eight-hour movement was defeated) an *Andover Review* editorial argued that centralized labor organizations (that is, the Knights of Labor) were the only social institutions that could counter such powerfully concentrated capitalist interests without involving politics

---

[11] Newman Smyth, "Use and Abuse of Capital," *Andover Review* 3 (May 1885): 423–36, and *idem*, "Social Helps," *Andover Review* 3 (June 1885): 508–19; Tucker, "Problems in the Pulpit," 298; see the Gladden selection from *Working People and Their Employers*, in *The Social Gospel in America, 1870–1920*, ed. Robert T. Handy (New York, 1966), 45.

[12] Henry F. May, *Protestant Churches and Industrial America* (New York, 1949), 91; Hopkins, *Social Gospel*, 89–97, 149.

in the economy (that is, without nationalization or strict regulation), a prospect that still frightened many Protestants leaders. Strikes and boycotts were justified for "fair causes," the review argued, and these causes were more plentiful since capital had become concentrated in so few hands.[13]

Echoing a dominant refrain in nineteenth-century labor ideology, the *Andover Review* closely associated industrialists' moral decline with the transformation of American manufacturing from early republican and Protestant ideals of artisanship and useful enterprise into corporate empire building. Luxury had led manufacturers to "moral hardening" and class "selfishness." They no longer understood or cared about the condition of work and life under an industrial regime, and they applied Christian values selectively to members of their own class. This self-absorption and class interest was in another editorialist's opinion "pre-Christian" and "pagan."[14] As industrial firms grew, manufacturers looked less like productive members of society and more like a leisured aristocracy or a distant financial oligopoly: "A great deal of capital to-day is simply restless fortune in activity, rather than sober wealth under well-directed energy. Hence the number of unnecessary and illegal enterprises." The review also explicitly attacked Gould: "Capital is equally busy in constructing and 'wrecking' railroads." Even before the Gould strike, Smyth chastized his congregation for personal luxury and indifference to their workers' welfare. Labor's complaints about large-scale industry, about mechanization and fragmentation of the work process, were, in Smyth's estimation, to be taken seriously.[15]

Beyond the programmatic statements by which ministers traditionally earned their bread, social Christians also explored new institutions that would minister the gospel to a changing society in innovative ways. Churches opened urban missions to proselytize as well as to cope with the overwhelming need for charitable services to the poor, and they flourished in industrial centers during the 1880s. Graham Taylor, whose Hartford congregation included some of the city's

---

[13] Editorial, "The Centralization of Labor," *Andover Review* 5 (May 1886): 532.

[14] Editorial, "The Insensibility of Certain Classes to Moral Obligations," *Andover Review* 5 (June 1886): 634, 637.

[15] "Centralization of Labor," 530; Smyth, "Claims of Labor," 310–11; as Gladden pointed out, this was not a choice between labor and capital but between good capitalists and bad ones; Handy, *Social Gospel in America*, 38–48.

poorest citizens, recruited student volunteers to help revive the laboring poor, materially and spiritually. Taylor, who would go on to found one of Chicago's most important settlement houses, at the time took a moderate position, urging the expansion of church activities into institutions such as temperance societies and charity organizations which would carry on the work of salvation through social service and reform. By the time he reached Chicago in 1892, Taylor advocated shifting responsibility for spreading the gospel far beyond the institutional reaches of the traditional Protestant churches: "Family, neighborly, industrial, civic, cultural, and other groupings and agences" are, he argued, "tributary to the whole endeavor to realize the ideals of religion."[16] In the late 1880s, Taylor gravitated toward the Nationalist movement inspired by Edward Bellamy's utopian socialist novel *Looking Backward* and promoted by Christian socialists such as Boston's William D. P. Bliss. It was during the 1890s that the socialist position toward which Taylor drifted became increasingly attractive for those schooled in social Christianity. Bliss's monthly *The Dawn*, established in 1889, proposed a broad social democratic program that included nationalization of railroads and utilities as well as municipal ownership and female suffrage. The most radical and unconventional Christian socialist of the era, Herron, struck responsive chords among the rural and urban poor, many of whom linked Christian redemption to the growing populist movement. Herron also enjoyed an increasingly critical middle-class readership during the 1890s.[17]

Dewey, Mead, and Social Christianity

In the 1880s and early 1890s, Dewey, one of the young academics rising in the new American university system, continued to defend liberal theology, playing a minor but increasingly important part in reexamining the relations of self and society and recasting the social role of the church. He wrote for the *Andover Review* and other

[16] Louise C. Wade, *Graham Taylor: Pioneer for Social Justice, 1851–1938* (Chicago, 1964), 33–34, 41–42; Taylor quoted on p. 95. See also Hopkins, *Social Gospel*, 154–60.
[17] Wade, *Graham Taylor*, 46, 93–94; Hopkins, *Social Gospel*, chaps. 10–11; on Herron, see also Robert Crunden, *Ministers of Reform*, 40–52.

theological journals and participated in religious organizations active on university campuses.

As an Andover liberal, Dewey shared a concern for the social conditions of spiritual growth. Individual character is morally and spiritually a product of society, Dewey argued in 1888. As "society concentrated," an individual "embodies and realizes within himself the spirit and will of the whole social organism." In this case, Dewey directed Christian social organicism against conservative individualist Henry Maine. Maine's authoritarian solution to problems of social disorder and civic virtue Dewey attributed to the anthropologist's lack of faith in the general population (for Maine just an aggregate of individuals, most of whom where not politically virtuous) and in democratic political institutions. Dewey argued that democracy is a "form of moral and spiritual association," a reflection of God's immanence in the social organism. This principle provided the basis for the moderate social Christian stand on the "social question" during the late 1880s: "The Kingdom of God is within us, or among us," Dewey proclaimed five years later. If this is the nature of revelation, then the pulpit must address the social issues of the day—especially economic issues. To do so it must restate religious doctrine and values in modern scientific, sociological, and political terms. Smyth's sermons to the working class had said as much.[18]

By 1893, however, Dewey directed this argument not only against individualists like Maine but against the established churches, some of which had raised the issue of social redemption in the notorious 1891 heresy trial of the moderately liberal Presbyterian Charles Augustus Briggs. Dewey was more uncomfortable than Smyth with the notion that the church should be the primary agency of social change. He maintained that standard clerical practices, based on biblical ("abstract") revelation, were suited only to anachronistic forms of government. The church, Dewey felt, must begin to "reveal" in ways suitable to democracy: "The function of the church is to universalize

---

[18] John Dewey, "The Ethics of Democracy" (1888), *Early Works* 1:236, 233, 243–44, "Christianity and Democracy" (1893), ibid., 4:7, and "The Relation of Philosophy to Theology" (January 1893), ibid., 4:367–68. For a contrary account of Dewey's relation to Andover, see Steven C. Rockefeller, *John Dewey: Religious Faith and Democratic Humanism* (New York, 1991), 129–30, 581n. My own interpretation is largely based on Bruce Kuklick, *Churchmen and Philosophers: From Jonathan Edwards to John Dewey* (New Haven, 1985).

itself, and then pass out of existence." But in 1893, Dewey was not clear about what this new democratic revelation would practically entail. And he still took established church practice seriously enough to attend services, send his children to Sunday school, and frequently address the Students' Christian Association at the University of Michigan.[19]

These ponderings over the role of established Protestantism in society reflected the broader dilemmas of the 1880s and 1890s. On the one hand, the Kingdom of God is immanent in history, and if, as most social Christians argued, that history culminates in American democracy, what role can traditional forms of revelation have in redemption? On the other hand, where in the array of supposedly democratic (and "Christian") institutions could American social Christians such as Dewey and his colleagues find the opportunity for a secular political practice equivalent to that of Green, who advocated a similar theory of immanent social redemption? In Great Britain the discourse of philosophical ethics could find an audience on the floor of the House of Commons, where Green defined and defended the new liberalism as a member of Parliament. American reform politics in the 1880s by contrast had fallen into relative disarray, undermined by the demise of radical republicanism in the 1870s, by the widespread corruption in the Republican party, then the party of regulatory reform, and by the chronic inflexibility of the American two-party system. Followers of social Christianity were only just establishing viable reform institutions in some of the major cities. None of the philosophers at Ann Arbor yet had the experience of the network of contacts and audiences to translate philosophical reconstruction into social reform.

Mead in Germany

Mead's experience in the late 1880s is instructive, and to some extent it exemplifies the political education on these and related questions gained by a substantial part of his generation of reformist academics.

[19] Dewey, review of J. MacBride Sterrett's *Studies in Hegel's Philosophy of Religion* (June 1890), *Early Works* 3:188–89, "Christianity and Democracy" (1893), ibid., 4:3–6, and "Relation of Philosophy to Theology," 367. For the most complete account of Dewey's Christian liberalism at the University of Michigan, see Rockefeller, *John Dewey*, chap. 3.

Once liberated from the confinement of Oberlin and the oppressive expectations of a career in the ministry, he even more enthusiastically than Dewey embraced a socialized and socialistic form of Christianity. As was true of many young scholars in the 1880s, Mead's conversion occurred in Germany, at the time the center of European socialism, both in the workers' movement and at the more conservative major universities. After years of isolation in the backwaters of the American Midwest, Mead enthusiastically absorbed German philosophy, political theory, and culture. There he began his efforts to fashion a synthesis of politics, apologetic philosophy, and psychology which would continue well into his tenure at the University of Chicago.

By the late 1880s young American scholars, discouraged by the doctrinal restrictions American churches imposed on higher education and by the limited postgraduate educational offerings at home, flocked to German universities in pursuit of relatively easy degrees, academic freedom, and the unsupervised cosmopolitan atmosphere of German university towns. Nine thousand Americans studied in Germany between 1820 and 1920, one-third of them in the 1880s alone. They attended Berlin University most frequently to study medicine with Rudolph Virchow and Emil DuBois-Reymond, physics with Hermann Helmholtz, philology with Jacob and Wilhelm Grimm, and the historical and social sciences with Heinrich Treitschke and Adolf Wagner. The theology and philosophy faculties at Leipzig, Heidelberg, and Halle attracted most of the remaining Americans during this period.[20]

From Germany, Americans brought back new approaches to higher education which helped create the specialized professional fields into which the American academy soon subdivided. With the new forms Americans borrowed new academic content. German academics introduced American scholars to philological and historical criticism of the Bible. At Berlin, Americans learned the principles of post-Hegelian *Naturphilosophie* from students of Friedrich Schleiermacher. Americans also became initiated into the "scientific" application of historicist and comparative principles to the study of ethics and society. Along with the "pure" approach to the natural sciences, this tradition of *Geisteswissenschaft* may well have been the most important intel-

---

[20] Jurgen Herbst, *The German Historical School in American Scholarship: A Study in the Transfer of Culture* (Ithaca, 1965), chap. 1.

lectual heritage from Germany and a major factor in the development of American social science. Finally, study in Germany exposed Americans to the European socialist tradition, particularly the municipal socialism that governed many of the German cities after Bismarck and the academic "socialism of the chair" that reigned in the *Social-wissenschaft* faculties at Berlin and Leipzig. Economists and reformers such as Ely and Henry Carter Adams emulated moderate German socialism while they borrowed from the historicist and statist economics taught throughout the German university system. In the years before World War I American social activists, radical and moderate, often traveled to study German municipal governments and social programs, returning with blueprints for municipal reform in American cities.[21]

Mead spent his first semester at Leipzig mastering German and going to the theater. He was joined in November 1888 by his friend Henry Castle, who studied economics and politics with Wilhelm Roscher, founder of the dominant, historicist school of "national economics." That following spring both men, having grown dissatisfied with Leipzig's offerings, shopped around. By that time Mead had decided on physiological psychology as a speciality, partly to avoid religious controversies in philosophy proper. Mead concluded, perhaps wrongly, that the field's newness protected it from interference by clerically partisan university administrations in the United States still wedded to conservative Scottish philosophy and the more orthodox forms of Calvinism. A chance encounter in Leipzig with G. Stanley Hall, then America's leading experimental psychologist, bolstered Mead's determination. Hall counseled against remaining in Leipzig to study at the world-renowned laboratory of Wilhelm Wundt, where Hall himself had apprenticed. Instead, Hall steered the young scholar toward study in Turin, Italy, but either because of language difficulties or a negative reply from Turin Mead ended up in Berlin, where he stayed for two years. Castle remained in Leipzig and eventually married the daughter of his landlady.[22]

---

[21] Ibid., chap. 3; Ross, "Socialism and American Liberalism." Chicago reformers often used Germany as a model for reform, for instance, in studies of employment agencies, factory inspection, and, most important for Mead's later reform experience, industrial and vocational education.

[22] Henry Northrup Castle to parents, February 3, 1889, Castle Papers. The reason for Hall's advice may have been that the demand for apprenticeship at Wundt's laboratory

Mead broadened and refined his thinking in Berlin's rich cultural and political climate. He arrived at the capital in 1889, the first full year in the reign of Kaiser William II, whose liberal labor sympathies precipitated Bismarck's resignation and led to the legalization of socialism. Mead and Castle, who rejoined his friend that summer, were caught up in the flow of German events. In their letters of this period social questions took precedence over philosophical and theological inquiry. But, following the fashion of Germany's idealist economics, which treated the national economy as an aspect of the social organism and an expression of Germany's cultural spirit, neither Castle nor Mead perceived any contradiction between social science and their earlier strictly philosophical concerns. Castle, who studied political economy (under Wagner) and ethics in Berlin, wrote his parents that the labor question was the "most pressing problem" and the "most imminent danger" of the day. The only solution was intervention by the state in industrial relations and the market. Society must "ameliorate social conditions,... elevate the working class and moderate the extremes of social inequality" through state intervention. The state, wrote Castle, is "the guardian of social as distinguished from private interests,... the organizer or reorganizer of society," taking over the role of the church, which is "out of sympathy" with the modern world.[23]

German economic theory and practice, especially programs for municipal planning and ownership, also inspired Mead, who attended socialist meetings in Berlin (before they were legal). Anticipating "a struggle between the great manufacturing barons and [the] arbeiterschutzbevegung" which would result in extensive tax, housing, and tariff reform, Mead looked forward to the winter 1890 seating of the Reichstag, to which the Socialists were sending thirty-five delegates. Caught up like many young American scholars in German conceptions of an orderly, rational, and interventionist state, Mead impatiently dreamed of applying back home what he had learned from his German

---

was so great that many students, especially Americans, were being turned away, as Mead's later colleague James Angell discovered in 1893; James Rowland Angell, "Autobiography," 10, typescript in Box 2, Folder 7a, Angell Papers, Sterling Library, Yale University.

[23] Mead's courses included political economy with Wagner and Treitschke and ethics and history of philosophy with Wilhelm Dilthey, who was to be one of Mead's dissertation readers. On Mead's studies in Germany, see Hans Joas, *G. H. Mead: A Contemporary Reexamination of His Thought* (Cambridge, Mass., 1985), 218. H. N. Castle to parents, April 7, 1889, Castle Papers.

experience and education. "The immediate necessity," he wrote Henry, "is that we should have a clear conception of what forms socialism is taking in [the] life of European lands especially of the organisms of municipal life—how cities sweep their streets[,] manage their gas works and street cars—their Turnvereins[,] their houses of prostitution, their poor[,] their minor criminals[,] their police[,] etc. etc. that one may come with ideas to the American work [*sic*]." City politics, Mead thought, would be the area in which to apply his and Henry's imported ideas because "city politics need men more than any other branch—and chiefly because according to my opinion the immediate application of the principles of corporate life—of socialism in America [—] must start from the city." He envisioned himself and Castle entering Minneapolis politics, he as a teacher at the University of Minnesota, Castle as a lawyer, the two of them taking over the Minneapolis *Tribune* and using it as a platform from which to expose urban corruption and launch a reform movement.[24]

This was no simple reform conception, "not reform for itself," Mead wrote, but part of a larger development, a "practical application of morals to life," and the "education of social ideas" in America, which, Mead lamented, is "horribly idealess." Politics was only a means of achieving a moral reform agenda that Mead conceived in strictly idealist terms. On that agenda Mead included "the psychology of moral development of [the] child" and "the vigorous organizing of movements for physical culture" which will "give the breath of new ideas where the air is now so thin." He considered his German training in physiological psychology the right sort of foundation for the political and moralizing work, as a scientific discipline and a means of livelihood.[25]

Organized Intelligence

Although Dewey and Mead had yet to engage directly in social reform, their synthesis of Hegel, physiological psychology, and social Christianity did find a practical outlet in an abortive project similar to the one Mead had hoped to undertake with Castle in Minneapolis. In

[24] George H. Mead to H. N. Castle, October 21, 1890, and August 1890 (typed transcript of letter), Mead Papers.
[25] Ibid.

1888, Dewey met Franklin Ford, an itinerant utopian syndicalist. A decade older than Dewey, Ford had worked for several years as a journalist in Baltimore, Philadelphia, and New York. Ford's visionary gospel of social reform called for the fuller incorporation of "thought" into social and economic life. Struck by the absence of systematic social investigation that could serve industrial, business, or political ends, Ford insisted that the conditon of modern America called for a great new scheme in which "intelligence," information ranging from economic forecasts to metaphysics, would be made readily available to guide anyone in their practical business endeavors.[26] Ford cast the problems in extravagant Hegelian terms that appealed strongly to Dewey and Mead. Society for Ford was an "organism" in which the "idea," spirit, was only partially expressed. In a dream he related to Dewey, Ford grandiosely imagined himself as a great mechanic who would restore the connections between spirit and society through his scheme to "organize" intelligence: "I have seen a immense spiritual belt revolving & unrolling in the swiftest & most powerful way. And I saw a great material pulley revolving too. I was caught in the belting myself, and I saw men standing around and yelled to them to help put the belt on that pulley. They wouldn't help & then I had to go back and study the belt—master the thought." Not caring anything about "the Idea as thought," Ford felt he must convince men to finish this spiritual task, to "put the spiritual belt about the earth's pulleys."[27]

While working as an editor for *Bradstreet's,* Ford tried to convince his employers to turn the publication into a news bureau that would report "intelligence." They would not, and he quit. After several years wandering the country in search of a sympathetic audience at universities, business establishments, and voluntary organizations, Ford landed in Ann Arbor, where his uncle, Corydon Lavine Ford, taught anatomy at the university. There the younger Ford found Dewey, at a time when the philosopher was particularly susceptible to a pseudo-Hegelian social vision. Dewey's relationship to Ford, which lasted

---

[26] For a full account of Ford's involvement in Dewey's personal and professional life at Ann Arbor, see Neil Coughlan, *Young John Dewey* (Chicago, 1975), 93–99; also Robert B. Westbrook, *John Dewey and American Democracy* (Ithaca, 1991), 51–58. For Ford's biography, see David H. Burton's introduction to *Progressive Masks: The Letters of Oliver Wendell Holmes, Jr. and Franklin Ford* (Newark, Del., 1982), 11–22.

[27] Dewey to Alice C. Dewey, June 6, 1891, Dewey Papers.

four years, was indeed peculiar, bordering on the kind of veneration people usually reserve for gurus or charismatic preachers. Dewey likened Ford's mind to a Corliss engine and attributed to it an uncanny ability to register social and spiritual truths. Ford "never stays wrong," Dewey wrote his wife. "It is wonderful his appreciation of the whole situation." Some of Dewey's entrancement rubbed off on Mead, who likewise saw in Ford a unique instantiation of the world spirit: "He has wrestled wholly unaided with the fact of organized intelligence— the meaning of Hegel—and the fact has succeeded in registering itself upon him—The thing is only the greatest that the world has ever seen." Ford's was the "sudden conscious recognition" that "he and all exist only as the expression of the universal self."[28]

It was not enough for Ford to convince Dewey and Mead that their ideas must be put to use. Ford wanted to see something tangible come of his preaching, preferably something that would earn money. In winter 1892 he and Dewey hatched a scheme, into which they drew Mead, for a philosophical newspaper that would "report thought" on a monthly basis or, as Ford himself put it, "report society in order that it may be seen to be an idea in motion."[29] Already the year before Ford had prodded Dewey to engage himself as a philosophical consultant to a Mr. Van Ostrand, a member of the Chicago Board of Trade who needed philosophical advice. Dewey's end of the bargain required finding a few students to go over Van Ostrand's own utopian ramblings ("The 'Mental Constitution' as the Organism of Social, Cosmical, and Physical Elements") for inconsistencies and invalid arguments. For his troubles Dewey received $100, a sizable sum in 1891, which Ford convinced him, against Dewey's better judgment, to keep. "So I've taken my first fee as a 'metaphysical healer'," Dewey wrote his wife. "If there are many men like [Van Ostrand] in Chicago, I'll resign & go out & hang up a sign 'Dr. Dewey, Metaphysical healer'." Dewey meant this seriously, but the scheme went nowhere. "Thought News," the newspaper, however, entered the final planning stages in February 1892. Its embarrassing extravagance became evident to Dewey only after final announcement of its publication received notice and ridicule in the Detroit and Ann Arbor press. The

[28] Ibid. Mead to H. N. Castle, Winter 1892, Mead Papers.
[29] Ford quoted in Coughlan, *Young Dewey*, 102–3.

newspaper did not appear as scheduled in April, and Ford disappeared from Dewey's life shortly thereafter.[30]

The "influence of the Ford vagary on Dewey" apparently caused some concern in the philosophical community, which, at Harvard at least, did not warm to Ford's kind of extravagant organicism. Ford was significant, however, not because he profoundly affected an emerging pragmatism, even though he influenced Dewey's and Mead's political perceptions. Instead, the Ford episode reveals how Dewey and his contemporaries struggled to expand a philosophical vision of spiritual immanence in the social and physical world, a vision that already implied social and political activism. Although "Thought News" involved some peculiar notions, they were not such a dissonant contribution to the fund of ideas and social programs from which Dewey's generation had to choose. The main difference between Ford's ramblings and social Christianity seems to have been the absence of a respectibility that only an institution like a church could provide. Ford's organicism was no stranger than Dewey's own to the religious and political discourses of the 1880s, and his theories on the socialization of credit and banking reflected some intriguing insights into the transformation of the American economy which were shared by other utopian thinkers of the era. Thus, Oliver Wendell Holmes ambivalently characterized Ford as either a crank or a genius yet took him seriously enough to maintain a regular correspondence from 1907 until Ford's death in 1918. In a sense Ford showed considerable savvy trying to ply his wares among university professors and businesspeople. Both social groups and their institutions, the university and the corporation, eventually employed projects similar to Ford's, though in more respectible social scientific forms.[31]

---

[30] Dewey To A. C. Dewey, May 31, 1891, Dewey Papers; Coughlan, *Young Dewey,* 102–8; Mead to H. N. Castle, February 28, 1892, Mead Papers. Ford resurfaced in New York City in 1897 where he opened a credit agency.

[31] The quotation is from a letter by James Angell, then president of the University of Michigan, to his son James Rowland Angell, October 2, 1992. According to the senior Angell, William James and George Palmer rejected a thesis by Dewey's colleague Alfred Lloyd because they found "traces of the same folly" in it. Ford's influence on Dewey's philosophy remained primarily a matter of presentation, to his students and the public. On the incorporation of Ford's ideas into Dewey's teaching, see Dewey to James Rowland Angell, March 11, 1892, Angell Papers (see note 22), and Dewey, "Introduction to Philosophy: Syllabus of Course 5" (February 1892), *Early Works* 3:211–35. For a different account, see Lewis Feuer, "John Dewey and the Back to the People Movement in American

Ford's utopianism appealed to the philosophers' hope to integrate mind, spirit, and body through social action, and to their belief that society was an organic expression of absolute spirit. "Thought News" was a failure, but it was consistent both with Dewey's and Mead's theological interests and with their later involvement in and perceptions of social reform. What the incident apparently taught them was that neo-Hegelian, spiritualist language did not hold much currency with the politically and socially conscious reading public or with the journalists, novelists, and essayists that public read. Nevertheless, Dewey continued to use Fordian locutions such as "organized intelligence" for several years, though the expressions took on slightly different meaning in the context of his mature philosophy.

Reconstruction

Dewey's discomfort with church membership and worship increased between 1892 and 1894, the year he moved to Chicago. Soon after his arrival he cut ties with Congregationalism, withdrawing his children from Sunday school and thereafter neglecting services. "Reconstruction," written in Michigan in 1894 and delivered before the University of Michigan Students' Christian Association, was virtually his parting statement. To his young audience Dewey argued that, although Christian reformers recognized the need for religious change in a "haphazard, disconnected way," they had not yet seen the "deeper forces which are at work," the "certain large tendencies" growing for centuries and coming to fruition at the end of theirs. Because of these historical sea changes the church needed "reconstruction." While authoritarian political institutions thwarted individual freedom and the brotherhood of man, the traditional church was necessary to preserve in its doctrines the "ideals" that could not be realized in society. Christianity was idealist, claimed Dewey, because its "thoughts" were

Ideas," *Journal of the History of Ideas* 20 (1959): 548. Feuer suits Ford up in the role of catalyst for Dewey's "revolt against formalism," in which the philosopher purportedly acquired a sociological approach. A substantial part of the Holmes-Ford correspondence can be found in Burton, *Progressive Masks*. A similar organicist language can be found in an early joint manifesto of the settlement house movement, made the same year as the "Thought News" fiasco: *Philanthropy and Social Progress* (New York, 1893); see especially the introduction by University of Michigan economist H. C. Adams.

stopped before they could become action—thought "was turned into an ideal. Because it was not true in act, it was held to be true only in emotion, or at some remote time, or by some supernatural means." But, Dewey continued, now that feudal aristocracy has died and the political and social context has changed, the church must reconsider its "idealism," that is, it must act instead of preach, and churchgoers must consider other institutions as vehicles of God's will on earth.[32]

Dewey borrowed the language of this declaration from the changing discourse of social Christianity. As several historians have noted, Dewey's generation increasingly drifted into Christian socialist politics as they became more familiar with the labor movement and the conflicts between labor and capital grew more irreconcilable. The shift to Christian socialism accompanied a larger movement away from the church and church-run institutions as the primary means of social redemption. The late 1880s and early 1890s were the years in which social Christians first experimented with settlement houses and the secularized "institutional" churches that replaced missionary work in the cities with new forms of Christian social work and sociology. Dewey followed this shift, but he addressed these remarks specifically at the iconoclastic sermons of Herron, whose well-known and radical Christian socialism provided a useful counterpoint to Dewey's own more moderate position. In his famous 1890 sermon "The Message of Jesus to Men of Wealth," Herron voiced a pessimistic assessment of late nineteenth-century industrial society, driven by an ethic of self-interest and competition. The pursuit of material gain does not serve Christian ends, Herron declared, nor do the institutions of public order. True Christianity needs a spirit of Christian "self-sacrifice," to which he exhorted his listeners. Herron repeated these exhortations for the University of Michigan Students' Christian Association in a series of lectures given in February 1894.[33]

Dewey's criticism of Herron underscored the dilemma inherent in the liberal conception of historically immanent redemption. In 1894, Herron still used the language of Christian revelation in which God's transcendent truths must be revealed to the unknowing and sinful. Herron's message that God's "law of human development and

---

[32] George Dykhuizen, *The Life and Mind of John Dewey* (Carbondale, 1973), 100; Dewey, "Reconstruction" (June 1894), *Early Works* 4:99.

[33] Published with the 1890 sermon as *The Christian Society* (Chicago, 1894).

achievement" was "self-sacrifice" and that each person must bear "the cross of absolute self-renunciation" did not suggest divine immanence in human hearts and lives, even if Herron simultaneously insisted that the spirit of Christian self-sacrifice was incarnate in humanity. Having argued that the realization of the individual self conforms to the larger spiritual design, it was hard for Dewey the psychologist to tolerate such an ethic of self-denial. Moreover, Herron's picture of American society suggested that it was far more unregenerate than Dewey's moderate brand of social Christianity could admit.

For Dewey, Herron missed the deepest of the "deeper forces at work" in American democratic culture: Herron's insistence that the church "sacrifice itself to the world" ignored the fact (not yet adequately reported) that "political, domestic and industrial institutions have become in fact an organized Kingdom of God on earth, making for the welfare of the individual and the unity of the whole." Modern democracy resembles the Kingdom of God on Earth so closely that Christian principles no longer need be preached as ideals—they should be recognized as "facts," as "revealed" in institutions other than the church. The church, argued Dewey, "has no monopoly on the organs of grace. . . . the means for lifting up the individual and binding men together in harmony are now found working in all forms of life." Therefore the church's role in society is to dissolve itself into the social milieu. Its present sacrifice is "not one in general, but one of detail," not "a sacrifice to some great mission in the future" but "a willingness to recognize accomplished facts and readjust itself accordingly." The church's duty is to "take its place as one among the various forces of social life, and to cooperate with them on an equal basis for the furtherance of the common end."[34] Herron called for the church to sacrifice because he had insufficient faith in the institutions of democratic renewal.

Dewey, in contrast, had concluded that American democracy was the most spiritually advanced, intrinsically Christian society yet to appear on earth: "It is in democracy, the community of ideas and interest through community of action, that the incarnation of God in man . . . becomes a living, present thing, having its ordinary and nat-

---

[34] Dewey, "Reconstruction," 101.

ural sense. This truth is brought down to life; its segregation removed; it is made a common truth enacted in all departments of action, not in one isolated sphere called religious." American democracy is essentially Christian, Dewey thought, because it is essentially classless. It is the "loosening of bonds, the wearing away of restrictions," and the "breaking down of barriers, of middle walls, of partitions . . . of isolation and class interest."[35] In 1891, Dewey argued with a "clever young Englishman" that "democracy has already gone so much further in this country than in England, it is so much in the atmosphere we breathe, in the currents in which we live" that upper and lower classes do not exist. Where there are no classes, where democracy is so thoroughly established as it is in America, the "mingling of classes" (as the Englishman advocated) is impossible.[36]

On the face of it, Dewey's was an extraordinarily naive and simplistic assessment of the American scene. Yet his views reflected the same paradox faced by other adherents to the new theology. As a philosopher and religious liberal he asserted the immanence of spirit in the real, in nature and society. Yet his world seemed unregenerate rather than redeemed: the history of the Gilded Age belied rather than confirmed Dewey's optimistic assessment of American social democracy. As the religious historian Henry May put it, by the 1890s the optimistic theories of liberal Protestantism, especially those concerning society and social progress, had to be reassessed "in the light of burning freight cars." How could the churches abandon abstract ideals, as Dewey put it, if social life conformed so badly to Christian values? Clearly those values were not readily found in actual social relations. Herron's position, although departing from the thoroughgoing liberal conception of an immanent spirituality, seemed the more realistic. To answer this question (or, better, to avoid answering it), Dewey, like others, equivocated and temporized. One argument was that the Christian spirit immanent in American life had unfolded more completely in political and cultural institutions than in economic relations. Politically and culturally America was democratic, classless and therefore Christian, even if economically it was not. There is no industrial democracy, Dewey wrote in 1888; distributive injustice still

---

[35] Dewey, "Christianity and Democracy," 8–9.
[36] Dewey, "The Angle of Reflection No. 4" (June 1891), *Early Works* 3:202–7.

thwarts the Kingdom of God on earth. "Society is still a sound aris-
tocrat," he lamented, "a democracy of wealth is a necessity" in which
all industrial relations will be "subordinate to human relations."[37]

But in a more general sense Dewey, like his liberal coreligionists,
struggled with the ambiguities of an organic theory of self-realization
in which the agency of historical change is immanent in the unredeemed historical moment. For religiously minded conservatives the
church was that agency, revealing God's message of salvation to the
unregenerate, redeeming humanity from above. Yet as religious writers came to view the church as one of many cultural institutions, each
of which manifested an immanent spirit, it became less clear from
what source redemption would flow. Social institutions were both in
need of change and the agencies of their own change. The members
of those institutions pursued both self-interest and a higher form of
self-realization. Thus, the popular association of Christianity with
democracy suggested that political institutions embodied higher spiritual principles and that the participants in democratic politics enjoyed
the capacity for self-redemption. Yet, as Herron observed, these institutions had repeatedly failed, and the world was still populated by
venal and selfish beings. What or who in humanity could be identified
as the agency of redemption?

This problem was left for Dewey, his colleagues, and their associates
to work out in a new context and in new terms in Chicago. Early in
1894, William Rainey Harper, president of the recently founded University of Chicago, offered Dewey the chair of the Chicago philosophy
department. Harper, hoping to build a strong philosophy faculty, had
failed to attract a more eminent, elder scholar for the position. He
settled on Dewey, partly on the prompting of Tufts, whom Harper
had hired in 1892. From Ann Arbor Dewey brought Mead as well
as James Angell, a former student in the Michigan department, to
teach experimental psychology and to help set up a psychology
laboratory.[38]

---

[37] May, *Protestant Churches*, 91; Dewey, "Ethics of Democracy," 246–47.
[38] Dykhuizen, *Life and Mind*, 74–78.

CHAPTER FIVE

Labor Is the House
Love Lives In

Dewey arrived in Chicago during the first days of the Pullman strike in July 1894. During the previous month, negotiations between the American Railway Workers Union (ARWU) and the Pullman Company, maker of luxury railway coaches, had broken down largely due to the company's refusal to ease economic burdens imposed on employees at Pullman, Illinois, the company town just south of Chicago. Within a few days after Dewey's arrival, the strike spread along the nation's rail lines as unionized railway workers refused to handle trains hauling Pullman cars. In Chicago's working-class and industrial districts violence broke out, leading to thirteen deaths and over $80 million in property destruction, including the burning on July 6 of much of the Chicago World's Fair buildings adjacent to the university (blame was never fixed). Within three days of the exhibition's destruction, President Grover Cleveland declared martial law in Chicago, marching several thousand federal troops down from Fort Sheridan over the objection of Illinois governor J. Peter Altgeld.[1]

Dewey at first responded enthusiastically to the strike: "My nerves were more thrilled than they had been for years," he wrote his wife, Alice, about a conversation with an ARWU organizer. "I felt as if I

[1] Ray Ginger, *Altgeld's America: The Lincoln Ideal versus Changing Realities* (New York, 1958), chap. 6; Chicago *Daily News*, July 7, 1894, 1. For an account of the Pullman strike in the packinghouse districts see James Barrett, *Work and Community in the Jungle: Chicago's Packinghouse Workers, 1894–1922* (Urbana, 1987), 127–31.

had better resign my job teaching and follow him around till I got into life." Dewey regarded the strike as an extraordinary event. "I don't believe the world has seen but few times such a spectacle of magnificent, widespread union of men about a common interest as this strike business. . . . its [*sic*] a great thing and the beginning of greater." But Dewey's excitement waned within a month. He was not put off so much by the destruction of property: "I think the few freight cars burned up a pretty cheap price to pay," he wrote his wife in the middle of July. It was, he felt, "the stimulus necessary to direct [the] attention" of the government and industry, "and it might easily have taken more to get the social organism thinking." And Dewey retained a strong antipathy to the "highest classes": "Damn them," he wrote. As the strike's failure became clear in mid-July, however, Dewey began to consider the ARWU's confrontation with the railroads "a most inconsiderate, unreflective thing, entered in at the worst of dull times with thousands out of work and not a chance in a thousand for success."[2]

Dewey's assessment did not fall far from that of many labor leaders, even those who led the strikes. Eugene Debs, the ARWU leader, had feared that the action against Pullman was premature. The union, fresh from its first major victory the previous year, was not prepared to handle the inevitable confrontation a strike and boycott would bring with the well-organized railway industry. Once federal troops appeared on July 4, Debs, realizing that the government sided with the rail corporations, tried to call the strike off. Union members, incensed at the appearance of troops on behalf of monopolists, persisted. By July 17, Debs and the union board were in jail, charged with contempt for violating a court injunction against the national boycott. They served three to six months in prison. As many as one-fourth of the ARWU members lost their jobs and suffered the blacklist. The strike was lost.[3]

Although it was a disaster for the union, the Pullman strike was an important turning point in the history of Chicago. Founded as a trading outpost on the shores of Lake Michigan, by 1870 Chicago stood at the hub of America's expanding railroad empire, serving the growing needs of the nation's westward-shifting population. The Chi-

---

[2] John Dewey to Alice Dewey, July 2, July 14, and July 28, 1894, Dewey Papers.
[3] Nick Salvatore, *Eugene Debs: Citizen and Socialist* (Urbana, 1982), 132–34.

cago fire of 1871, although devastating two thousand acres of the
city's prime real estate, only briefly delayed its rapid development as
an urban center. Between 1871 and 1890, Chicago's population grew
by more than 250 percent, from 298,000 to over a million residents,
making it the second largest city in North America. To accommodate
the burgeoning population, the city spread from 35 to 185 square
miles, absorbing surrounding townships and unincorporated land.
Ideally situated at the crossroads of rail and lake transportation, Chicago industry and commerce soon dominated the seemingly endless
markets and resources of the Midwest. In the city's exchanges, merchants traded lumber, grain, and meat in huge quantities. The largest
corn market in the United States, Chicago also provided the nation's
largest grain depository in the massive elevators and warehouses that
dotted the lake shore. By the 1890s, Chicago meat packers had perfected their far-flung systems of transporting western cattle and hogs
to be butchered for eastern and foreign markets; they took over the
nation's meat processing. By the late 1880s, only Pittsburgh led Chicago in steel production, and the combined output of the city's manufacturers placed it third after New York and Philadelphia.[4]

Chicago's development involved the transformation of industry as
well as its growth. In selected industries firm size grew dramatically:
the average clothing manufacurer, for instance, employed twice as
many workers in 1890 as in 1870; the average meat-packing firm
increased more than fourfold. The city's major manufacturers used
the most advanced production methods, mechanizing to an unprecedented extent and revolutionizing the labor process. Late Victorians
had viewed the end of the nineteenth century as the culmination of
the factory system, but these years also brought the elements of mass
production that were to characterize the twentieth century. Factory
managers applied an intensive division of labor that methodically and
minutely broke craft down into assembly line drudgery. This transformation of work remade the American laborer. Chicago's industries
demanded fewer skilled craftspeople, replacing them with unskilled
immigrants, many of them women and children, adequately trained
to the tasks of machine operation and cheaper to pay.[5]

[4] Bessie Louise Pierce, *A History of Chicago,* 3 vols. (New York, 1937–57), 3:3–20, 50,
65, 73, 93, 146, 154–63.
[5] Such was the case in meat packing, Chicago's largest industry and the center of much
labor activism; see Barrett, *Work and Community,* 3–5, chap. 1. On Chicago, see also

This industrial transformation took a predictable toll on social harmony. Chicago was Josiah Strong's most unregenerate city, populated and led by foreigners and "romanists" recruited to work in the city's factories and sweatshops. By 1890, 78 percent of the population reported foreign parentage, largely Catholic, to Strong's and others' chagrin. A disharmonious crazy quilt of ethnicity, Chicago had the largest concentration of Swedes in the world and the second largest of Bohemians after Prague. The dominant ethnic group, first- and second-generation Germans constituted a full third of the population in 1884. Only a quarter of the city descended from Anglo-European settlers. Residents spoke countless languages, and one could walk in some districts without hearing English on the streets.[6]

The Pullman strike was the third great industrial conflagration to tear apart the city since the Civil War. The first, the Great Railway strike of 1877, centered in the rival industrial cities of Pittsburgh and St. Louis, spread along the rail lines to Lake Michigan's growing metropolis, bringing sympathy walkouts and street fights. For a few days at the end of July, Chicago's economic activity halted, until the local elite mobilized police and armed guards. At least thirteen people (most of them workers) died in armed confrontations. The Haymarket "riot" nine years later revealed the violence with which the new industrial capitalism could respond to public protest, in this case the eight-hour movement. Political hysteria in the aftermath of viclence between police and strikers led to the imposition of an extended period of unofficial martial law on the city. The trial, appeals, and execution of the "conspirators" drew the confrontation out over the rest of the decade. When in 1893 reform governor Altgeld pardoned the remaining Haymarket prisoners, the discord that lurked just below the surface of the city's life revived. By 1894, Chicago had established

---

David Hogan, *Class and Reform: School and Society in Chicago, 1880–1930* (Philadelphia, 1985), Preface, and Bruce C. Nelson, *Beyond the Martyrs: A Social History of Chicago's Anarchists* (New Brunswick, 1988), 10–15. According to Nelson, industrial modernization was not a uniform process, especially in its effects on employees. On the introduction of machine production and deskilling, see Harry Braverman, *Labor and Monopoly Capital* (New York, 1974), chaps. 4–5; David Montgomery, *Workers' Control in America: Studies in the History of Work, Technology, and Labor Struggles* (Cambridge, 1979), chaps. 1, 5.

[6] Josiah Strong, *Our Country* (New York, 1885), 129; Pierce, *Chicago,* 3:22; Nelson, *Martyrs,* 15–23.

itself not only as the stockyard and railroad capital of the United States but also as the national focal point of industrial confrontation.[7]

That year's strife over Pullman served as a lightning rod of public opinion and a major catalyst for social reform. The public response in Chicago to the strike and to the broader economic and social crisis, however, was not uniform. Consider, for example, the conflicting currents in Chicago's working class. Chicago labor had a long tradition of radical political activism, which supported the election of several local politicians during the late 1870s. But the labor movement in Chicago also deeply divided along craft and ethnic lines, building rival organizations that jockeyed for ideological and political leadership throughout the latter decades of the nineteenth century. After the Pullman strike, more conservative labor leaders closed ranks around the defense of unions and contracts, and, promoting machine politicians who respected labor's minimal rights, they managed labor until the reemergence of progressive leadership around 1900. Debs and some of his followers, in contrast, viewed the failure of the strike as a blow against the American republic: the domination of corporations in American life and the corruption of political leadership had been at stake. Debs hoped for a regeneration of American life and culture through the reestablishment of a republic of productive citizens. The strike's failure led him and others into increasingly radical criticism of American industrialism, in the Socialist party and in the Industrial Workers of the World.[8]

But if much of Chicago's working class developed new attitudes toward socialist revolution, they were increasingly negative and apathetic. The laboring poor, having joined the ARWU in open battles with the police and soldiers in the summer, by fall were demoralized by the strike's suppression and the prolonged economic depression. They continued to enter the anarchist and socialist organizations active in the ethnic neighborhoods of west and south Chicago, but in fewer numbers. Those organizations, linked to the German *Turnverein* and ethnic marching and singing clubs as well as the city's early trades and industrial unions, had built a rich political culture of pa-

---

[7] On the 1877 strike, see Pierce, *Chicago*, 3:244–52. The details of the Haymarket incident can be found in many sources, including Paul Avrich, *The Haymarket Tragedy* (Princeton, 1984); Nelson, *Martyrs*, chaps. 8–10.

[8] Nelson, *Martyrs*, chap. 3; Salvatore, *Eugene Debs*, chap. 6.

rades, picnics, educational institutions, and newspapers which was sustained in some form into the twentieth century. But in the repressive aftermath of the Haymarket affair, and as the ethnic and occupational composition of the city changed, that culture faltered. After the battle with Pullman, a smaller percentage of the city's working class joined socialist organizations and even fewer voted for socialist candidates in municipal elections.[9]

The city's educated and civic-minded elite also divided over events such as the Pullman strike and the labor conflicts that followed. Dewey, whose enthusiasm was unusual for a person of his social standing, came to a more moderate position within a year after the great strike, praising Jane Addams's pale chastisement of Pullman (in her famous "Modern Lear" essay) as "one of the greatest things I ever read both as to its form & its ethical philosophy." By then his attitude was more akin to that of his colleague Tufts, who recalled years later that the strike left a "grim and deep impression" on him and that he and his neighbors, sympathetic with yet frightened by the "embittered, homeless and hungry men," armed themselves against a group of Independence Day revelers they mistook for rioters.[10]

Even Tufts's mild sympathy for the Pullman strikers was unusual. Most of Dewey's and Tufts's contemporaries responded to the labor problem with a mixture of wrath and terror, cheering on federal troops in Chicago and arming college students in Cambridge. The middle-class press excoriated workers for precipitating confrontations and self-righteously defended the industrial regime and wage labor, reasserting the principles of free-market entrepreneurialism, free labor, and Protestant faith, the hallmarks of northern republicanism which dominated American social commentary after the Civil War.[11]

By 1894, however, a significant part of Chicago's civic and cultural leadership began to respond to industrial conflict in a more concili-

[9] Nelson, Martyrs, 228–42.

[10] Dewey to Jane Addams, January 19, 1896, Addams Papers; Jane Addams, "A Modern Lear," Survey 29 (November 1912): 131–37. Dewey read Addams's article in 1896, the year she wrote it. Publishers initially rejected the essay as too sympathetic toward unions and too personal about George Pullman; see, for example, H. E. Scudder to H. M. Wilmarth, April 18, 1896, Addams Papers; James Hayden Tufts, "Autobiography," unpublished typescript, Tufts Papers, Chicago.

[11] Ginger, Altgeld's America, 36–39, 41, 49, 162; James Gilbert, Work without Salvation: America's Intellectuals and Industrial Alienation, 1880–1910 (Baltimore, 1977), chap. 2; Richard Hofstadter, Social Darwinism in America (Boston, 1955), Introduction, and The Age of Reform (New York, 1955), chap. 4; Hogan, Class and Reform, 22–23.

atory fashion. The American religious leaders who had begun to reexamine social policy in the 1880s broadened their search for alternatives as the problems of industrialism deepened. The groundwork for a more thorough reexamination of social values had already been established by the critical theology of the liberal Protestant churches and the closely related social Christian movement, both of which questioned the hyperindividualism of orthodox Calvinist social theology. Meanwhile, social Christian and Christian socialist activism influenced parallel intellectual movements in the growing American university system, in the new discipline of sociology and in academic political economy led by revisionists such as Richard Ely and the University of Michigan's Henry Carter Adams, who increasingly borrowed from the historicist, statist, and socialist traditions of the European continent.[12]

This critical perspective developed in new industrial cities such as Chicago. There, for instance, Henry Demarest Lloyd used social Christianity and Jeffersonian republicanism to attack monopoly and privilege and to defend trade unionism and government regulation. By the mid-1890s the more practical of Chicago's religious-minded reformers, such as Graham Taylor and Addams, had already established settlement houses in the poorer districts of the city and, in response to civic corruption and the dismal conditions of urban life, initiated reform projects. When the depression of 1893 devastated the city's working poor, Addams and her colleagues at Hull House provided relief but found that the mechanisms of the urban political machine did not adequately suit their programs of social and moral reform. That summer Lloyd and others joined the state labor movement in an abortive effort to forge the Labor-Populist Alliance to promote socialization of production and challenge "Clevelandism" and corruption in the Democratic party.[13]

Generally, the depression spurred social Christians and secular reformers to attack public institutions and leaders for callous treatment of the city's poor. When popular British journalist William T. Stead arrived in Chicago in 1893, he found the squalor and deprivation,

---

[12] Dorothy Ross, "Socialism and American Liberalism: Academic Social Thought in the 1880's," *Perspectives in American History* 9 (1977): 5–79.

[13] Henry Demarest Lloyd, "Lords of Industry," *North American Review*, June 1884, reprinted in *Lords of Industry* (New York, 1910), 116–47; Jane Addams, *Twenty Years at Hull-House* (New York, 1929), 159–75; Hogan, *Class and Reform*, 23.

the licentiousness of the city's red light and saloon district, so shocking
that he convened a public meeting in the Central Music Hall to discuss
the effects of the depression on the moral life of the city. At that
November meeting, Stead delivered his famous address "If Christ
Came to Chicago!" in which he scathingly attacked the city's elite
for heartless indifference to the poor, the prostitutes, the intemperate,
and the working class. Anticipating the complete breakdown of social
order, those present (including Addams, Taylor, and business and
labor representatives) formed a "civic church" to save the "public
conscience" of the city. The Chicago Civic Federation (CCF), incorporated in February 1894, soon turned toward arbitration of labor
disputes, which in the earliest phases of the CCF's existence involved
entreating employers to recognize unions and employees to avoid
violent strikes. The CCF brought together some of the most resonant
voices in Chicago's moderate reform community, yet it did not represent the sum total of progressive activity in the Pullman strike's
aftermath. Local CCF chairman Ralph Easley turned Stead's impas-
sioned plea into the stereotypical "corporate liberal" organization,
building a business alliance with conservative labor leadership which
promoted progressive industrial and social reform as the means of
stabilizing and legitimating business and government. Meanwhile,
local progressives, including those in the Chicago philosophers' network of acquaintances, traveled in a more ambiguous world of labor
and social activism. Several political discourses intersected in that
milieu, and only some of them could accurately be described as "corporate" or "liberal."[14]

The Work Ethic and the "Labor Problem"

One of the focal points of public concern among progressive activists
and elsewhere was the erosion of traditional work values under the

---

[14] William T. Stead, *If Christ Came to Chicago!* (Chicago, 1894), 465–71; Louise C.
Wade, *Graham Taylor: Pioneer for Social Justice, 1851–1938* (Chicago, 1964), 73–78.
The CCF helped establish a state board of arbitration in 1895, but under Easley's leadership
it soon lost its credibility with progressives in the local labor movement. Activists such as
Addams and her friends in the Chicago philosophy department had less to do with the
CCF after 1900, shifting their involvement to other municipal reform organizations, some
of them, such as the Municipal Voters' League, emerging from the original CCF efforts.
See Hogan, *Class and Reform*, 37–38.

factory system. In earlier nineteenth-century secular and religious beliefs, work provided the cement that held America together and bound
one's character to one's divine destiny. In the years after the Civil
War, it became apparent that factory production was transforming
work into industrial drudgery, from an artisan enterprise that reinforced social responsibility and built good character. Modern factories
turned crafts into labor done for wages and turned workers' minds
from the intrinsic value of labor to extrinsic rewards. This transformation occurred partly in fact and partly in the mythological history
of the American experience presented by middle-class shapers of public opinion. The most evangelically pastoral and nativist of these writers believed that industrialization drew men and women into a
demoralizing and corrupting urban environment and sullied the population with alien laborers. More temperate analysts characterized
the America left behind as something of a rural paradise of democratic
communities led by honest republicans, lost with industrial development and the closing of the frontier in 1893.[15]

As Daniel Rodgers has argued, in this changing context of industrial
practices the work ethic lost much of its earlier sense and meaning.
If factories morally degraded work, and if the factory system increasingly dominated American industry, then one could hardly believe
that through work itself people achieved or demonstrated any kind
of social or spiritual grace. Adding to this concern, the increasing
domination of the ideally free market by trusts and corporations raised
even wider doubts about the almost mythologically conventional wisdom that individuals could achieve prosperity and self-fulfillment
solely on the basis of their own resources. So, in the 1880s and 90s,
in conjunction with their condemnations of industrial violence and
monopolization, publicists, moralists, ministers, and academics in-
tensively reexamined work values. Some tried to rehabilitate the individualistic work ethic. Others sought substitutes for it.[16]

The Chicago philosophers entered the United States' fastest growing

---

[15] A good example is Strong, *Our Country*. The frontier's passing was mourned by
Fredrick Jackson Turner in his famous 1893 address to the World's Columbian Exposition
in Chicago. For an extended reexamination of the frontier thesis (and western history in
general) as a form of mythology, see Patricia Nelson Limerick, *Legacy of Conquest: The
Unbroken Past of the American West* (New York, 1987).

[16] Gilbert, *Work without Salvation*, chaps. 5, 7, 8; Daniel Rodgers, *The Work Ethic in
Industrial America, 1850–1920* (Chicago, 1978).

industrial city at a time when national attention was turned toward the "labor problem." They too reassessed work values, hoping thereby to help reconstruct a society fractured by industrial conflict and demoralized by industrial drudgery. Factories, they argued, brought moral decline by intensifying the division of labor, by automating, by elevating pecuniary over moral incentives for work, and by increasingly separating manual labor from the intellectual control and planning of the production process. Like many of their contemporaries, however, the Chicago philosophers increasingly abandoned moralistic language when analyzing social disintegration. They tried to reinterpret the ethical meaning of work in the industrial age, seeking a new language for their moral concerns and a basis for social integration other than an individual's commitment to his or her vocation.

In the writing of the Chicago philosophers on work and industry in the late nineteenth century, one finds as well the unmistakable traces of an overlapping yet broader social and political tradition— what historians have identified as "producer republicanism." Like the related Protestant work ethic, producer republicanism tied social order to industrious and rewarding occupations. Unlike the Calvinist orthodoxy, however, producer republicanism concerned itself primarily with the secular foundations of a worldly polity, the American republic founded in 1776 and codified in the Constitution of 1787. In a tradition (also somewhat mythological) stretching back through the Italian renaissance to the original republic of Rome, republicanism established certain necessary conditions for the maintenance of a stable representative government. Recognized citizens, those community members allowed to choose political leadership, required economic and social independence to have the civic virtue necessary for sound political judgment, that is, they could not owe allegiance to someone with economic or social privilege, who would use that power to maneuver voters into a political tyranny. Independence traditionally hinged on the availability of land, a contingency Thomas Jefferson took quite seriously during his presidency. The seemingly endless supply of arable land on the American continent promised an inexhaustable natural economic resource for the independent citizenry. With yeoman farmers, skilled and independent small business and craftspeople would provide the backbone of representative government.[17]

---

[17] Since Machiavelli, western political theorists recognized that even the best-constructed

The especially "producerist" version of American republicanism emerged in the late eighteenth century as part of the revolutionary movement. The ideological and political unity that helped the republican movement survive the war with Britain was short lived. As early as the 1790s, former revolutionaries and patriots in port cities like New York found themselves divided over political, economic, and cultural issues, concerning the roles of deference and wealth in politics, the franchise, and the French Revolution, even over the meaning of civic virtue. The politics of the new nation, still uniformly premised on republican principles, took on more of a class character, pitting artisans and mechanics against merchants and patricians. If merchants believed that wealth was the prerequisite for and true measure of responsible citizenship, then the cordwainers and blacksmiths believed that only honest productive labor made one civic-minded and reliable.[18] A version of traditional republicanism emerged which cast suspicion on unearned wealth, invested trust in independent artisanship, and identified the spirit of the republic with a loosely defined notion of productive labor. As factory production developed along the Atlantic seaboard after the 1810s, creating new forms of production while simultaneously undermining traditional crafts, the American public continued to divide over the meaning of civic virtue—factory owners identifying it with economic and social accomplishment and political respectability, artisans, workers, and farmers with skilled craft, economic independence, and freeholding. By the Civil War, one could identify a distinctly producerist current within the republican mainstream, associated with an emerging working class.[19]

Like other nineteenth-century public discourses, producer repub-

---

republics tend to disintegrate under the forces of the marketplace and imperial expansion. The literature on the republican tradition is vast; central arguments for the role of Machiavellian republicanism in American politics can be found in J. G. A. Pocock, *The Machiavellian Moment: Florentine Political Thought and the Atlantic Republican Tradition* (Princeton, 1975); Gordon Wood, *The Creation of the American Republic, 1786–1787* (New York, 1972). Joyce Appleby, *Capitalism and a New Social Order: The Republican Vision of the 1790s* (New York, 1984) provides a counterargument. See Hogan, *Class and Reform*, xxi–xxiv, for a discussion (siding with Appleby) pertinent to Chicago reform.

[18] See Howard Rock, *Artisans of the New Republic: The Tradesmen of New York City in the Age of Jefferson* (New York, 1984), chaps. 1–2, on voting behavior and ideology among artisans in New York City; Sean Wilentz, *Chants Democratic: New York City and the Rise of the American Working Class, 1788–1850* (New York, 1984), chap. 1, on the general issue.

[19] Wilentz, *Chants Democratic*, 15–18.

licanism developed along the uneven lines of fracture so typical of American political culture. For many labor advocates, such as Debs, producer ideology carried a critical message, challenging the development of large, corporate firms, the industrial division of labor and machine production, even the economies of scale provided by factory production. The defense of the craft skills and workplace autonomy which were eroding under the advance of factory production involved, for many, a defense of one foundation stone of American democracy, the ability to choose and control one's occupation without being under the arbitrary authority of a nonproducing hereditary elite. When conjoined with a continental European republicanism, forged in the revolutionary period of the late 1840s and imported to the United States by succeeding waves of immigrants, producerism often moved in radical directions. Chicago was famous for this political tradition, espoused by European and American anarcho-socialists and syndicalists during the last half of the nineteenth century, many of whom fought as "1848ers" in the Civil War, often counting themselves simultaneously as Jeffersonians and socialists. This critical republicanism would play a continued role in the city's labor movement into the twentieth century in numerous strikes, planned and spontaneous, reasserting worker control of the workplace.[20]

A different set of political actors, however, espoused a more conservative producer republicanism. Some versions were purely nostalgic, in reaction to the evolution of American society, as was the case, for example, with middle-class sentimentalization of preindustrial culture in the Arts and Crafts movement.[21] Producerism could be conservative in another sense as well, especially when espoused by captains of industry who claimed that the management of capital and labor constituted a paramount contribution to the productive enterprises of the nation. Conservative producer ideology assumed that a community of interest potentially existed between workers and their employers, because many capitalists emerged out of the working-class and engaged in productive occupations. This view of productive cit-

---

[20] Montgomery, *Workers' Control*, chap. 1, and "Labor and the Republic in Industrial America: 1860–1920," *Le Mouvement Social*, no. 111 (April–June 1980), 201–15 (especially 215); Salvatore, *Eugene Debs*, chap. 3; Nelson, *Martyrs*, 156–65.

[21] This interpretation is argued well in T. J. Jackson Lears, *No Place of Grace: Antimodernism and the Transformation of American Culture, 1880–1920* (New York, 1981), 60–96; see also Frank Lloyd Wright's famous essay, "The Art and Craft of the Machine," in *Eighty Years at Hull House*, ed. Allen Davis (Chicago, 1969), 85–88.

izenship could be found in working class quarters as well. Even in militant labor organizations such as the Knights of Labor, which saw its goal as the achievement of a cooperative commonwealth of productive citizens, skilled and presumably class-conscious workers believed in the community of interest. Their paragon was the producer, not the worker or the proletarian.[22]

Industrial Democracy

The belief in a community of interest characterized many of the arguments for "industrial democracy" that captured the attention of reformers in the 1880s and 1890s. One root of this shared and ambiguous reform discourse extended back into the social Christian movement. From his position as a national spokesman for the emerging social gospel, Washington Gladden exhorted Americans to Christianize industry, moving it into a higher stage of social and economic "cooperation." While for Gladden this evolutionary understanding of industrial history licensed workers' "combination" in unions against capitalists (especially monopolists), he argued that cooperation ultimately must lead to conciliation between labor and management within the framework of capitalist market relations. Thus, Gladden opposed Christianization to socialism, which he rejected as faulty economics.[23] Lyman Abbott similarly understood industrial democracy as a stage in social evolution (after slavery, feudalism, and individualism), using the term explicitly and stressing popular participation in economic decisions. Yet Abbott too defined industrial democracy in conciliatory terms, as a rapprochement between the warring parties of labor and capital who would otherwise destroy each other and society in militarily organized confrontation. Both Abbott and Gladden advocated informal and formal means of conciliation and arbitration, in the public interest as well as in the respective interests of employers and employees. Both preachers tended as well to conflate the problems of control and power with the related

---

[22] Leon Fink, *Workingmen's Democracy: The Knights of Labor and American Politics* (Urbana, 1983), chap. 1.

[23] Washington Gladden, in *The Social Gospel in America: 1879–1920*, ed. Robert T. Handy (New York, 1966), 39, and *Applied Christianity: Moral Aspects of Social Questions* (Boston, 1892), 98, 121, 144.

issues of redistributing wealth and meeting the economic terms of organized labor. Thus profit sharing, ranging from employee stock ownership to the gain sharing (or productivity raises) of the Towne plan, often replaced true participation as a popular solution to industrial autocracy.[24]

Although often conciliatory and meliorative, the rhetoric of industrial democracy nevertheless sent more radically democratic messages. Secular advocates echoed the Christian language heard from pulpit thumpers such as Gladden, promoting as well new forms of community between labor and capital. In Chicago, Lloyd and Addams pursued arbitration as the solution to strikes and industrial warfare, both of which would end with the application of the principles of democracy and the rule of law to the workplace. But Lloyd's notion of industrial democracy included the demand for full participation of workers and the public in the governance of industry, a position he shared with more radical labor activists. Lloyd increasingly adopted the rhetoric of the British labor movement and Fabian socialists, including the collectivist demand for socialization of the means of production, which he and moderate labor socialists (such as Chicago's Thomas Morgan) pushed first in the American Federation of Labor with moderate success and later in the short-lived Labor-Populist Alliance of 1893–94.[25]

This line of argument for industrial democracy extended back into the earlier history of the term's use in the 1870s. Labor advocates of industrial democracy defined it as some combination of worker participation in management, the formation of producer cooperatives, and collective bargaining. Their descendants among progressive labor activists in the Chicago Federation of Labor would continue to advocate participatory forms of industrial democracy which included municipal ownership, eventually expanding them into a political program for a labor party. And it is important to recognize that their middle-class supporters, like Gladden, Lloyd,

[24] Lyman Abbott, *Christianity and Social Problems* (Boston, 1896), 59, 283; Milton Derber, *The American Idea of Industrial Democracy, 1865–1965* (Urbana, 1970), 8, 68–70.
[25] Henry Demarest Lloyd, "Servitudes not Contracts" (1889), in *Lords of Industry*, 156, and *A Country without Strikes* (New York, 1900), 175–76; Chester M. Destler, *Henry Demarest Lloyd and the Empire of Reform* (Philadelphia, 1963), 205–7, 263–79; Jane Addams, "The Settlement as a Factor in the Labor Movement," in *Hull-House Maps and Papers* (New York, 1895), 196–200.

and Addams, considered the right to bargain collectively (to "combine") central to the defense of democracy in the new world of
monopolistic industry. At a time (the 1890s) when management
refused to negotiate with employee representatives, the demand for
union recognition did not seem particularly conciliatory. It was
largely on the question of compulsory arbitration that labor separated from middle-class reformers such as Addams, but this was by
no means always the case and positions regularly changed. So too
did the terminology. Between the 1870s and World War I, industrial
democracy evolved from the ambiguous advocacy of greater participation, collective bargaining, socialization of the means of production, and income redistribution to the mainstream promotion of
profit sharing and employee stock ownership. But the 1920s was
not the 1890s; earlier reformers such as Lloyd did not necessarily
have management-controlled corporatism in mind when they first
championed workplace democracy.[26]

Within this twisting and tangled web of ambiguous rhetoric, the
Chicago philosophers formed their own notions of how to extend
democracy from the ballot box to the workplace. As we see in the
next few chapters, Chicago pragmatism contained both radical and
conservative elements, the "two souls" of late nineteenth-century reform. In demanding a practical and theoretical reconciliation of head
and hand, they offered a philosophically sophisticated version of the
producer ethic, challenging fatalistic estimates of human worth and
condemning the exploitation of human creativity. They called for
democratic participation on the part of employees—in the interest of
their full self-activity and self-realization and not just in the name of
industrial peace and order. At the same time, like many of the most
radical of American labor leaders, Dewey and his colleagues simultaneously promulgated a more conservative work ethic, one that clung
to the belief in a community of interest between capital and labor
and avoided the rhetoric of class conflict.

As Dewey arrived in Chicago, he and his colleagues were already
exploring the politics of industrial democracy and social reconstruction. But, as for much of the literate middle class, 1894 marked an
important turning point for Chicago philosophy. With the move to

---

[26] I am following Derber, *American Idea of Industrial Democracy*, here. Although uncritical of the movement, Derber's account gives a good sense of the variety of meanings
for the term "industrial democracy."

Chicago, the philosophers grouped around Dewey at Ann Arbor entered a new phase in their political experience that would have a dramatic effect on their political outlook and on the development of their philosophy. Although they were no strangers to the social turmoil of the 1880s and 1890s, and in Mead's and Dewey's cases eager for political involvement, the intensity of social conflict in Chicago and the scope throughout the city of social and political reform surpassed the experiences of any of the new department's members. This was the kind of problematic environment Dewey and Mead had sought in Ann Arbor. It would, they hoped, provide them a chance to bring America's immanent "organic intelligence" to fuller expression. They would immerse themselves in Chicago's municipal reform movement (as Mead had hoped to do in Minneapolis) and link their ideas with social activism. "The town seems filled with problems holding out their hands and asking somebody to please solve them—or else dump them in the lake," Dewey wrote Alice. He described Chicago as "hell turned loose, and yet not hell any longer, but simply material for a new creation."[27]

After 1894 philosophical discussion at Chicago shifted its extraphilosophical focus. The philosophers' arrival in Chicago did not put an end to the effort to attain religious reconstruction. Dewey, Mead, and their colleagues, however, worked out their mature theories in the process of directly addressing, in popular forums and in scholarly journals, the problems of the city rather than the problems of the spirit and the church. Their efforts took new form as they, like many of their contemporaries, drifted toward secular means of realizing Christian values in modern industrial society. While never fully abandoning the Christianity of their social commitment, Chicago philosophers, following other reformers, increasingly perceived and described fin de siècle social crisis in secular terms. Here we can claim for the Chicago pragmatists only academic leadership in a broad intellectual and social movement that united the crusade of a socialized Christianity with the critique of an industrial system that degraded productive work, rewarded unproductive wealth, and undermined independent citizenship.

[27] Dewey to A. Dewey, August 25, 1894, Dewey Papers.

Settlement Houses

The University of Chicago philosophers found issues of secular reconstruction ready-made in two nonphilosophical contexts: the culturally oriented reform activities of Chicago's settlement houses, and
the educational crisis that beset Chicago schools at the turn of the
century. It was largely through settlement activity that they encountered Chicago's labor movement, and one can argue that the settlement reform culture formed, or at least mediated, their perceptions
of the labor problem.

Reformers such as Addams built settlements on the fringes of institutions that Dewey and his colleagues knew well, churches and
universities. In 1889, she and her friend Ellen Gates Starr established
Hull House, the city's first bona fide settlement, in a formerly sub-
urban mansion on the west side which had become engulfed by the
immigrant working-class neighborhoods of the new industrial city.
Others soon followed: University of Chicago sociologist Charles Zueblin opened Northwestern University Settlement in December 1891
in the city's Polish section on the northwest side. Two University of
Chicago graduate students established the University Settlement in
January 1894. That same year on the near west side Taylor founded
Chicago Commons, "to provide a center for a higher civic and social
life." By 1911 settlement pioneer Robert Woods counted nearly three
dozen settlements and similar institutions in Chicago alone.[28]

Settlement houses were in large part founded as a humanistic response to the terrible social conditions of late nineteenth-century
America. American cities had always been squalid.[29] Rapid industrial,
commercial, and urban growth after the Civil War, however, com-
pounded the hardships that had long congested American urban centers. Leading American cities in population growth, industrial
capitalization, and concentration of factory employment, Chicago
seemed to lead as well in chronic urban misery. One decade before
the new century, Chicago sprawled across the plains southwest of
Lake Michigan, a chaotic grid of inadequately cleaned and maintained
streets lined in many wards with overcrowded, filthy, and hazardous

---

[28] Robert A. Woods and Albert J. Kennedy, eds., *Handbook of Settlements* (New York,
1911), 37–80.

[29] See, for instance, Christine Stansell's description of early nineteenth-century New York
City in *City of Women: Sex and Class in New York, 1789–1860* (Urbana, 1987), 4–10.

frame houses and tenements without internal plumbing or adequate ventilation. The streets, only one-third of which were paved, were covered with manure, garbage, and the contents of chamber pots, as well as untended children who on occasion had to be fished out of the open sewers that ran along some gutters.

In many districts a dominant industry defined the social and natural environment, employing a major percentage of its residents and spewing out the noise, smell, and wastes of industrial production. Most notorious for sending the odors of butchering and decomposition throughout the city, and waves of flies and vermin into the surrounding neighborhoods, the stockyards, located west and south of downtown, defined neighborhoods in which the University Settlement operated. In the immediate vicinity of Hull House the garment industry literally took over the quarters of near west side residents, subcontracting vast amounts of production to the sweatshops housed in tenement apartments throughout the district.[30] This industrial ecology took its toll on the health and welfare of workers and residents alike. Epidemics periodically swept through the city's population, reflecting inadequate administration of public health and the overtaxation of the primitive infrastructure of refuse collection and street cleaning. As a whole, the city suffered terrible mortality rates. In 1882 one-half of Chicago's children died before the age of five. Worklife too could be grim, even during economic prosperity. Manufacturers throughout the city exploited child labor, enforced twelve- and fourteen-hour days, housed production in creaky firetraps, and dictated inhumane work rules.[31]

The dreadful material conditions of rapidly industrializing urban America presented an objective need for the commonsense solutions a settlement house might supply. Thus, the settlement houses began to provide the basic human services that eventually became absorbed by municipal, state, and federal government: aid to the indigent, child care, and adult education, for example. Perhaps more important was

---

[30] Contemporary descriptions can be found in Addams, *Twenty Years at Hull-House*, 198–205, 294–96; Florence Kelley, "The Sweating System," in *Hull-House Maps and Papers*, 27–45; Abraham Bisno, *Abraham Bisno, Union Pioneer* (Madison, 1967), 81–89. See also Steve Fraser, *Labor Will Rule: Sidney Hillman and the Rise of American Labor* (New York, 1991), 26–29.

[31] In 1886, one-third of the city population still used outhouses and privies. Officials did not provide sanitary inspection of buildings until 1880; Pierce, *Chicago*, 3:54–55; Ginger, *Altgeld's America*, chaps. 1–2.

the changing perception of those objective needs in the eyes of a new generation of the American middle class. The "subjective necessity" for settlement houses, wrote Addams in 1892, was the belief, born of dissatisfaction with the established church, that Christianity "has to be revealed and embodied in a line of social progress." The same concerns and expectations that led Newman Smyth to address sermons to the working class also compelled some churches and seminaries to establish urban settlements. Taylor's work in Hartford and Chicago grew out of his seminary work; so did Woods's Boston project, Andover House. The church had failed to act in the true Christian spirit of brotherhood and unity as originally preached by Christ. Many young, middle-class Protestants expected more effective church action on social problems. Alienated from the established churches, the settlement, according to Addams, was the "nearest approach they could find to an expression of their religious sentiments."[32]

The settlement house expressed in institutional form the principles of liberal Christianity much as overseas missions and revivals were established in the spirit of an earlier evangelicalism. Settlements also carried further the process of secularization begun by social Christianity. Religious language and church orientation became increasingly problematic when reformers tried to introduce them in ethnically alien immigrant communities.[33] To be effective, settlement houses had to abandon explicit reference to institutions and theologies that Jews and Catholics found objectionable and oppressive. Secular language was particularly necessary to compete with anticlerical political ideologies that had intrinsically greater appeal to working-class communities than did elite religious doctrine.

Chicago settlements soon became institutional vehicles for applying Christian social ethics to labor issues and remained centers of middle-class sympathy and support for the labor movement until World War I. "At Hull House one got into the Labor movement as a matter of course," observed Alice Hamilton, one of the settlement's residents. Several unions were organized and met regularly at Hull House, es-

---

[32] Allen Davis, *Spearheads for Reform: The Social Settlements and the Progressive Movement, 1890–1914* (New York, 1967), 3; Addams, *Twenty Years at Hull-House*, 123, 152, 270–71. On earlier charitable reform in Chicago, see Hogan, *Class and Reform*, 13–17.

[33] Daniel Day Williams, *The Andover Liberals* (New York, 1941), 150; Davis, *Spearheads*, 15.

pecially fledgling women's trade unions that found little support among male workers. Addams frequently spoke in support of the right to organize and defended strikes, for which Hull House workers frequently organized meetings and raised funds.[34] One should not underestimate the sincerity or commitment of the settlement house activists to labor's cause simply because they espoused a middle-class Christianity. Residents frequently joined strikers on the picket lines, and when necessary in the jail cells as well. Led by Florence Kelley, Hull House residents organized Chicago's antisweatshop campaign of 1891–93, winning passage of the landmark Illinois Factory Inspection Act in 1893, limiting child labor, and setting health standards for certain workplaces. The city's factory inspectors, led by Kelley and Alzina Stevens, one of the settlement's few working-class residents, worked out of an office across the street. They began each work day over coffee in the Hull House coffee shop. At the University Settlement, Mary McDowell was indispensible in organizing female packinghouse workers during the stagnant years after 1894.[35]

Adopting the rhetoric of earlier Christian activists and the homiletic wisdom of Russia's Leo Tolstoy, settlement reformers guided their labor activism by Christian humanist beliefs in universal equality, brotherhood, and the right to spiritual and material fulfillment. Settlement workers often perceived industrial labor in terms of a sentimentalized Christian spirit of brotherhood, unification, and love. As Addams and Starr saw it, labor brought individuals together in a common enterprise and spiritually transformed the secular world, despite the evidence of industrial Chicago. Ideally, labor was "the house love lives in," wrote Addams, borrowing from a Russian proverb that dignified the toiling of farmers and artisans while simultaneously romanticizing it: "No two people nor group of people can come into affectionate relations with each other unless they carry on together a mutual task." For her, as for the many settlement activists influenced by Tolstoy, labor could be as sacred as prayer.[36]

---

[34] Hamilton quoted in Davis, *Spearheads,* 103, see also 106, 118; Addams, *Twenty Years at Hull-House,* 212, and "Settlement as a Factor," 189.

[35] Ellen Gates Starr was arrested on at least two occasions. On Kelley, see Katherine Kish Sklar, "Hull-House in the 1890's: A Community of Women Reformers," in *Unequal Sisters,* ed. Ellen DuBois and Vicki Ruiz (New York, 1990), 109–22; Dorothy Rose Blumberg, *Florence Kelley: The Making of a Social Pioneer* (New York, 1966), chap. 12. On McDowell, see Barrett, *Work and Community,* 135–37, 143.

[36] The proverb is related in Addams, *Twenty Years at Hull-House,* 271, see also 152.

Settlement activists were middle class, however, and for all their labor sympathies they had a different stake in social reform than the members of the communities they served. Above all, settlement workers committed themselves to peaceful nonconfrontational solutions to social problems, considering the settlement house a mission of sociological and ethical enlightenment in the strife-torn city. Settlements, contended McDowell, must be "a method and not a partisan organization standing for any religious, political or social system." Despite her strong commitment to building militant unions through the Women's Trade Union League and the packinghouse unions, she believed that ultimately the settlement would be a neutral place "where values may be weighed." Likewise, Addams thought settlements could "take a larger steadier view" than a worker "smarting under a sense of wrong" or a capitalist "ignoring human passion." The settlement's duty, as Addams saw it, was "in keeping the [labor] movement from becoming in any sense a class warfare." She hoped that as labor became more established it would discover "the larger solidarity which includes labor and capital." It is not surprising that key settlement activists favored labor arbitration, as a guarantee of union recognition and collective bargaining but also as a means of avoiding potentially violent or economically damaging confrontation.[37]

This institutional and philosophical commitment to mediation did not close settlement house doors to people with more radical socialist and anarchist perspectives. Some settlement house residents actively supported local and national socialist parties. Kelley, an active revolutionary socialist in the 1880s and 1890s, maintained membership in Debs's party during the 1910s. Starr supported the socialist movement up until World War I, giving speeches at Socialist party conventions and running as a socialist candidate in the 1916 municipal elections. She perceived no contradiction between her membership in the party and her commitment to Christian social redemption.[38]

[37] Graham Taylor, *Religion and Social Action* (New York, 1913), 17; Mary McDowell, "Beginnings," autobiographical essay in Mary McDowell Papers, Chicago Historical Society, Box I, Folder 3; Addams, "Settlement as a Factor," 196, 200, 202; see Wade, *Graham Taylor*, 110, 144–45, 203–4 on Taylor's role as labor mediator, for example, in the building trades strike of 1900 and the Teamsters strike of 1905.

[38] Kelley maintained an earnest (if somewhat sporadic and sometimes painful) correspondence with Friedrich Engels until his death and translated his *Condition of the English Working Class;* see Blumberg, *Florence Kelley,* especially 158. On Starr, see Josephine Starr's

Settlements also attracted to their gatherings many revolutionary socialists and anarchists from the surrounding communities. Every year from October to June, Chicago Commons offered a weekly Tuesday evening "free floor" at which an invited speaker introduced a topic for open discussion. The absence of limits on speech (except for the advocacy of violence) attracted local radicals and revolutionaries as well as faculty and students from local colleges and universities. At its height in the late 1890s, these gatherings filled the Commons auditorium with up to three hundred people. Hull House had similar gatherings, such as the Working People's Social Science Club.[39] They cultivated an air of confrontation, but such encounters served more to sharpen settlement activists' mediating abilities than to influence them one way or the other. The settlements thus provided unusual forums for verbal exchange, drawing academics into the midst of discussions they would otherwise not have heard. Dewey and his colleagues, who frequently spoke at these sessions, were thus forced to defend their ideas before contentious audiences and to compete with radical political rhetoric and arguments. Addams viewed these labor and economic discussions as conflicts between diverging points of view, which made it difficult for the settlement "to be liberal in tone, and to decide what immediate measures are in the line of advantage to the labor movement and which ones are against it."[40]

One such confrontation involving Dewey took place during a conference titled "Social Reconstruction" jointly held at the Commons and Hull House in December 1896. From the dais an impressive collection of speakers elaborated on Dewey's social Christian theme of two years earlier: true Christianity reconstructs society as the means of redemption, and true social reconstruction is Christian at heart. Gladden used the Sermon on the Mount as his starting point, and

typescript biography of her aunt in Box 3, Folder 27, Starr papers, Sophia Smith Collection, Smith College Library.

[39] Wade, *Graham Taylor*, 127. Taylor suspended the free floor in 1902 because discussion became too intemperate for his comfort; Addams, "The Objective Value of a Social Settlement," in *Philanthropy and Social Progress* (New York, 1893), 52–54.

[40] "Hull-House: A Social Settlement," in *Hull-House Maps and Papers*, 217; Dewey to J. Addams, October 12, 1898, Addams Papers. For the perspective of a working-class socialist who frequented Hull House, see Bisno, *Abraham Bisno*, 115–24. On Tuesday night free floor at the Commons, see Wade, *Graham Taylor*, 127–28; also J. P. Gavit to A. M. Simons, March 21, 1898, Taylor Papers, Chicago Commons Collection, Box 1, Newberry Library.

other speakers similarly focused on the religious nature of social reform. "The man who discovers the religion of democracy," declared
Lloyd, "will save the world." From the floor, however, "the bitterest
and most violent [denunciations] were directed against the church."
A conflict emerged as well between "the evolutionary majority and
the small revolutionary minority," who argued that the means of
gradual, "constitutional" reform no longer existed in the American
political system. Dewey expressed the "prevailing sentiment" of the
gradualists when he declared that "education is *par excellence* the
method of social reconstruction." But this position did not lack in
deference, though patronizing, to the working-class section of the
audience: manual training and industrial education must be incorporated into a common school system, reconstructed to serve the
needs of all classes. Taylor concurred: "Those of us who have been
educated in the schools have very much to learn from those who have
been educated at the work bench." Social reconstruction, then, though
decidedly unrevolutionary, sought common ground between the
classes in a manner which, at least for a time, accepted working-class
perspectives on their own terms.[41]

It was this mediating social role that Dewey found so attractive in
settlement activism. He wrote his wife of Addams's settlement philosophy, which he described as "wonderful." The settlement was not
"a thing, but a way of living—hence had the same aims as life itself."
Its purpose was "the unification of the city's life or the realizing of
the city's unity." Dewey's conversations with Addams in fall 1894
were a great revelation to him. Addams's insistence that confrontation
was harmful and unnecessary led Dewey to rethink his philosophical
stance: "I can see that I have always been interpreting the dialectic
wrong end up—the unity as the reconciliation of opposites, instead
of the opposites as the unity in its growth, and thus translated physical
tension into a moral thing."[42]

Mead concurred. Writing in 1907, he described the settlement as

[41] "Economic Conference at Chicago Commons and Hull-House," typed summary transcript by George Hooker, Reel 50 (the original is in Folder A–2, Box 9, Series 13a), Addams
Papers. The conference took place December 7–10, 1896. Conference participants included
Taylor, Dewey, Addams, Gladden, Lloyd, Fabian socialist John Graham Brooks, and University of Chicago sociologist C. R. Henderson. A pamphlet announcing the event is in
Taylor's scrapbook, Taylor papers, (see note 40).
[42] Dewey to A. Dewey, October 9 and 10, 1894, Dewey Papers.

an "outgrowth of the home, the church and the university," surpassing all three in its ability to deal "intelligently" with urban problems. It was the settlement's unique role as a home for intelligent and inspired people, rather than as a mission of God or a scientific outpost, that Mead considered its unrivaled strength. The settlement enabled its residents to become an understanding part of city life, self-conscious intelligence in the midst of the incomprehensible urban landscape. In this sense it transcended detached science. In Mead's mind, the settlement embodied the ideal of an engaged "social" science guided by "working hypotheses"—provisional rather than absolute or dogmatic knowledge. For this reason, the settlement outdid the church as a forum in which to make moral judgments that would deal with changing social problems, such as "the right of the employer to use his property rights to control and exploit the labor of children and women [or] the justice of the union in its effort to advance the wage."[43]

The Chicago pragmatists did not limit their involvement in settlement activities to moral and intellectual support. Dewey was a member of Hull House's first board of trustees, and other department members (Mead, Tufts, James Angell, and A. W. Moore) sat on the board of directors for the University Settlement at various times over a twenty-year period. Most of the Chicago philosophers lectured regularly at the settlements, particularly in Hull House's philosophy and social science clubs, and in extension courses. Although most department members regularly appeared at settlement functions, only Tufts took up residency for any length of time, a summer at Hull House spent learning "labor's views and conditions," the attitudes of immigrants, and Addams's interpretation of urban issues. Both Mead and Tufts collaborated closely with Addams on school issues after Dewey's move to New York. Personal relationships with settlement residents were also quite close. Department members regularly invited Addams for dinner and appeared at the settlement dining table themselves. The Dewey family maintained strong personal ties to Hull House even after leaving Chicago. Their children played and took classes in the Hull House kindergarten. Addams held a memorial service for eight-year old Gordon Dewey after his death in 1904. And the Dewey's named their daughter Jane after Addams. The Mead

[43] George Herbert Mead, "The Social Settlement: Its Basis and Function," *University of Chicago Record* 12 (1907–8): 110.

family sustained a similar relationship with those at the settlement on Halstead Street. Over the years, members of the vastly extended Mead family could be found in residence with Addams.[44]

Through their close involvement in settlement activities, the Chicago philosophers were drawn into the periphery of the labor movement, acquiring a distinctively settlement house perspective on class conflict. As many reformers saw it, settlements were of a type with labor unions. Both were the kind of secondary institution social activists and academic radicals believed would mediate the individual's relations to the social whole, providing ethical guidance and group identity as industrialism and urbanization destroyed older communitarian forms. Addams, like Ely and the social Christian preachers before her, considered unions necessary in an age of "combination" for employees to hold their own against their corporate employers.

Mead, who eventually became one of Chicago labor's most reliable academic supporters, and who held more sophisticated views on the subject than his fellow department members, considered unions an essential stage in the evolution of labor-management relations. Like the settlement, the labor union channeled the unorganized energy of the labor movement and working-class discontent, usually expressed in the "programist" form of revolutionary political ideology, into manageable, achievable demands to be presented at the bargaining table (essentially "working hypotheses"). As an alternative to revolutionary socialism, "organized" labor (the adjective was an important hallmark of social responsibility) directed the workers' primitive impulses against their employers (or against capitalism as a social system) "toward immediately possible achievements, with a vivid

---

[44] Dewey's and Mead's participation in the settlement movement is well known and well documented. See Davis, *Spearheads*, 58–59; also Robert M. Crunden, *Ministers of Reform: The Progressives' Achievement in American Civilization, 1889–1920* (New York, 1982), chap. 2; Lewis Feuer, "John Dewey and the Back to the People Movement in American Thought," *Journal of the History of Ideas* 20 (1959): 545–68. On the role of department members in the University Settlement, see list of directors in Box I, folder 3b, MacDowell Papers, Chicago Historical Society. Additional details on the involvement of Chicago philosophers in the settlements can be gleaned from their correspondence: Mead to Helen Castle Mead, June 27, 1901, Mead to son, December 19, 1914, Mead Papers; Jane Addams to James Hayden Tufts, October 15, 1907, and February 22, 1908, Tufts Papers, Amherst. See also Tufts, "Autobiography," and "After 50 Years," in reunion book for Yale Divinity School Class of 1889, in Tufts Papers, Amherst. A limited picture of their participation at Chicago Commons can be reconstructed from Graham Taylor's scrapbooks, Taylor Papers (see note 40).

sense of the present reality of the means used and their necessary parity with the methods of the employer." As with the churches' idealism, born of frustrated attempts to remake the real world, the laboring class's desires and impulses had become projected into an abstract future (as ideology or "program"). Like the reconstruction Dewey envisioned connecting the church with the actual, social world, labor organization restored (or created) an "organic" relation between workers as a group and their social environment, which included employers and the public.[45]

[45] Henrika Kuklick, "Professionalization and the Moral Order," unpublished manuscript, University of Pennsylvania, 1984; Addams, "Settlement as a Factor," 184, 188; Mead, review of Gustave Le Bon's *The Psychology of Socialism,* in *American Journal of Sociology* 5 (1899): 411, and "The Philosophical Basis of Ethics," *International Journal of Ethics* 18 (1908): 318.

CHAPTER SIX

The Educational Situation

Although consistent supporters of trade unionism throughout their tenures at Chicago, Dewey and his colleagues at first limited their labor activism to participating as experts on psychology and pedagogy in the movement for educational reform. That movement, a comfortable alternative to the harder world of industrial conflict, nonetheless addressed distinctly class issues, often from the perspective of the laboring poor.

It was in large part the opportunity to participate in the educational reform movement that attracted Dewey to Chicago in the first place: president William Rainey Harper offered him (in addition to a substantial salary increase and the ability to hire his own department) the direction of the pedagogy department, under which Dewey hoped to create an experimental school for applying and testing his educational and psychological theories. By 1894 the University of Chicago already promised to become one of America's preeminent research and teaching institutions. Begun by Baptist elders with money supplied by John D. Rockefeller, the university in truth was controlled, and its future decisively formed, by Harper, its first president. University policy, partly to offset a reputation as the university of Standard Oil, stressed the importance of social service by faculty, an obligation encouraged by the broader context of Chicago politics and social activism. The social activist experience would be crucial in the development of Chicago pragmatism. But, although the university provided one institutional framework within which Chicago pragmatism would flourish, it was in many ways restrictive. Harper ruled his faculty and students autocratically, placing limits on political outspokenness and on at least one occasion dismissing a teacher for antimonopolistic speeches. Dewey and his colleagues enjoyed relative freedom to form their department's curriculum, but relations with Harper were frequently strained. Harper's arbitrary imperiousness, especially on matters concerning the department's efforts to build a progressive pedagogy program around the University Laboratory School, forced Dewey's departure in 1904. A residue of hostility remained, especially with Mead, until Harper died in 1906.[1]

The School and Society

In 1894, Dewey had little doubt about the socially reconstructive potential of education and the role psychology could play in guiding educational (and thereby industrial) reform. Over the previous two years he had developed the general outlines of a primary school curriculum that soon would earn him the reputation as America's preeminent progressive educator.

The main features of Deweyan pedagogy are well known, but they have suffered some misunderstanding at the hands of later critics and supporters alike. As perhaps the most innovative feature of his curriculum, Dewey introduced actual social relations as the foundation of learning at his University Laboratory School. Set up in a series of Hyde Park locations, the school opened in 1896 with less than three dozen students, three teachers, and a few tables and chairs. By the time it reached its final setting in an old house on Ellis Avenue, one hundred forty children were enrolled, taught by twenty-three teachers and ten assistants from the university graduate school. And, although

[1] Laurence R. Veysey, *The Emergence of the American University* (Chicago, 1965), 366–80; Steven J. Diner, *A City and Its Universities: Public Policy in Chicago, 1892–1919* (Chapel Hill, 1980), 17–20. On academic freedom at Chicago, see documents in Clarence J. Karier, ed., *Shaping the American Educational State, 1900 to the Present* (New York, 1975), 31–47. The University Laboratory School as Dewey envisioned it ended operations in 1904, when it was absorbed into a larger conglomeration of university educational programs. On the Dewey school and Dewey's resignation, see George Dykhuizen, *The Life and Mind of John Dewey* (Carbondale, 1973), 74–81, 108–15; also Katherine Camp Mayhew and Anna Camp Edwards, *The Dewey School* (New York, 1936), 17–19.

still barren of traditional furnishings, it was soon full of the artifacts and tools, constructions and experiments, of a cooperative learning environment. Six-year-olds built models of community life on a sand table, seven-year-olds practiced culinary chemistry in the kitchen, and fourteen-year-olds built an admirable clubhouse in the yard, complete with a darkroom under its mansard roof. The participants and their activities brought together an extended community of reformers, academics, and parents who shared Dewey's commitment to "democratic" education. They shared as well a chronic need for funding to keep the school alive, for despite Harper's initial commitment the school never received much financial support from the university.[2]

The Lab School teachers carefully cultivated a schoolroom community life around "occupations" and practices familiar to the child from everyday life. Beginning with home life, the instructors gradually expanded the children's social universe to include more diverse occupations, other cultures, and other historical periods, all the while encouraging them to investigate the subject matter collectively. With the tools and artifacts of industrial and agricultural production in their hands, children were trained to contribute to the common goals of learning and producing in cooperative ventures such as gardening, cooking, and simple building projects.

Lab School students acquired intellectual skills by applying them practically, learning mathematics through the measurements necessary for carpentry and building, learning botany by raising gardens, learning chemistry in the kitchen as well as in primitive laboratories. As in all things Deweyan, each part of the curriculum was integrated with other parts in an organic conceptual unity worthy of the name "Hegelian." Practical arts facilitated the learning of history, introducing children to the social and economic relations of various epochs and cultures via their industrial arts and agricultural practices. Children would learn about early textile production by first learning to weave. They would then also learn about the cultivation and processing of flax and cotton. This became an opportunity to learn many other things: the social division of labor, the relations between the city and the countryside, the botanical classification of fibrous plants,

---

[2] The Dewey school's history is well chronicled. See Dewey's own accounts in John Dewey, *The School and Society,* in *The Child and the Curriculum and the School and Society* (1902, 1915; rpt. Chicago, 1956); Mayhew and Edwards, *Dewey School,* chap. 1.

the chemistry needed for the processing of raw materials in the textile industry.

Critics of progressive education have consistently derided Deweyan pedagogy by misrepresenting its "child centered" focus as indulgent and undisciplined. Yet, the process of building a curriculum at the Lab School was neither ad hoc and nor chaotic. Deweyan teachers planned the course of studies around the core subject (or activity) of industrial arts and history, "coordinating" diverse lessons, loosely timing the study of historical epochs to coincide with analogous stages in child development. In proposing that the child be the center of early education (the main complaint of progressivism's critics), Dewey meant two things. First, he argued, as did many other psychologists and pedagogues of his time, that teachers must know children—their capacities and incapacities for learning at different stages in childhood, their individual strengths and weaknesses—to teach them effectively. As Dewey understood child development, it proceeded through stages of intelligence and ability linked to the biological development of the body and brain. Second, Dewey maintained, on strongly argued philosophical grounds (as we see below), that the best way to teach children was to capitalize on their own interests rather than force them to learn information and disciplines for extrinsic rewards. So, although Deweyan teaching did indulge the interests of the child, it did so only on the assumption that interest was a necessary prerequisite of well-disciplined and energetic education.[3]

Dewey can be credited with devising a unique, experimental program in elementary education. His ideas and techniques, however, were not entirely innovative. Child-centered education had long been promoted in the teachings of Friedrich Froebel and Johann Pestalozzi, central European proponents of the Rousseauian tradition. German immigrants brought Froebellian and Pestalozzian theories and methods to the United States in the 1850s, which they and their American followers put to work after the Civil War in the new kindergartens and day schools that became increasingly popular with the middle class. William Torrey Harris and Susan Blow promoted kindergartens

[3] For descriptions of the curriculum at the University Laboratory School, see Mayhew and Edwards, *Dewey School,* chap. 2; Dewey, "Plan of Organization of the University Primary School," *Early Work* 5:224–43, and *School and Society.* On the history of progressive education, see Lawrence Cremin, *The Transformation of the School: Progressivism in American Education, 1876–1957* (New York, 1961), chaps. 2–4, 9.

as part of the American Hegelian movement in the 1880s. Harris, who guided a younger Dewey toward graduate study at Johns Hopkins in the early 1880s, espoused a conservative Hegelianism that treated psychological development as an element in spirit's historical unfolding. Although they shared key terms and principles, Froebellianism bore only a faint resemblence to Deweyan pedagogy. Like Dewey, the Froebellians engaged children through play and "occupations" in the larger social world. But the Froebellians tried to achieve socialization in a more schematic formal manner, theorizing that individual children grew intellectually and morally by interacting with the objective manifestations of spirit in history. Using specially designed geometrical blocks, or "gifts," the Froebellians led children through the early stages of spiritual "self-realization," engaging them in carefully controlled versions of "play" and "occupations" that would help internalize spirit's presence in the object world. By playing with spherical blocks, children, according to Harris, would not only internalize the concept of a sphere, or sphericity, but also other forms of unity and wholeness such as social and moral order.[4]

Froebellian romanticism fit nicely with new images of childhood in liberal Protestant and reform communities, changed as Christian nurture edged out orthodox Calvinist notions of original sin. By the 1890s younger psychologists and pedagogues, who accepted many of the teachings of the Froebellian movement about the role of play and self-activity in learning, believed they were carrying the romantic tradition a step farther when they challenged Harris's leadership of the educational reform movement and abandoned the heavily spiritual organicism of the orthodox Hegelians. Dewey, who at the time was reexamining his relation to institutional (and idealist) Protestantism, joined the American followers of Johann Friedrich Herbart in the schismatic Hegelian avant-garde of educational reform. Dewey sat on the first board of the National Herbart Society and contributed several articles to the Herbart *Yearbook*, although they indicated little about the degree to which he subscribed to Herbartian doctrine.[5] The Amer-

---

[4] Dom Cavallo, "From Perfection to Habit: Moral Training in the American Kindergarten, 1860–1920," *History of Education Quarterly* 16 (1976): 147–61; on Harris, see Merle Curti, *The Social Ideas of American Educators* (New York, 1935), chap. 9.

[5] *The First Yearbook of the Herbart Society* (1895; rpt. New York, 1969), 204. The Chicago Froebel Society was long connected with Hull House; see Evelyn Weber, *The Kindergarten: Its Encounter with Educational Thought in America* (New York, 1969), 47.

ican movement allowed broad latitude in interpreting the German philosopher's writing. The Herbartian employment of a core curriculum, suited to the role of apperceptive mass in Herbartian psychology, caught on among kindergarten and other educational reformers. Dewey borrowed the Herbartian principle of correlation directly, though he preferred the word "coordination" and a core of historical studies instead of the Herbartian use of literature. This terminological preference partly reflected Dewey's deeper criticism of Herbartian theory, for example, the advocacy of a rigid "culture epoch theory," a theory of pedagogical and cognitive stages, and the orthodox Herbartian inclination, as Dewey put it, to treat the child "as *pupil,* rather than as human being."[6]

It was largely, however, in the Herbartian spirit that Dewey wrote "Interest in Relation to Training of the Will" for the Herbart *Yearbook* in the winter of 1895/96, which he revised and reprinted for the next several decades. This essay provides a far more sophisticated and revealing statement of Dewey's educational philosophy than his brief enunciation of principles in "My Pedagogical Creed" (1895) or his 1899 address to University Laboratory School parents and supporters, *The School and Society.* "Interest in Relation to Training of the Will" addressed philosophical issues with which Dewey had struggled since Ann Arbor: the problem in neo-Kantian ethics of explaining how the will mediates between desire and obligation, the related contradiction between utilitarian hedonism and the social and political moralism of its major proponents, and the elusive meaning (and often transcendental implications) of post-Kantian idealist notions such as self-realization and self-activity. But the essay went far beyond the philosophical roots of the new pedagogy to engage the issues of citizenship and industry in a troubled republic.

Dewey presented the educational controversies of his time as a "lawsuit" between two psychologies, a traditional "psychology of effort" and Dewey's own "psychology of interest." Traditionalists argued that children are motivated to learn only when disciplined to study and will absorb even the most uninteresting bodies of knowledge with the proper effort and enough extrinsic moral and punitive in-

---

[6] Harold B. Dunkel, *Herbart and Herbartianism: An Educational Ghost Story* (Chicago, 1970), chap. 14; Weber, *Kindergarten,* 10, 18–20, 36–38, 46–47, 56; Dewey, "Educational Ethics: Syllabus of a Course of Six Lecture-Studies" (1895), *Early Works* 5:297.

centive. In the end, not only will the child benefit by acquiring knowledge but society also will gain by instilling greater discipline and better intellectual habits in its future citizens. As was often his custom, Dewey did not name these advocates of effort even if he labeled them. He certainly meant the Gadgrinds, established practioners of a rationalist pedagogy centered around learning literary classics, classical languages, logic, history and civics, and abstract mathematics by recitation, lecture, and reading. His contemporaneous writings indicate that he also meant Harris, then U.S. Commissioner of Education, who for all his Hegelian and Froebellian romanticism placed great stock in discipline, effort, and the moral imperatives of the work ethic.[7]

A Crusade against "False Hegelianism"

Dewey traced the effort psychology to a neo-Kantian dualism between desire and reason, a philosophy that held that one can achieve reason only by overcoming or ignoring desire through a willful effort. Children's immediate interests, based in the emotions and the desire for pleasure, can never lead them to superior knowledge. Education based on interests will only indulge childish inclinations, never cultivate adult rationality. Since the most outspoken critic of the interest psychology was Harris, supported by other conservative Hegelians and idealists who dominated the National Education Association (NEA), Dewey used a device similar to one in his earlier arguments against T. H. Green: Harris was in reality a "neo-Fichtean." Harris, although a confirmed believer in self-realization theory, simply perverted, according to Dewey, the Hegelian way of thinking. Harris turned self-realization into a moral ideal, detached from the true process of realization, which Dewey claimed could be understood only in terms of the interest psychology.[8]

For Dewey the traditional emphasis on effort brought unwarranted separation of means and ends on a psychological as well as an edu-

---

[7] Curti, *Social Ideas*, 318, 325, 330, 346; Cremin, *Transformation of the School*, 19–20.

[8] Dewey, review of William Torrey Harris's *Psychologic Foundations of Education* (June 1898), *Early Works* 5:372–85, "The Psychological Aspect of the School Curriculum" (April 1897), ibid., 5:164–76, and "Self-Realization as the Moral Ideal" (November 1893), ibid., 4:42–53; W. T. Harris, *The Psychologic Foundations of Education* (New York, 1898), chap. 31.

cational level. On the educational level, teachers focused on inculcating a set of values and ideas—established knowledge—without addressing the means by which those ideas would be introduced to the student, that is, without adjusting to the child's psychological and emotional ability to absorb, attend to, or understand the subject matter. On the psychological level, since the child had no interest in the ideas in the recitation book, that is, had no sense of their intrinsic value, he or she learned those ideas for other reasons: for grades, for teachers' praise, to avoid punishment, and so on. The ideas which from the educators' point of view were the purpose of education became, from the child's perspective, mere means to artificial, extrinsic ends. When learned in this fashion, ideas were easily forgotten, once gratification was achieved or the disciplinary environment of the classroom removed.[9]

The psychology of interest, by contrast, integrated desire and reason, the main theme in Dewey's psychological writing since the mid–1880s. Dewey claimed for the interest psychology what he denied the advocates of effort: a true Hegelianism, which described an organic self unfolding through self-activity or self-realization, without falling prey to the "neo-Fichtean" inclination to view the individual self as merely an element of the idealized heavenly spirit. "Self-activity" and "self-realization" were the terms used by Harris and other conservative Hegelians, but Dewey meant them differently. Like Harris, the younger philosopher sought to cultivate a process of objectification in the child, involving a realization of the psychological self in the larger natural and social world. This process began with the child's own voluntary action in its primitive self-activity. Individual self-activity, they both believed, constituted the heart of human agency, the self-caused action of a free and morally responsible being, that part of character and experience undetermined by external forces.[10]

Here the similarity ended—or, rather, Dewey consciously ended it, for in the 1890s he struggled to distance himself from Harris's brand of Hegelianism, a philosophical and pedagogical system that Dewey found formalistic (as he would later describe it) and antidemocratic (as we see below). Although established Froebellians such as Harris placed the child at the center of the curriculum, they did so with

[9] Dewey, "Interest in Relation to Training of the Will" (1899), *Early Work* 5:111–50.
[10] Harris, *Psychologic Foundations*, chap. 3.

authority and control. The child was a savage, according to Harris and many of his contemporaries, driven by irrational passions and impulses, in need of social constraints in order to achieve true self-activity. Social institutions, created by man as he "ascends out of nature," structured "the world of human passions and desires, of human arbitrariness and caprice," into an orderly community in which the childish will was subordinated to the adult common good.[11] Social order facilitated individual self-activity, but only through right education, "the process of adoption of this social order in place of one's mere animal caprice." To attain true freedom (which "has the form of eternity"), the individual must make "the passage from impulse to obediance to social order." On this psychological foundation Harris reserved a prominent spot for play, but he also denigrated the self-active impulses play expressed, opposing play to cooperation as a private pursuit of "immediate gratification" which had to be controlled. The child always stood in need of socialization, which began with the imitation of adult practices, customs, and language, forming the basis for social relations.[12]

Dewey also viewed the child as primitive. But, if the child was a savage, there was something to be learned from and in this savagery. Childish impulses did not differ in kind from rational self-control, only in sophistication and the extent of cooperation. Dewey abhored the opposition of social order to individual self-activity and felt that conservative Hegelians, following Green in Great Britain and Harris in the United States, had allowed a neo-Kantian dualism to intervene between the passions and reason. The child, Dewey argued, just like the "savage" begins with cooperative, social impulses that need only the proper conditions to develop. The school therefore should assume that the child's play is already social in nature, already inclined to recognize primitive responsibilities to others, and should allow the child to learn in self-active cooperative "occupations"—not formalized manipulative regimens—engaging his or her interest on its own terms.[13]

[11] Here Harris referred to the growth of the state in history, but the same applied to the growth of responsibility in the child, whose life history recapitulated the history of humanity; ibid., 260–61.
[12] Ibid., 282–83, 300.
[13] Dewey, "Froebel's Educational Principles" (February 1900), *Middle Works* 1:222–24. Dewey expressed, with remarkable diplomacy, some of his differences with Harris over

Like Harris, Dewey expected the individual's self-activity to follow a path toward greater cooperation and social responsibility. Yet Dewey conceived of self-activity as "always a concrete *specific* activity" in which no idealized self (such as a "moral motive," Harris's ultimate ethical good, or a spiritual object, God) is pursued as a goal. True educational self-realization involves, according to Dewey, an inherently productive and self-cultivating set of schoolroom occupations, which are pursued both for their own sakes and as means to a further end. The integration of means and ends in the act of self-realization constitutes the active interest a child will sustain in the learning process. As Dewey was fond of pointing out, interest means standing between, that is, between self and object as activity, or between self and goal as means to an end. For example, when playing, the simplest and most direct form of truly human activity, children identify self, activity, and object in a way that sets no larger goals and does not differentiate means from end. In most other activity, however, means and ends are separate in time and space. To learn and develop properly, according to Dewey, the self has to identify with both the end of action and with the means, such that the latter is "organically bound up with the end as to share in its value."[14]

The interest psychology called for tailoring the curriculum to the current intrinsic interests and inclinations of the child, discerned in part by scientific psychology and in part by commonsense observation of children's habits. When the purpose of childish activity is to learn something as well as to play, then interest must be sustained by other means than simply the child's natural playfulness. The self must be involved in the process of attaining the ultimate object of knowledge. This did not mean enticing children by appealing to their basest pleasures (as some advocates of effort claimed). Rather, Dewey called for using interest to guide education, coordinating the curriculum in such a way as to help the child identify her self with the goals of learning. Originally the child's family engages her interest, Dewey argued,

---

the question of interest in "The Psychological Aspect of the School Curriculum" (April 1897), *Early Works* 5:164–76.

[14] Dewey, "Interest in Relation to Training of the Will," *Herbart Yearbook* for 1895, 2nd supp. (Chicago, 1896), 223. This original edition contained considerable material excised by Dewey from his 1899 edition. When appropriate, my page citations are to the 1896 edition rather than to the copy-text emendations in the *Early Works*. See also Dewey, "Self-Realization as the Moral Ideal," 43, 46, 52.

through the network of emotional relationships that are also productive and educational. Children learn language, skills, customs, and cooperation (as well as obedience to just authority) out of a natural desire to help achieve commonly held family goals that are tangible and often immediate. The imagined picture of the rural family sustained by Dewey and his colleagues did not include incest, alcoholism, the exploitation of children by their parents, or religious extremism. It was instead a well-knit, cooperative productive unit, independent of political authority, governed by a set of implicit rules and values, and directed toward the readily accepted goals of survival, cohesion, mutual support, and, if possible, prosperity.

Educational Democracy

The conflict between the dualistic idealism of such traditionalists as Harris and the interest psychology reflected a deeper institutional and political conflict in the schools, one between a conservative authoritarianism and the democratic potential of a common school education. The key to educational authoritarianism, and the key to its removal, was the child's relation, at once psychological and ethical, to the objects of knowledge or, as Dewey preferred, the activity of learning. Would the child, Dewey asked, identify with the goals of education, make them a part of himself or herself, and see the purpose in the schoolwork? Or would the child be isolated from the goals of learning, unable to understand the significance or purpose of recitation, and perceive schooling as alien and therefore uninteresting except as a token to exchange for approval and power? The former, according to Dewey and other Chicago educational reformers such as Colonel Francis Parker, constituted truly democratic self-activity in which the child participates in establishing the goals and creating the tools of learning. The latter imposed educational ends and means on the child, in disregard for his or her natural desires and impulses.[15]

[15] Parker was emphatically Pestalozzian in calling for a democratic classroom that allowed children to participate in constructing the curriculum. The Herbartians, in tying curricular development to the psychological and historical growth of the apperceptive mass, also tended to leave the direction of education up to the child and thus viewed themselves as inheritors of the Pestalozzian tradition. See Francis W. Parker, *Talks on Pedagogics* (1894; rpt. New York, 1969), v, 411; Charles De Garmo, *Herbart and the Herbartians* (New York, 1912), 3–11; Dunkel, *Herbartianism*, 30–35, 40.

Schoolwork that does not engage the child's interest is merely drudgery, Dewey argued, in which immediate tasks are unrelated (as means) to educational and personal goals with which the child identifies (or, which the child identifies as part of his or her self-activity). School lessons are "necessary evils, accidentally and externally attached to something we want, so that we can't get one without the other. They are not regarded as in the same process of self-expression as is the end." Traditional schoolwork fails, Dewey believed, because it separates the means and ends of education, contriving goals of learning extrinsic to the learning process itself. By doing so, traditional education and the philosophy that justifies it on ethical (and to a lesser extent psychological) grounds divides the child's character between a commitment to the educational system and his or her own intrinsic interest and motivation.[16]

Much more was at stake here than the organization of classroom activities. The authoritarian separation of means and ends in education reflected, Dewey thought, the absence throughout society of productive activity done for its own or self-expression's sake. Thus, Dewey's model for schoolroom drudgery was factory wage labor in which the worker does not identify self with industrial goals and works simply for remuneration. Factory work thwarts self-realization, Dewey argued, by separating means and ends, relegating one to the worker and the other to the manager or owner. From the worker's point of view, "the day's task is to him only incidentally, accidentally, not intrinsically, a means to the end." He works only for a "physical" end, the wage, not a "psychical" end organically related to his task and his personal aspirations.[17] Factory work and classroom recitations were, for Dewey, instances of the same psychological and ethical failure: in each someone works for a goal not of her own choosing, with which she cannot identify, in which she has no stake. For Dewey this was no better than slavery, if only on a psychological level: "Plato somewhere speaks of the slave as one who his actions does not express his own ideas [*sic*], but those of some other man. It is our social problem now, even more urgent than in the time of Plato, that method, purpose, understanding, shall exist in the consciousness of the one who does the work, that his activity shall have meaning to himself."[18]

---

[16] Dewey, "Interest in Relation to the Training of the Will" (1896), 223.
[17] Ibid.
[18] Dewey, *School and Society*, 23.

Mead made this connection much more strongly in "The Relation of Play to Education," presented at Graham Taylor's Chicago Commons in May 1896 as part of the settlement's open lecture series. In his speech, probably delivered to a socially and ethnically mixed audience of settlement and community residents, Mead attacked the work ethic enforced in the factory and promoted through a dreary and regimented common school curriculum. Like Dewey, he identified a common psychology in factory work and rote learning. Traditional schooling had been based erroneously on the extrinsically goal-directed and controlled "work phase" of human activity, to the exclusion of its two other phases, "play" and "art." This kind of education merely reflected modern work values, reinforcing the alienation, frustration, and self-denial engendered by wage labor and factory work. Mead defined work in general as "an endeavor, in which a definite end is set up, and the means are chosen solely with reference to that end." Although work is a natural part of human life, it allows a separation of immediate occupation from the goals of that activity, such that especially in industrial work "intelligent interest in the product to be attained is not the immediate motive power in holding the laborer to his work." The product attracts the employer's interest but the worker is occupied only with the wage.[19]

To restore the right relation to work, Mead argued, means and ends must be reintegrated such that work becomes its own reward: "It is ... impossible to get beyond this incomplete and unnatural character of work until the whole man responds immediately to the product upon which he is working, and is not required to seek for impetus in his labor from an interest that lies completely outside his shop or factory and its activities." By reintegrating means and ends in this manner, one turns work into something akin to art, activity the purpose of which is intrinsically connected to the form and means of execution. "It is an unfortunate workman who is in no sense an artist," Mead wrote, "and a sorry artist who never works."[20] Similarly, Dewey held up sculpting as the paradigmatic opposite of drudgery in classroom and factory:

The sculptor has his end, his ideal, in view. To realize that end he must go through a series of intervening steps which are not, on the face of it,

[19] George Herbert Mead, "The Relation of Play to Education," *University of Chicago Record* 1 (1896): 141–42.
[20] Ibid., 142.

equivalent to the end. He must model and mould and chisel in a series of particular acts, no one of which is the beautiful form he has in mind, and every one of which represents the putting forth of personal energy on his own part. But because these are to him necessary means for the end, the ideal, the finished form is completely transferred over into these special acts. Each moulding of the clay, each stroke of the chisel, is for him at the time the whole end in process of realization. Whatever interest or value attaches to the end attaches to each of these steps. . . . A genuine interest in the ideal indicates of necessity an equal interest in all the conditions of its expression.[21]

Mead's and Dewey's idealization of art and artisanship echoed the pre-Raphaelite aestheticism so influential among middle-class settlement activists in the 1890s. With the genteel expectation that an exposure to "high" western European art and collegiate American culture would humanize and civilize members of their working-class, immigrant community, Hull House activists spent much of the settlement's first years creating galleries, sponsoring talks on the classics, and trying to get their neighbors to participate. Jane Addams and her colleagues undertook these activities in the elitist spirit of John Ruskin and Toynbee Hall, the British equivalent of (and inspiration for) the settlement house. Their frustration, however, at engaging the interest of the community led to projects more in keeping with the guild socialist aesthetics of William Morris, such as the Hull House Labor Museum, a historical gallery opened in November 1900 to display the industrial arts and crafts of the many immigrant cultures found on the near west side. Approximating an adult version of Dewey's Lab School classes (Hull House residents initially considered calling the museum the Labor School), Addams and her colleagues brought local women in to demonstrate spinning and weaving methods from their respective lands of origin, including Italy, Syria, Russia, and Ireland. While Hull House made industrial history the primary object of its lessons, residents supplemented the industrial arts demonstrations with songs, European prints depicting weavers, and lectures on the history of the labor movement. After a successful first year in which previously disinterested older members of the community took part in Hull House activities for the first time, the settlement planned to expand the museum to include wood and metal work, pottery, and

[21] Dewey, "Interest in Relation to the Training of Will" (1899), 128.

bookbinding. By this time art, for the settlement residents, represented an expression of the community, of its customs, its habits, the characteristics acquired in its long history, and its dignity. If Addams and her colleagues initially hoped to assimilate the diverse immigrant subcommunities into a true American civilization, they soon recognized that they could not simply impose a genteel culture on their neighbors. They increasingly appreciated immigrant folkways on their own terms, even if they continued their attempts to ease immigrant assimilation.[22]

The Hull House Labor Museum displayed a Morrisite conviction that art and work, as Mead had argued, must be restored to the right relation enjoyed in artisan economies. Art, wrote Hull House's Ellen Gates Starr in 1895, could "set the leaven of the beautiful in the midst of the ugly. . . . It is only when a man is doing work which he wishes done, and delights in doing, and which he is free to do as he likes, that his work becomes a language to him. As soon as it does so become it is artistic."[23] Art was a reformer's tool, something more than a "fringe . . . on the end of the day," insisted Addams. It was the interjection of humanist, Christian values into the drudgery and conflict of industrial life. Likewise, Dewey believed it possible "to extend the idea of artistic production to all kinds of work." Settlements, argued Starr, by "holding art and all good fruit to be the right of all," would help overcome the "impious warfare of the children of God."[24]

Manual Education

By restoring more organic relations among art, play, and work, the Chicago pragmatists hoped to reestablish rewarding occupations and

[22] "First Report of a Labor Museum at Hull House" (n.d.), pamphlet in Hull House Papers, University of Illinois at Chicago; Rivka Shpak Lissak, *Pluralism and Progressives: Hull House and the New Immigrants, 1890–1919* (Chicago, 1989), chaps. 2–3.

[23] Ellen Gates Starr, "Art and Labor," *Hull-House Maps and Papers* (New York, 1895), 165, 167, 179.

[24] Dewey, "Imagination and Expression" (September 1896), *Early Works* 5:202; Helen Lefkowitz Horowitz, *Culture and the City: Cultural Philanthropy in Chicago from the 1880's to 1917* (Lexington, Ky., 1976), chap. 6 (Addams quoted p. 135); see also T. J. Jackson Lears, *No Place of Grace* (New York, 1981), chap. 2; Starr, "Art and Labor," 179; "First Report of a Labor Museum"; Frank Lloyd Wright "The Art and Craft of the Machine," in *Eighty Years at Hull-House,* ed. Allen F. Davis and Mary Lynn McCree (Chicago, 1969), 85–88.

crafts in the new industrial order of factories and cities. Dewey and his colleagues envisioned and promoted a radical transformation of the educational system which eventually would eliminate the tendency in modern society to divide intellectuals from workers, and ethical consciousness (concerned with ends) from practical execution (the employment of means). "The most interesting and vital problems in educational practice today," declared Dewey to an art and manual training convention in 1906, "are such as concern the connexion of play and work, of the intellectual and informational and the dynamic and motor factor; of instruction from books and teachers and from self-guided productive activities; such as concern in short the development of a type of education which shall make at once a man or a woman and a worker." The ability of these new citizens to build an egalitarian society would depend on their ability to achieve a psychological wholeness akin in form to the union of the mental and manual in the experience and activity of the craft worker.[25]

Dewey and his colleagues built the foundation for this expected transformation in the coordinated curriculum, with one cornerstone the teaching of industrial and cultural history and another the instruction in practical arts and crafts. At the heart of this second cornerstone lay manual education, the training of children in the use of crafts and their tools, especially, though by no means exclusively, woodworking. Manual education was to produce the new "democratic" man and woman, who would no longer live divided by social barriers or within rigidly hierarchical classes.

Dewey made a career out of promoting manual education. Within a few years after his arrival in Chicago he achieved recognition as the country's leading proponent and theorist of nonacademic training in the public schools (especially after Parker's death in 1902). When Harper annexed the Chicago Manual Training School in 1902, he and Dewey made the University of Chicago's pedagogy department one of the few places in the United States for the training of manual education teachers. Mead acquired his reputation as an advocate of manual education after Dewey's departure from Chicago, and by 1910 he led the local movement for an equitable, single-track industrial education program.[26]

---

[25] Dewey, "Culture and Industry in Education" (1906), *Middle Works* 3:290–91.
[26] Dewey, "Plan of the Proposed Pedagogy Department," typed manuscript, University

Like child-centrism and the coordinated curriculum, Dewey's and Mead's industrial program also had ample precedent. American educators had advocated the inclusion of manual education in some part of the common school curriculum at least since 1879, when the tools and methods used in Victor Della Vos's "instruction shops" at the Moscow Imperial Technical School were exhibited at the Philadelphia Centennial Exhibition. Americans initially borrowed the Russian technical training system as a solution to problems encountered in engineering education and as a means to train students in lower-level industrial skills. Within a short time, American businesspeople began to promote manual education, hoping that technical training would help circumvent established, union-controlled apprenticeship traditions as a means to train skilled labor. During the 1880s several manual training schools were established in major American cities with the support of national and local business organizations; Chicago's Commercial Club founded the Chicago Manual Training School in 1884. By the 1890s manual education advocates had overcome Harris's staunch resistance in the NEA.[27]

Manual education attracted conflicting groups of supporters, with different conceptions of its role in the broader curriculum and of its relevance to the social and political problems of the day. In the hands of its business proponents, manual training was almost entirely vocational, part of a strategy to introduce into American schools a two-track, European-style curriculum which would train the working class in technical skills in one set of schools and teach the middle and upper classes liberal arts in another. There were, however, those who considered manual education an instrument of moral and social adjustment that transcended narrow vocationalism. Between 1895 and 1904 reformers put a great deal of weight on the introduction of manual training into the common school curriculum as the means to revitalize moral education in America and tailor it to the needs of a factory-centered industrialism.

Much of this concern focused on order rather than justice and on the moral economy of skilled and civically responsible labor, which

of Chicago President's Papers, Box 30, Folder 23, Regenstein Library, University of Chicago; Mead, *Report of the Committee on Industrial Education* (Chicago, 1911), Introduction.

[27] Editorial, *Manual Training Magazine* 2 (1900–1901): 59; Cremin, *Transformation of the School*, 23–34; Sol Cohen, "The Industrial Education Movement, 1906–17," *American Quarterly* 20 (1968): 95–110.

manual education promised to maintain. Addams, for example, traced social conflict to the proliferation of unskilled laborers, who, because they "[feel] constantly the restriction which comes from untrained power," cannot "keep [their] sense of proportion" and rebel. "There is no more dangerous agency in modern civilization than the demogogue, with ignorant labor at his back," declared Charles H. Keyes, the supervisor of the NEA's Department of Manual Training. "He can do little or nothing with the intelligent mechanic or artisan, but no tyranny is so unreasonable as the tyranny of illiterate labor." Mead also observed that "labor troubles are comparatively absent from these [skilled] callings." Finding ways to restore skills or provide adequate substitutes for the artisan work ethic became something of a cottage industry among educators and social activists. Manual training advocates considered tool exercise the necessary tonic for an ailing work ethic, standing, as one writer put it, "for a large measure of that which is the general nature and idea of work." Mead similarly contended that the "intelligence of the artisan who made the whole article made of him an admirable citizen of the older community." This "intelligence," Mead believed, "very largely . . . made the success of our early democratic institutions."[28]

While few believed they could actually restore artisans to their former role in the American republic, many manual training advocates hoped to reconstitute some kind of similarly virtuous citizen out of the fragmentary elements of the modern character. Most advocates claimed the moralizing effects on psychological grounds. Irene Sargent, a professor of art history at Syracuse University and an outspoken leader of the Arts and Crafts movement, warned that without manual education or some similar palliative to mindless work a factory operative "will develop morbidly, and his mind will offer a resting-place for destructive and chaotic ideas." He might become "an insurrectionist, perhaps even a pervert and criminal."[29] Charles Ham, the first director of Chicago's Manual Training School and author of

[28] Addams, "The Settlement as a Factor in the Labor Movement," in *Hull-House Maps and Papers*, 195; Report on Charleston National Education Association convention, 1900, *Manual Training Magazine* 2 (1900): 46; Mead, "Relation of Play to Education," 142; A. W. Richards, "The Thought Side of Manual Training," *Manual Training Magazine* 3 (1902–3): 65–66; Charles R. Henderson, "The Manual Training School as a Factor in Social Progress," *Manual Training Magazine* 2 (1900–1901): 5; Mead, "Industrial Education, the Working-Man, and the School," *Elementary School Teacher* 9 (1908–9): 371.
[29] Sargent quoted in Lears, *No Place of Grace,* 71.

a widely read treatise on manual training, argued that manual education would right an "ill-balanced mental constitution," the product of urbanization, with "the essential element of rectitude [physical development or skill]." "May not the two systems of training [intellectual and manual] be so connected in the schools," he asked, "as to cause the manual to react upon the mental, with the effect of greatly strengthening the ethical side of the mind?" University of Chicago sociologist Charles R. Henderson considered manual training essential in "the unfolding of every human being." Others simply believed manual instruction would teach respect for work, revitalizing a dying work ethic and combating the evils of sloth and idleness. It "opens up" activity that facilitates moral growth, thereby helping remove "the disposition to riotousness, to self-abasement," argued one speaker before the NEA in 1901.[30]

As Ham's remarks suggest, some support for manual education evoked pastoral nostalgia for a mythological rural America. Manual education advocates believed that as families moved to cities children lost contact with facets of life necessary for proper moral upbringing and adequate social and political awareness. The traditional emphasis on formal literary and scientific learning was considered ultra-intellectual and one of the many aspects of city life corrupting American "manhood" by isolating it from its rural source of vitality. The city, reported president William DeWitt Hyde of Bowdoin College, "tends to breed a race of mental dwarfs and moral cripples" who "come to school with flabby minds as well as flabby muscles, with undeveloped wills as the counterpart of unused hands." The loss of "motor activities" provided by farm chores and the loss of practical engagement in productive work isolated the child from fundamental aspects of the learning process. Immigration exacerbated this problem with a new influx of what G. S. Hall called "the great army of incapables" into public schools. Nativist educational and social reformers considered immigrant students of lower caliber than their "native"

[30] Charles H. Ham, *Manual Training: The Solution of Social and Industrial Problems* (New York, 1886), 132, 137. Charles R. Henderson, "Manual Training School as a Factor"; "The Value of the Sloyd Idea as a Basis for Educational Manual Training"; report of address by William DeWitt Hyde, "The End of Education," at Connecticut State Teachers Association; and report on paper of R. Charles Bates at the NEA's Department of Superintendent (February 1901), *Manual Training Magazine* 2 (1900–1901): 5–6, 40, 109–10, 169–70.

schoolmates and in need of supplementary vocational and manual training. It became even more urgent to decrease the dropout rate as states began to consider child labor laws that would force young workers out of the factory and, many feared, into the street.[31]

Yet it would be a mistake to trace back the interest in manual education to nothing more than a fear of moral and civil disorder. At least a significant minority of manual education advocates, many associated with the same institutions and networks as the Chicago pragmatists, hoped that in addition to restoring the rabble to order manual education would cultivate the other features of civic virtue, which would benefit the poor and working class: cultural enrichment, greater control over work life, cooperation, and equality. In Chicago, for instance, the interest in educational alternatives grew with concern over the problem of child labor. Led by the most labor-oriented and socialist members of the Hull House community, Florence Kelley, Alzina Stevens, and Abraham Bisno, the Chicago reform community made child labor a central issue, thereby focusing attention as well on the inadequate schooling provided the city's working class. During the 1890s child labor became a hot issue among social reformers, who believed factory work morally debilitated adolescents and helped create, with cyclical and structural unemployment, juvenile delinquency and antisocial behavior. Reformers considered manual education the necessary complement to compulsory attendance laws as a way to keep in school working-class children, who, it was believed, took little interest in intellectual work.[32]

On the face of it, the concerns of reformers' were not those of the people they hoped to serve. But the pursuit of social order and less riotous dispositions did involve a genuine concern for the enrichment of working-class lives. Reformers hoped manual education would recreate the "whole man" by restoring the lost connection between

[31] Hyde, "End of Education," 109–10; David E. Gordon, "Manual Training for Negro Children," *Charities and the Commons* 15 (1905): 84; Hall quoted in Cohen, "Industrial Education Movement," 99; editorial, "Child Labor and the Schools," *Chicago Teachers' Federation Bulletin*, October 6, 1905, 4; Mead, *Report of the Committee on Industrial Education*, Introduction.

[32] On Kelly's work, see Florence Kelley and Alzina Stevens, "Wage-earning Children," in *Hull-House Maps and Papers*, 49–78; Dorothy Rose Blumberg, *Florence Kelley: The Making of a Social Pioneer* (New York, 1966), chaps. 9, 11. For a critical appraisal that sets "child saving" in the broader structure of changing social relations see David Hogan, *Class and Reform* (Philadelphia, 1985), chap. 3.

intellectual and manual aspects of human endeavor, a psychological balance of head and hand. It was believed that the social divisions of industrial society created analogous divisions in the human psyche. Resulting social problems could be attacked through schooling and psychological readjustment. This was seen in part as a matter of reducing the tensions of the marketplace by redirecting the child's focus from competitive academic achievements toward self-fulfillment and self-realization. Manual training motivated the child by noncompetitive means, by appealing to the child's nonintellectual interests and, through them, drawing the child into intellectual study gradually. More often manual training was seen as the basis for the child's introduction to the complex interdependencies of modern society. For Dewey this meant using the child's motor instincts to initiate him "into the laws of human production and achievement, and into the methods by which man gains control of nature, and makes good in life his ideals." Far more than instruction in industrial history, this education was designed to help children become aware of and assume their various roles or functions in society (as worker, family member, citizen). Manual training would provide the requisite "trained and sound body, skillful eye and hand, habits of industry, perseverance, and, above all, habits of serviceableness."[33]

At times even reformers' pastoral longings transcended simple nostalgia. Dewey promoted manual training with a sophisticated argument about the effects of changes in social production on individual psychology. As the family moved to the city, it became less an organic productive unit in which all members participated in social and industrial activity centered in the rural home. There the child had benefited morally and mentally, acquiring "self-reliance, independence of judgement and action," as well as "habits of regular and continuous work." The factory system's intensive division of labor and the consequent disintegration of the rural or semirural household changed all that. The home was changed "from a workshop into a simple dwelling-place" in which the child lost contact with useful occupations and "the practical and motor training necessary to balance his intel-

[33] Mead, "Relation of Play to Education," 143; C. Hanford Henderson, "The Manual Training Outlook," *Manual Training Magazine* 2 (1900): 65–75; Dewey, "The Place of Manual Training in the Elementary Course of Study" (1901), *Middle Works* 1:236, and "Ethical Principles Underlying Education," in *Third Yearbook of the National Herbart Society* (Chicago, 1897), *Early Works* 5:59, 65, 66.

lectual development." Urban children, though they absorbed more information during increased school hours, lost the "power of using it."[34]

Both Dewey and Mead feared the political consequences of over-intellectualized schooling. As the division of labor removed tasks from the home, children lost contact with those functional parts of human industry that became divided up between different occupations and socioeconomic groups. This narrowed the child psychologically, but also morally. Like many, Dewey and Mead considered psychological fragmentation a major contributing factor to class tensions of the late nineteenth century. Mead argued that industrial conflict boiled down to the inability of workers and capitalists to understand each other's functional position in society, divided along psychological lines between manual and mental occupations. The first step toward removing industrial disagreements from the vicious circles of ideological and political contests, Mead argued, "is the recognition that it is the incompleteness with which the different social interests are present that is responsible for the inadequacy of the moral judgements [relating to industrial negotiations]." Addams, in an article supporting the Chicago Teachers Federation entrance into the Chicago Federation of Labor, made a similar argument. Children with manual training will have a different attitude toward labor than those without. Not only will students acquire knowledge of and experience with manufacturing through classroom reenactment of industrial history, but they will also learn about the lives of workers, past and present. Students, Addams argued, thus will acquire an empathy for and understanding of the "habits, needs and hopes" of America's laboring classes. This sensitivity would provide the basis for a more democratic, experimental approach to contemporary social problems. Students so educated might in the future "be able to restore a genuine relation between the workman and the scholar without all the groaning of the spirit which now afflicts the classically educated individual, when he attempts to restore a balance between the cultivation of his hand and brain."[35]

[34] Dewey, "The Primary Education Fetich" (May 1898), *Early Works* 5:258–59.
[35] Mead, "Philosophical Basis of Ethics," 318; Addams, "On the Humanizing Tendency of Industrial Education," *Chicago Teachers' Federation Bulletin*, July 3, 1903, 4; Dewey, "Primary Education Fetich," 267; Richards, "Thought Side," 68.

Conservative and radical advocates alike believed that these social influences and the therapeutic effects of manual training penetrated to the neurological level. By 1900 a new orthodoxy had emerged in educational reform that linked manual training regimens, particularly the Swedish *sloyd* series of woodworking exercises, to stages in the child's neurological development. Manual training, it was believed, connected positively to the central nervous system, improving overall coordination, developing neurological complexity, exercising talents, and establishing habits that transferred automatically to other physiological and neurophysiological activities.[36]

In this way, manual training figured significantly in the Child Study movement of the 1890s. Proponents of Child Study argued that, once psychologists and physiologists could learn the patterns of childhood development, they could devise a science of teaching that would closely guide grade school instruction. Of course Child Study enthusiasts differed sharply on what *sort* of patterns the scientist would discover in the child. Most agreed, however, that children follow uniform or nearly uniform stages of growth. Many Child Study advocates proposed "recapitulation" theories according to which children develop through stages that parallel the stages of human evolution. Some drew pedagogical lessons from similarities they perceived between supposedly retarded children and "races" that most educated Americans considered physiologically and psychologically primitive. Retarded children, the physiologists insisted, exhibit the characteristics of lower species or "races," such as webbed hands, "mongoloid" eyes, or "negroid" facial features. "Normal" children display similar features but grow out of them. To help the child grow out of those stages and to avoid any possible educationally induced retardation or regression to a primitive stage, teachers, it was argued, must pay close attention to the level of the child's development. Older children can handle "fine work," for instance, such as writing in books at their desks. Young children's primitive physiology, however, with its limited coordination and neurological refinement, requires that they engage in projects that resemble the primitive art of South Sea

---

[36] Walter J. Kenyon, "Spirit and Purpose of Manual Training in the Elementary School," *Manual Training Magazine* 3 (1902): 82; reports of conference of Eastern Manual Training Association in Cleveland (June 1900), *Manual Training Magazine* 2(1900): 40, 42, 44.

Islanders or, for slightly older children, industrial crafts. Manual training specialists found their niche in the work provided at these early
stages of childhood development.[37]

Followers of Child Study typically applied manual education's approach to neurological development and *sloyd*'s conveniently stagist
program to the treatment of the insane, pioneering the use of occupational therapy. University of Chicago psychologist James Angell,
for example, lectured in 1908 for Taylor's Chicago School of Civics
and Philanthropy on "The Value of Occupations in Improving the
Minds of the Insane." The course, for insane-asylum attendants, combined instruction in the use of manual training (paper construction,
clay molding, basket weaving) with instruction in applying play techniques. As stated in the school's promotional leaflet, the purpose of
the course was to find new methods to "restimulate" the "warped
and dull" minds of the insane "by occupation, instruction and amuse-
ment following much the same lines which the best teachers of little
children find most effective." In keeping with the developmental
model championed by Child Study, which presented insanity and
"feeble-mindedness" as arrested development, Angell and Taylor's
school believed that treatment of the insane was essentially the same
as early childhood education, particularly in the methods to train the
nervous system and motor coordination.[38]

Even those who, like Dewey and Mead, felt uncomfortable with
the strict stagist developmentalism of the *sloyd* series or recapitulation
theory, accepted the correlation between neurological development
and manual training. The new neurophysiology's antidualistic model
of the relation of mind and body also fit comfortably with the Chicago
philosophers' psychological and social organicism. During the 1890s,
the Chicago pragmatists accepted a broadly construed Hegelian version of recapitulation theory in which the child's ontogenetic development roughly paralleled human phylogeny. Dewey welcomed manual
training's recognition that "a motor factor is so closely bound up

[37] Frederick Burk, "From Fundamental to Accessory in the Development of the Nervous
System and of Movements," *Pedagogical Seminary* 1 (October 1898): 34–36; Francis
Parker, "Editorial," *Transactions* of the Illinois Society for Child Study 3 (January 1899):
205; G. Stanley Hall, "Child-Study: The Basis of Exact Education," *Forum* 16 (December
1893): 432; H. H. Donaldson, *The Growth of the Brain* (1895; rpt. New York, 1914).
[38] Course description in Chicago School of Civics and Philanthropy, Box II, 1903–8
folder, Graham Taylor Papers, Newberry Library, Chicago; course description in *Survey*
20 (1908): 388–89.

with the entire mental development that the latter cannot be intelligently discussed apart from the former." In "attitude" the child is "primitive," being "decidedly motor" in its activity. Manual training, by directing children's "motor powers to recapitulate social industries," will lead them through social and industrial progress and the full history of human knowledge. Viewed in neurophysiological terms, the student is a "reservoir of motor energy, urgent for discharge upon his environment." Nervous energy expends itself most likely and most beneficially, Dewey felt, as a recapitulation of the history of "social occupations." The order of the recapitulation, while only approximate, must be respected, with special care taken not to force small children to engage in tasks too refined for their primitive motor and sensory skills.[39]

Democracy in Education?

The championship of a revitalized work ethic and the crusade against neurological decay were by no means separate issues. They converged with a genuinely humanitarian desire to improve working conditions, emancipate factory operatives from enslavement to their machines, and return social and political power to the uprooted denizens of the industrial landscape. To be sure, the treatment of the child as a biological organism subject to scientific study and control, and Child Study's penetrating inspection of the child's behavior, had their repressive implications, especially in the writings of the many physiologists and educators who envisioned public education as an extensive system of social control and rehabilitation. The temptations of child anthropometry lured even Dewey, who at times characterized students as objects infinitely malleable for the benefit of social order. His and Mead's notions of self-realization through progressive training conformed to traditional ideals of an educated and essentially conservative citizenry who would define their self-activity primarily in terms of service to society rather than dissent or rebellion.[40]

There is, in fact, no simple way of categorizing Mead's and Dewey's

[39] Dewey, "Place of Manual Training," 232–34, 236; Kenyon, "Spirit and Purpose," 80–87; Dewey, "Criticisms Wise and Otherwise on Modern Child-Study" (1897), *Early Works* 5:210.

[40] Dewey, "Interest in Relation to Training of the Will" (1899), 118–19.

work on educational theory and practice. Both philosophers tried to build social and psychological order on a foundation of humanistic and, they believed, democratic values. Dewey spoke for the need to train children for self-direction, adaptability, leadership, and control over their circumstances so that they "may take charge of [them-selves]; may not only adapt... to the changes which are going on, but have power to shape and direct those changes." This especially applied to children of the laboring class who had lost any "fixed station in life" and faced careers subject to the vicissitudes of tech-nology. Dewey viewed manual training as a method of social unfold-ing in which institutional setting fostered the individual enrichment that in turn enriched society as a whole. Manual education, thus, would "give play, give expression to [the child's] motor instincts, and ... do this in such a way that the child shall be brought to know the larger aims and processes of living."[41]

Mead was more definite than his older colleague, favoring a new apprenticeship system in which all children would learn adaptable industrial skills supported by theoretical knowledge of industrial, so-cial, and economic organization. This, Mead believed, would allow the apprentice to adapt to a variety of tools and situations and would free future workers from enslavement to machines and automation. "The school and the shop must go hand in hand in modern artisanship. Their lack of connection in the old system spells the disappearance of the old-time system as the old-time artisan has disappeared. There can be no question that the modern artisan demands schooling if he is not to be a mere creature of the machine."[42] An integrated manual and academic curriculum, Mead argued, would also form the basis of truly democratic labor-management relations, which would be more efficient without falling prey to the enticements of technocracy. At some times Mead sounded almost like British guild socialist Morris in his advocacy of worker participation and shop floor democracy. By 1908 he tied a moderate form of codetermination to his proposed apprenticeship system, calling for direct consultation and empower-ment of employees. But his argument was ambiguous, however com-mitted he was to creating a humane workplace: "The expert even in

[41] Dewey, "Ethical Principles Underlying Education," 59–60, and "Place of Manual Training," 235.
[42] Mead, "Industrial Education, the Working-Man and the School," 372.

industry demands not blind obediance but intelligent co-operation, and the more intelligent the co-operation can be, the higher the efficiency of the expert. What is wanted in an ideal machine shop, where the tools are made to do certain work, is that the man who uses the tools should be able to criticize the tools."[43] Writing in terms acceptable to the moderately liberal businesspeople to whom he appealed, Mead put distinct limits on industrial democracy and stressed its efficiencies over its ethical and political virtues. Although attributable in part to the audience he addressed, Mead's ambivalence typified his and Dewey's writing before 1904. It became even more pronounced after 1904, as Mead entered the leadership of the progressive reform movement, and was especially evident in the philosophy and social reformism emanating from the Chicago philosophy department of that period.

Reformers had limited success transforming work into craft or injecting art into what must have seemed an enveloping factory culture. Settlement workers directed much of their energy into union support and factory legislation, neither of which did much to change the basic relations or attitudes of workers to their work. They were somewhat more successful outside the workplace, in forcing access to cultural institutions for lower-class Chicagoans. Mead, like many others, also advocated profit sharing, ostensibly as a means to encourage worker interest in company fortunes.[44]

As Mead realized, however, the direct liberation of work from tedium and alienation was an "improbability," due only at the "millennium." Only in education, which in its current form both reflected and reinforced the bifurcation of means and ends in society as a whole, could something be accomplished: "We are not able to reconstruct our whole industrial system so that the labor shall be always an expression of the whole man, but we are able to banish this slavish dwarfing method from our school rooms."[45] As we have seen, the Chicago pragmatists and their circle strongly supported unionization. Unionization, however, was only one answer to the social and psy-

[43] Ibid., 375.
[44] Horowitz, *Culture and the City,* chap. 6. For a particularly dismal failure at early factory welfare reform involving both Addams and Dewey, see Robert W. Ozanne, *A Century of Labor-Management Relations at McCormick and International Harvester* (Madison, 1967), 41–43; Mead, "Relation of Play to Education," 142.
[45] Mead, "Relation of Play to Education," 143.

chological problems of modern society. Many problems existed beyond the reach of the mediating power of trade unions. As Mead saw it, the effects of industrial change penetrated to people's fundamental attitudes, so that while legislation could meliorate social hardships, and while ostensibly neutral parties could arbitrate industrial conflict, neither could guarantee necessary moral and psychological development. In theory, with unions came greater responsibility on the part of workers, and with the challenge presented by unions corporate power would be checked. But Mead and Dewey noted that collective bargaining had limits and that strikes and union solidarity also encouraged conflict and rigid class boundaries. For institutions like unions to work, there must first be a concerted effort on the part of academics and the public to arbitrate differences. There must also be a change in attitudes, in social psychological roles, which only education could provide, either through cultural programs designed to enrich laborers' lives and inform the middle class about slum and factory conditions or through curriculum reform designed to break down social barriers of class and occupational status.

Dewey, in fact, though a strong union supporter, wrote little during his tenure at Chicago to justify his support on philosophical or sociological grounds (except in defending teacher autonomy vis-à-vis the Chicago superintendent of schools). For him social mediation was most effectively achieved through the broader ethical training that only school could provide, and that unions could in fact hinder by forcing individuals into class roles. Showing a distinct change of allegiance from the heady July days of 1894, Dewey exclaimed in 1899 that teachers would minister the new Kingdom, not trade unionists. Reformers such as Addams seemed to treat trade unionism as necessary only given the context—as a defense against factory production rather than as the organizational basis for democracy (as a socialist like Eugene Debs believed). Although Addams and other settlement workers strongly supported the trade union movement, their commitment occasionally wavered. This wavering became especially evident in later struggles between the teachers union and the superintendent of schools, in which Addams sided with the superintendent.[46]

---

[46] Dewey and James H. Tufts, *Ethics* (New York, 1908), chap. 12; Mead, "Industrial Education, the Working-Man, and the School," 370–77; Dewey, *School and Society*, 60–

Indeed, most of the labor reform with which Dewey or Mead had contact before 1910 was educationally oriented. Though education would not change the workplace directly, it could change, so it was believed, the mentality of employers about their social and moral responsibilities. Instruction could also transform the attitude of employees toward their work. In some cases this change involved the palest sort of industrial meliorism that tolerated the fundamental evils of factory work, letting psychological reform displace a genuine alleviation of working conditions. Some of Addams's statements justifying manual training disclose a relative lack of interest in the actual relations of production in the factory. Her main concern was with the psychological adjustment of workers to their plight as factory operatives: "A man who makes, year after year, but one small wheel in a modern watch factory, may, if his education has properly prepared him, have a fuller life than did the old watchmaker who made a watch from beginning to end."[47] Nor did Dewey challenge the basic hierarchy of authority in the workplace. "Some are managers and others are subordinates," he wrote. The proper education would socialize them to a common sense of purpose, enabling each "to see with his daily work all there is in it of large and human significance." "How many of the employed are today mere appendages to the machines which they operate!" Dewey exclaimed, suggesting that this was "due in large part to the fact that the worker has had no opportunity to develop his imagination and his sympathetic insight as to the social and scientific values found in his work." Dewey even suggested that marriage, by providing employees greater stake in their jobs, would thereby make them see "new meaning" in their tasks and encourage "steadiness and enthusiasm previously lacking."[48]

Slowly the Chicago philosophers reached a more sophisticated understanding of the labor problem than the one they applied under the tutelage of Franklin Ford at Ann Arbor. But theirs was an unhappy consciousness about work and industry. On the one hand, their educational psychology addressed even more basic questions of social reorganization than did political rhetoric grounded in structural social

---

61. On Addams's disputes with Haley, see Julia Wrigley, *Class Politics and Public Schools, Chicago 1900–1915* (New Brunswick, 1982), 115–17.

[47] Addams quoted in Lears, *No Place of Grace*, 80.

[48] Dewey, *Child and Curriculum*, 24, and "Interest in Relation to Training of the Will" (1899), 127–28.

analysis (for instance, Marxist socialism). The Chicago pragmatists wanted to build industrial democracy on a reconstruction of social relations that penetrated to the roots of social injustice in the daily relations and attitudes of teachers and children, workers and managers. Their "radically" democratic stance extended to support for organized labor, directly and through educational reform, a risky position in the 1890s at a university that tolerated little criticism of industrial capitalism. On the other hand, in their emphasis on attitude and psychology, the Chicago philosophers missed just as deeply rooted structural causes of social inequality and injustice, an absence of thought that would undermine their ability to critically respond to the rapidly changing terrain of economic and political life. This divided consciousness did not result from an effort to hide political radicalism from the university administration, a "politics of protective coloration."[49] Rather, it resided in the Deweyan model of human action, at the root of pragmatist psychology and social theory, the heart and divided soul of their "radical" democracy.

[49] Robert B. Westbrook, *John Dewey and American Democracy* (Ithaca, 1991), 86–92.

CHAPTER SEVEN

The Reflex-Arc

Two years after arriving at Chicago, Dewey published "The Reflex-Arc Concept in Psychology." He claimed that his essay, an attack on mechanistic versions of the "new" physiological psychology, met the "greater demand for a unifying principle" in a field disoriented by its own accumulation of facts. "The material is too great in mass and too varied in style to fit into existing pigeon holes," Dewey wrote, "and the cabinets of science break down under their own dead weight." Although the "reflex-arc" concept had adequately unified the science until then, it was no longer sufficient in 1896.[1]

Few escaped Dewey's criticism. In "The Reflex-Arc Concept" he openly attacked the dominant schools of Anglo-American and German experimentalism and the reflex-arc model they applied to experience and behavior. Dewey had in mind any theory that in his estimation depicted mind as a sequence of discrete reflexes, including the functionalism of William James and James Mark Baldwin as well as the psycho-physics of Wilhelm Wundt and the mechanistic reductionism of Herbert Spencer. As an alternative Dewey proposed, first, that mind is continuous and active and that mental activity traces a "reflex-circuit," an unbroken "coordination" of functionally differentiated activity. Second, Dewey contended that the contents of mind—ideas, percepts, affects—are "functions" constructed to facil-

---

[1] John Dewey, "The Reflex-Arc Concept in Psychology" (July 1896), *Early Works* 5:96.

itate survival in a problematic environment. Finally, Dewey argued that human activity and thinking follow a "doubt-inquiry" pattern in which doubts emerge when obstacles and novel events interrupt habitual activity, stimulating inquiry and ideation, the projection of "working hypotheses."

Idealism and Functionalism

The 1896 essay may not have done all that Dewey claimed for it, but it did codify a new set of terms with which to describe and analyze human action and it was crucial in establishing the direction of the Chicago philosophy department. Historians have marked the article as a turning point in Dewey's intellectual development. It was, according to the standard histories of psychology, the first statement of the functionalist psychology for which the department became famous, beginning the gradual ascent toward the mature instrumentalism found in the *Studies in Logical Theory* published seven years later.[2]

Dewey's intellectual biographers often note as well that by this time he had abandoned the absolute spirit and other conventional elements of his earlier idealism. This may be one of those historical issues that misdirects our attention away from a richer understanding of the philosophical strategies Dewey, his colleagues, and most important their broader network of associates employed to address the problems and audiences of their era. Certainly Dewey was able to find the language that would convey his previously idealist arguments about mind without entangling him and his psychological teleology in the web of transcendental or absolute idealist theories. The change in terminology, however, obscured important continuities between Dewey's instrumentalist functionalism and his earlier philosophy. As in his earlier expositions on the New Psychology, in his reflex-arc article Dewey sought to demonstrate, incontrovertibly and scientifically, the thoroughgoing immanence of mind in the neurological functioning

---

[2] Edna Heidbreder, *Seven Psychologies* (New York, 1933), 209; Edwin Boring, *A History of Experimental Psychology* (New York, 1950), 554; Robert B. Westbrook, *John Dewey and American Democracy* (Ithaca, 1991), 67–71. On the centrality of the department's psychological research, see James Rowland Angell, unpublished autobiography, pp. 30–31, Box 2, Folder 7a, Angell Papers, Sterling Library, Yale University.

of the body and the presence of telos in the biological functions of human existence. With this new language of immanent teleology as a starting point, guided by the principle that mind is a self-active, creative force in the construction of experience, the Chicago Pragmatists fashioned a model of social action on which they and others could hinge a new reformist politics.[3]

In many respects Dewey simply gave new language to old ways of thinking, achieving his 1886 goal of forming a rhetorical bridge between idealist philosophy and nascent evolutionary psychology. The new terminology that characterized Dewey's mature instrumentalism bears a strong resemblance in meaning to concepts he used in his earlier, explicitly idealist work: they preserved the earlier organicism, and, although one cannot find such idealist hallmarks as the doctrine of internal relations, they restated rather than rejected the central principle of teleological immanence. Many of the key terms and concepts were the same, for instance, "interest," "action," and "attention." Others, such as "habit," "reflex," and "impulse," which were common to most psychology of the period, Dewey used with idealist meaning. Finally, Dewey found equivalents of earlier idealist terms which allowed him to avoid the transcendental implications of the idealist tradition. Where in 1886 Dewey used such idealist terms as "redintegration" and "apperceptive mass," in 1896 he and his colleagues wrote of "reconstruction" and "coordination" or adapted the physiological notion "habit" to the idealist concept of apperception.[4]

One thing Dewey accomplished through his reconstruction of psychological terminology was to claim the mantle of science for a philosophical tradition in danger of being closed out of the experimental

---

[3] The standard text on this transition is Morton White, *The Origins of Dewey's Instrumentalism* (New York, 1943), especially chaps. 8 and 9. White does not focus on the reflex-arc critique. Dewey, "From Absolutism to Experimentalism," in *Contemporary American Philosophy: Personal Statements,* 2 vols., ed. George Plimpton Adams and William Pepperell Montague (London, 1930), 2:13–27; George Dykhuizen, *The Life and Mind of John Dewey* (Carbondale, 1973), 83–94; Bruce Kuklick, *Churchmen and Philosophers: From Jonathan Edwards to John Dewey* (New Haven, 1985), chap. 16, traces idealism further into Dewey's career than does White or Dykhuizen.

[4] The term "coordination" was widely used in the era's educational psychology, expecially among Herbartians; see Charles De Garmo, *Herbart and the Herbartians* (New York, 1912), pt. 3, chap. 4. The terms "apperceptive mass" or "apperception mass" continued to be used by Chicago anthropologists and sociologists into the 1920s; see Rivka Shpak Lissak, *Pluralism and Progressives: Hull House and the New Immigrants, 1890–1919* (Chicago, 1989), 26.

laboratory. The reflex-arc critique based human psychology on a synthesis of physiological response and mental action, which from Dewey's perspective (as in the judgment of others) united idealist
philosophy with Darwinian biology and speculative faith with experimentation. The fact that he cut his evolutionary psychology from
idealist cloth did not mean, Dewey insisted, that he stood in reaction
to scientific progress: "In criticizing this conception it is not intended
to make a plea for the principles of explanation and classification
which the reflex arc idea has replaced."[5] Any mental science that did
not recognize mind's constructive role in experience, Dewey argued,
simply dealt in abstractions from actual experience. Any science that
did not accept mind's immanence in the world we perceive could not
be fully empirical.[6]

After Psychology

Dewey and his colleagues sorted out the terminology and substance
of the reflex-arc critique over the course of the early 1890s. A syllabus
written for Dewey's spring 1892 introduction to philosophy at the
University of Michigan continued to attribute the organic unity of
consciousness to the telos permeating all aspects of human action.
Rather than explain mental activism in terms of apperception and
redintegration, however, Dewey substituted the reflex-arc as the central principle of psychology (and therefore philosophy), referring to
the organic unity of action (and therefore of mind) as a coordination.
The psychological substratum of reality, for Dewey, ceased to be
"knowledge as such" and became "action." Whereas the reflex-arc,
Dewey argued, is the "unit of nervous action," the term applied not

---

[5] Dewey, "Reflex-Arc Concept," 96.

[6] Dewey made this case in another form against the pessimistic appraisals of humanity
by Darwin's most successful popularizer, Thomas Huxley. Interpreting Darwin in the most
orthodox and deterministic manner, Huxley dissociated ethical judgments from human
evolution and consequently the evolutionary science of psychology. Dewey countered that
Huxley misinterpreted the dynamics of evolutionary change, providing a classic American
version of evolutionism that depended heavily on neo-Lamarckian concepts of biological
development. See Richard Hofstadter, *Social Darwinism in American Thought* (Boston,
1955), 95–96. Dewey, "Evolution and Ethics" (April 1898), *Early Works* 5:34–53. The
argument resembled one used at the time to support the so-called Christian sociology as
well as Christian socialism; for example, see George Herron, *The Christian Society* (Chicago, 1894), chap. 1.

just to automatic reflexes but to "every unified action," from a child's impulse for food to philosophical theories, from the movement of an amoeba to a "virtuous act."[7]

For Dewey each reflex-arc was "a coordination of certain experiences; ... an *expression,* more or less direct, more or less explicit, of the whole of life; ... the manifold circumstance of the Universe attaining a unity in action." The reflex-arc thus had a double meaning. It still referred in the conventional sense to the central nervous system's "minor reflexes," automatic responses to external stimuli. But it also referred to the unity of action—coordination—provided, Dewey argued, by the will. The reflex-arc, in Dewey's terminology, became a synonym for the will, a "moving equilibrium of actions" which like the will is a "unity of action; this unity being constituted by the relationships of subordinate activities." By introducing purpose to activity the will established an order to the multitude of responses and perceptions available to the mind. As a neurological equivalent of the will, Dewey's conception of the reflex-arc bore little resemblence to the reflex of Spencer or Alexander Bain. It more closely resembled the apperceptive processes discussed by Johann Friedrich Herbart, Hermann Lotze, and Wundt. All minor acts within a reflex-arc, whether a philosophical theory or the baby's grab for food, became subordinate to the act's overall purpose or, as Dewey now more frequently called it, its function.[8]

Dewey's commitment to physiological psychology did not change over the next three to four years and was in fact the main attraction Mead found in the Ann Arbor department. But apparently Dewey's first uncritical appropriation of the reflex-arc as the unit of psychological and philosophical analysis began to trouble him. In two articles written for *Psychological Review,* he criticized a more conventional reflex theory, the celebrated James-Lange theory of emotion, the view of James and Danish psychologist Carl Lange that emotions are simply the secondary reflections of automatic responses to external stimuli. According to James and Lange, one's emotions do not cause one's actions but represent reflections on specific behaviors that respond to specific stimuli. When one sees a bear in the woods, one does not first

[7] Dewey, "Introduction to Philosophy: Syllabus of Course 5" (February 1892), *Early Works* 3:212. On the history of reflex-arc psychology, see Robert M. Young, *Mind, Brain, and Adaptation in the Nineteenth Century* (Oxford, 1970), chap. 5.

[8] Dewey, "Introduction to Philosophy," 212, 214–15.

feel fear and then prepare to run. Rather, fear is an emotional reflection on whatever response one makes to the stimulus. The bear, not the fear, is the stimulus to which one responds by running away. Dewey explored the possibilities of uniting the James-Lange theory with a more teleological conception of emotional development taken from Charles Darwin's *Expression of the Emotions in Man and Animals.*[9]

Although Dewey's most obvious concern was to synthesize the two theories, his true purpose was to demonstrate the unintended idealist implications of the James-Lange thesis: "It furnishes this [Dewey's] old idealist conception of feeling, hitherto blank and unmediated, with a medium of translation into the terms of concrete phenomena." The problem with the James-Lange theory, however, was that it did not go far enough. In many instances the teleological and evolutionary character of affect (as an activity) was lost. Many affective responses, for example, the cold sweat of fear, were simply "idiopathic" for James, arbitrary responses to stimuli having no evolutionary value or explanation. Although no direct survival value is evident for such responses, Dewey argued, they are nonetheless "teleologically conditioned," representing "disturbances, defects, or alienations of the adjusted movements" which have evolutionary value.[10]

Dewey in fact introduced a new element into James's theory. Agreeing with James that evolution selects actions, not ideas or feelings, he construed activity in an entirely different manner, one consistent with his position in 1886. He had problems with the mechanistic quality of activity under James's theory—it was not organic enough and needed "reconstruction." James characterized action as a sequence of stimuli and responses (what Dewey later pejoratively called the reflex-arc). The idea or object acts as a stimulus, the behavior is a "discharge" of the stimulus, a neurological response, and emotion is the "repurcussion" of the discharge. Against James's view Dewey proposed a

[9] Charles Darwin, *The Expression of the Emotions in Man and Animals* (London, 1872); Dewey, "The Theory of Emotions," *Early Works* 4:152–88; William James, *The Principles of Psychology,* 2 vols. (New York, 1890), 2:482. Dewey agreed with Darwin but did not accept that emotions could be independent of behavior and therefore cause it in the manner Darwin proposed. The James-Lange theory, in contrast, treated emotion as a corollary of action. This was the position Dewey himself "laid down quite schematically" in 1886, that "feeling is the internalization of activity or will"; Dewey, "Theory of Emotions," 170, 171n.
[10] Dewey, "Theory of Emotions," 170, 160.

model similar to the one he offered in his 1886 *Psychology,* but with different terminology. He maintained that "the mode of behavior is the primary thing, and that the idea and the emotional excitation . . . represent the tension of stimulus and response within the co-ordination which makes up the mode of behavior."[11] With a few minor exceptions, emotion occurs when the coordinated totality of action, the reflex or habit, breaks down. A tension arises between the tendency to act habitually and a perception that is incongruous with preexisting activity. The incongruous perception, when viewed as part of a broader coordination, signifies for the individual the possibility of future action different from the present habit. The perception, signifying the future, is ideal. This, argued Dewey, is the true nature of stimulus and response. In this complex process, contended Dewey, the emotion "stands for the entire effort of the organism to adjust its formed habits or co-ordinations of the past to present necessities as made known in perception or idea. The emotion is, *psychologically, the adjustment or tension of habit and ideal,* and the organic changes in the body are the literal working out, in concrete terms, of the struggle of adjustment."[12] Emotion, then, occurs when coordinated activity breaks down and adjustment between parts of activity is necessary to recoordinate action. One only feels emotion, to use James's example, when one has no automatic response to the bear encountered in the woods. If we are in the habit of petting bears and .this one bites, we feel fear as we change our habit and run away. Habitually running from bears (as most of us do), by Dewey's argument, entails fear only when the bear disturbs our coordinated habit of walking in the woods (without bears) and we must adjust the activity of strolling with the perception of the bear.

The Chicago Experiment

Dewey did not explicitly repudiate the reflex-arc concept underlying the James-Lange theory until his 1896 article, but on his move to Chicago he suggested experiments for the new psychology lab that

[11] Ibid., 174, emphasis removed.
[12] Ibid., 185. See also George H. Mead, "Herr Lasswitz on Energy and Epistemology," *Psychological Review* 1 (1894): 172–75, for a similar statement concerning perception of objects.

were designed to challenge all psychology that took the reflex as its unit of analysis. The experiments were the work of James R. Angell and Addison W. Moore. At Ann Arbor, Angell had written a diligent masters thesis on mental imaging and memory which fit neatly into a small corner of James's and Dewey's psychological territory. Following an itinerary quite similar to Mead's, Angell studied in Germany after a year at Harvard. After a one-year stint at the University of Minnesota, Dewey appointed him instructor at Chicago. Far more successful academically than Mead, Angell additionally took the directorship of Chicago's experimental psychology laboratory, a position Dewey originally had sought for Mead. Moore, after having received his doctorate from the department in 1895, stayed on as a teaching fellow and later as a professor.[13]

Angell and Moore's 1895 study contributed to a vast literature on reaction-time. Reaction-time experiments were an indispensible part of the psychological studies perfected by Wundt and his students in Leipzig. In such experiments, subjects pressed a key or some other device under varying conditions in response to visual, aural, or tactile stimuli. The particular kind of study conducted at Chicago called for the subject to vary the focus of attention in preparation for the signaling stimulus, either on the organ of reception (the ear, when the stimulus was aural) or on the organ of response (usually a finger). The experiment's goals were to test the effects of attention on perception and to determine any variations in response time. Some of Wundt's students discovered that when the subject focused on the hand (called a "motor reaction"), response time was on average quicker than when he or she focused on the ear (a "sensory reaction").[14]

The existence of a regular pattern became a matter of dispute between the "structuralist" psychology of the German school (repre-

---

[13] When compared with young Mead's informal philosophical explorations, Angell's thesis seems constricted, assimilating a vast psychological literature but without Mead's agonized insights. The thesis can be found in Box 25, Folder 307, of the Angell Papers at Sterling Library, Yale University. Neither Mead nor Angell finished their doctorates. A reluctant William R. Harper hired Mead at Dewey's insistence, probably without a sterling recommendation from James Angell, Sr., who thought him a poor teacher and was glad to see him leave Michigan. See James Angell to James R. Angell, June 3, 1994, Angell Papers, Box 3, Folder 18; Dewey to W. R. Harper, March 27 and April 10, 1894, University of Chicago Presidential Papers, Box 17, Folder 11, Regenstein Library, University of Chicago; Dykhuizen, *Life and Mind*, 77–78.

[14] James Angell and Addison Webster Moore, "Reaction-Time: A Study in Attention and Habit," *Psychological Review* 3 (May 1896): 245–58.

sented in the United States almost exclusively by Edward Titchener at Cornell) and the "functionalist" theories that were beginning to dominate American psychology. The dispute centered on the interpretation of experiments such as the reaction time studies, but the theoretical implications went much deeper.

The discovery of a reaction-time pattern sufficed for most followers of the Leipzig paradigm, especially Titchener. Structuralists like Titchener and other adherents to Wundtian psycho-physics were inheritors of that part of the associationist tradition that held the mind to be composed of mental elements. A British student of Wundt's, Titchener reduced all higher cognition to two psychological "elements," the sensation and the affect. There is, Titchener insisted against the idealist tradition, no conative element, no initial involvement of the will in the psychological process. He maintained that mind is a concatenation of sensations and feelings, a reflex-arc, discrete psychological events linked by laws of association. It is unclear whether Titchener considered this an accurate picture of the mind, or whether he considered it only a model that one must accept for the sake of rigorously scientific investigation. At the very least, though, structuralist psychology, in excluding the study of telos, only studied mind abstracted from actual cognition, practice, or circumstances. The psychological laboratory was for structuralists a refined atmosphere for the sudy of mental essences. Titchener admitted the abstract nature of this undertaking but insisted that one could and must study psychological parts, the elements of sensation and affect, before the whole of action.

Baldwin at Princeton challenged Titchener's findings on empirical and theoretical grounds. His lab work revealed the existence in the general population of two "reaction types," motor and sensory. With these results Baldwin challenged the Leipzig assumption that in studying the responses of an individual subject (through such experiments and trained introspection) psychologists studied mind as such. Baldwin's introduction of individual psychological differences suggested that mind does not have a universal structure. That, and the fact that a subject's responses changed over time (without simply converging to the norm), also suggested to Baldwin that both voluntary and involuntary reflexes are functions, not, as Titchener argued, "structures" of thought.[15]

---

[15] This famous exchange in the history of psychology can be traced through the following articles: E. B. Titchener, "Postulates of a Structural Psychology," *Philosophical Review* 7

Angell and Moore finished their study as the Baldwin-Titchener dispute unfolded acrimoniously on the pages of *Mind* and *Psychological Review*. Based on their own rather inauspicious empirical findings and on Mead's and Dewey's "dynamo-genetic" model of action, Angell and Moore argued that Baldwin's irregular time differentials did not signify different types of responses but instead represented a relation between habit and attention. Each person had idiosyncratic, habitual coordinations that they "customarily employed in the everyday business of life." Those coordinations "would afford pathways peculiarly pervious to rapid nervous discharges, i. e. they would form paths of least resistance." Changes in reaction time were due to a complicted relation between attention and the degree to which a particular aspect of an act was habitualized.[16] All psychological events, they held, emerged with the disruption of a coordination; just as in Dewey's remarks on James's theory, emotion accompanied action rather than motivated it.

Like Baldwin, the Chicago department viewed the mind as functional to survival. Unlike Baldwin, they argued that the mind cannot be divided into mental elements, be they structures as Titchener argued or functions as Baldwin interpreted them. The smallest unit of psychological analysis, argued Dewey, is an act or coordination (what two years earlier he labeled a reflex-arc). The structuralists began with "rigid distinctions between sensations, thoughts and acts" and tried to construct a "sensori-motor circuit," really a "patchwork of disjointed parts, a mechanical conjunction of unallied processes." Baldwin's "incomplete" functionalism similarly divided action into discrete elements, stimuli, responses, and so on. A complete functionalism recognizes that even the distinction between stimulus and response, or sensation and affect, is merely functional. Titchener's elements were in fact not separate, distinct entities but "divisions of labor, functioning factors, within the single concrete whole." The distinctions between stimulus and response are "distinctions of func-

(September 1898): 449–65, "Structural and Functional Psychology," *Philosophical Review* 8 (1899): 290–99, and "Simple Reactions," *Mind*, n.s. 4 (1895): 74–81; James M. Baldwin, "Types of Reaction," *Psychological Review* 2 (1895): 259–73; Titchener, "The Type-Theory of the Simple Reaction," *Mind*, n.s. 4 (1895): 506–14; Baldwin, "The 'Type-Theory' of Reaction," *Mind*, n.s. 5 (1896): 81–90; Titchener, "The 'Type-Theory' of the Simple Reaction," *Mind*, n.s. 5 (1896): 236–41; Baldwin, "Types of Reaction," *Psychological Review* 2 (1895): 265–73. See also James R. Angell, "The Relations of Structural and Functional Psychology to Philosophy," *Philosophical Review* 12 (May 1903): 243–71.
[16] Angell and Moore, "Reaction-Time," 246, 254.

tion, or part played, with reference to reaching or maintaining an end." They are coordinated with each other to achieve that end and cannot be treated outside the purposive act without losing their functional definitions.[17]

It is only when the coordination breaks down, when an obstacle or incongruous, difficult object interferes with habitual action, that conscious stimuli and responses emerge from the stream of habitual experience. Normally an act "functions" without awareness. It is habitual. One becomes aware of a stimulus only when one's habit of acting is somehow disturbed. The disturbance draws attention to the act itself; one then has the stimulus to action "in mind." Someone walking does not think about walking but rather about something else or nothing at all. Walking requires attention only when something like a hole in the sidewalk or a debilitating affliction interferes. "The sensation or conscious stimulus is not a thing or existence by itself; it is that phase of a co-ordination requiring attention because, by reason of the conflict within the co-ordination, it is uncertain how to complete it."[18] In the first case, the hole becomes a stimulus to change one's path. In the second, the affliction requires constant attention to all the minutiae of locomotion (including holes).

Dewey borrowed the oft-used example of a child reaching for a flame to illustrate his argument. The child's habit of reaching for bright objects is disrupted by the burning of the flame. The originally unconscious habit suddenly turns into a painful awareness of the habit, the stimulus, and an array of possible responses. The child doubts both what she sees and her usual response, and it is this doubt "which gives the motive to examining the next act." The first response in this case is inquiry, a complex act that leads (ideally) to a better definition of the stimulus, the event that has just taken place. The child learns (ideally) that her act of reaching her hand into the bright object was an act of passing her hand into a flame. In "response" to her need for a new response to bright objects, the child discovers a new, more specific stimulus ("flame," not just "bright object") as well as a new, more prudent practice in the presence of candles.[19]

---

[17] Dewey, "Reflex-Arc Concept," 97, 100, 104.

[18] Ibid., 106–7; Angell, whose widely used 1904 textbook popularized Chicago's functionalism, put it more clearly: "Consciousness appears at those points where the purely physiological mechanisms of the organism prove inadequate to cope with the requirements of its life"; *Psychology* (New York, 1904), 176.

[19] Dewey, "Reflex-Arc Concept," 107.

The dynamic Dewey perceived was no different than the one he read into Darwin, James, and Lange and likened to his own position of ten years earlier. In 1886 he wrote of dissociated perceptions that represented aspects of experience incongruous with the apperceptive given. In 1896 he wrote of doubts that arose with the interruption of a habit or the breakdown of a coordination. In 1886 he argued that feelings and other psychological elements were the products of a continuous process of active cognition which was also practical and biologically adaptive. In 1896 he presented those elements as the products of a continuous activity in a problematic environment.

Dewey had revised his psychology considerably since the publication of the 1886 textbook. He and his colleagues refined his original understanding of how cognition functions in evolution and how perceptions, feelings, and ideas emerge from the seamless line of activity. They also stressed the physiological basis of action more and emphasized the role of motor activity in cognitive development. And they dropped almost all reference to spiritual absolutes. But, as becomes evident in the next chapter, what they retained from Dewey's earlier explicitly idealist philosophy was at least as important as what they changed, for philosophy and for social reform.

CHAPTER EIGHT

The Working Hypothesis
and Social Reform

Chicago pragmatism did not enjoy the longevity or depth of its counterpart in Cambridge. With Dewey as its central figure, the school had an institutional life of merely ten years, barely a moment in the history of philosophy. If the department had an historical focus, however, it hovered between its institutional location at the university and the more amorphous set of contacts, networks, and activities of Chicago's reform movement. As a school of thought, Chicago pragmatism wore the traces of earlier theological and academic discourses, but it was the city that dressed it up for the twentieth century, providing its distinctive character and determining its substantial relation to American culture and politics. While bracketing Chicago pragmatism's brief institutional life, the decade after the Pullman strike amounted to a far more important formative period for a set of broader social and discursive links that outlived Dewey's direct leadership. Quite unlike Harvard's golden age of philosophy, which defined itself within ivy-covered institutional walls, Chicago pragmatism inscribed itself in the industrial and political life of the city, a task that took several decades to accomplish.

In this setting, the publication date of the reflex-arc critique takes on extraphilosophical significance. In 1896, the nation watched the disappointing absorption of the Populist movement into the perennially unworthy Democratic party and their joint failure at the polls in November. The rhetoric of Christian socialism rose to higher and higher levels of anticapitalist indignation, in frustration over the business class's indifference to the message of Jesus. Locally Chicagoans no longer suffered the deepest hardships of the depression, but they dealt with an informal political repression in the aftermath of the strike, renewed when an unstable anarchist assassinated President McKinley in 1901. Socialist parties and movements were still present in the city's intellectual and political life, but they had lost considerable momentum. Dissident voices suffered in the academy as well. The 1895 firing of University of Chicago economist Edward Bemis for advocacy of trade unionism and bimetallism and for criticism of John D. Rockefeller, the university's founder, sent a clear message to faculty members that public expressions of political radicalism would be dealt with harshly at Harper's university.[1]

Department members continued to occupy their comfortable niche in the reform culture, between what appeared to them to be warring ideological parties of the left and right. It was during this period that Dewey, Tufts, Mead, James R. Angell, and some of their students regularly attended settlement events, lecturing on topics in philosophy and psychology: "the evolution of intelligence" (Mead), educational psychology (Dewey and his students), Epictetus (Dewey). Mead gave a stereopticon presentation on Hawaii at Hull House, Dewey met with the Chicago public school teachers and provided kindergarten training, and Angell gave workshops at Chicago Commons for asylum attendants. While the rest of Chicago seemed mired in the problems of class and industrial conflict, the settlement culture must have seemed a safe haven from which to explore the intersecting discourses of reform, revolution, and repression.[2]

From this vantage point, the reflex-arc article served as something of a quiet manifesto, one of many. "The point of this story is in its application," Dewey insisted, and he and his collegues would continue to make that point in a series of articles written between 1895 and

---

[1] On the Bemis case, see Mary O. Furner, *Advocacy and Objectivity: A Crisis in the Professionalization of American Social Science, 1865–1905* (Louisville, Ky., 1975), chap. 8.

[2] The ancestral homestead of the Castle family was in Hawaii. Mead supported the planters in the 1893 liberal coup against Hawaiian Queen Liliuokalani. See issues of the Hull House *Bulletin* in Addams Papers (microfilm), and Graham Taylors scrapbooks, in Taylor Papers, Newberry Library, for a record of the department's activities. The Chicago School of Civics and Philanthropy ran the asylum attendant classes in 1908. They are described in Louise Wade, *Graham Taylor, Pioneer for Social Justice* (Chicago, 1964), 170.

1910 which addressed the problems of the city as problems in psychology. The pragmatists hoped this psychological view of social disorder would substitute for what they called the "class view," the representation of social conflict as an irreconcilable contest between classes (or in premodern societies, castes) that would end only with the defeat of one class by another. While Dewey and his colleagues fit many perspectives under the rubric of "class view," they were especially critical of the revolutionary socialism and anarchism they heard from the working-class participants in settlement house activities. Not only did the pragmatists hope to convert revolutionaries to a reformist political program, but they hoped to demonstrate that the intersecting forces of social disorder, when properly understood, could be balanced within the organic coordination of the reflex-circuit. Only then, they argued, could the irrationalities of class politics be abandoned and a reasonable, experimental program of reform put in place.

In this historical context, the new psychology's power lay in its demonstration of mind's immanence in history and human action, in finding "the meaning of the spiritual in the whole process of realizing the concrete values of life."[3] And this search became a common project among department members. Higher cognition emerged, they argued, phylogenetically and ontogenetically from the most primitive, biologically based behavior. Not only reason but those attributes and products of reason that late Victorian social Christians cherished as the message of Jesus also inhered in the circuit of coordination: cooperation, compassion, brotherhood, reciprocity, sociality. The reflex-circuit—unbroken, barriers and walls taken down, with a coordinated division of labor between the psychological functions—represented the hope of reconstructing society on the real foundations of human behavior as described by the science of psychology.

By theoretically integrating ideas in the circuit of adaptive behavior, the Chicago pragmatists provided themselves and others with a point of departure for a social psychology of knowledge that worked much like Hegel's philosophy of history: it offered a critical framework from which to analyze previous theories, and it justified the cultural and political engagement of the Chicagoans' own philosophy. For the pragmatists the highest order of thinking functioned on a historical

---

[3] John Dewey, "The Reflex-Arc Concept in Psychology" (1896), and "Psychology of Effort" (January 1897), *Early Works* 5:109, 159.

scale much as elemental ideas functioned for the individual, as reflections on the problems of current behavior and as signs of future
action.

Thus, Chicago functionalism subsumed all branches of knowledge
into psychology, viewing each discipline as an aspect of human action,
a position for which they were both credited and criticized. "All
reflective thought," argued Mead in 1900, "arises out of real problems
present in immediate experience, and is occupied entirely with the
solution of these problems or their attempted solution" Each philosophical discipline represents on a grand scale a stage in the effort to
solve a practical problem, much as the individual creates conceptual
tools to solve problems encountered in individual experience. Metaphysics is an abstract statement, "in permanent form," of the problem
on a level of analysis reached only when the conflict between hypo-
thetical solutions "persists and cannot be ignored." Deductive logic
is the study of what the Chicago philosophers liked to call the "past
meaning of the object," which is to say the way problems of perception
and conception have been solved in the past (in the manner that the
child in the reflex illustration determined that the shiny object was a
flame). The future meaning of objects and the establishment of new
concepts or universals is the subject matter of psychology and inductive logic, the logic of experimental science. Finally, the general theory
of logic is "the general theory of the intelligent act as a whole."[4]

These were the principles that guided Dewey's contribution to the
Studies in Logical Theory, which, viewed in the context of his and
his colleagues' earlier writing, is somewhat anticlimactic. In four essays devoted to the logic of Hermann Lotze, Dewey argued that the
German logician interpreted logical notions as absolute because he
failed to "define logical distinctions in terms of the history of readjustment of experience." Dividing the subject matter of logic from
that of psychology, Lotze also divided the material of thought, its
antecedents and sensory stimuli, from thought itself. This distinction
posed the same problem for Lotze as that between noumena and
phenomena had for Kant: if thought is something different from its
antecedents or subject matter, how can the antecedents of thought

[4] George Herbert Mead, "Suggestions toward a Theory of the Philosophical Disciplines,"
Philosophical Review 9 (January 1900): 1, 2, 4.

cause thought? How can thought "know" ontologically different subject matter or construct a coherent experience around those "objects"
which is not abstract, subjective, and meaningless? Outside the circuit
of functionalist action, dualistic philosophers presumed, as Angell
observed many years later, "an incredible and unceasing miracle."[5]

As he did with many of his philosophical benefactors, Dewey re-
translated Lotze into the terms of the reflex-circuit: Lotze's distinctions between thought and its subject matter were actually only
functional "divisions of labor" arising in the course of reflective inquiry into problematic experience. The overall evolution of human
acts subordinated ideas, including logical categories, and objects to
the more inclusive psychological whole of which ideas and objects
were a part. As Hegel had subsumed Kant, so the new functionalism
subsumed those who preceded it.[6]

Ethical judgments occupied a similar place in the circuit of coordination as the propositions and axioms of logic: they inhered in
biological development as expressions of the ever-changing telos of
behavior. Ethical judgments, Dewey argued in *Psychology,* are a natural part of an individual's activity, and moral development occurs
as the individual matures, biologically and socially. In early Deweyan
ethics, judgments of a socially responsible individual emerge out of
the initially impulsive pursuit of self-gratification. The individual does
not pursue pleasure as such, as the hedonists argued (Dewey followed
T. H. Green here), but seeks out specific objects of gratification, requiring an increasingly refined intelligence to know those objects and
the means of obtaining them. Reason and consciousness increase in
sophistication as the objects of desire recede in time and space. To
be truly reasonable, desire must imply "a consciousness which can
distinguish between its actual state and a possible future state, and is
aware of the means by which this future state can be brought into
existence." Impulses can never reach ends by working blindly, argued
Dewey. "They must be directed along certain channels by the intel-

[5] Dewey, with the cooperation of members and fellows of the Department of Philsophy,
Studies in Logical Theory (Chicago, 1903), 20, 26, 36–37; James R. Angell, unpublished
autobiography, p. 28, Angell Papers, Box 2, Folder 7a, Sterling Library, Yale University.

[6] See also Simon Fraser McLennan, "Typical Stages in the Development of Judgement,"
128–42, and A. W. Moore, "Some Logical Aspects of Purpose," 341–81, in *Studies in
Logical Theory.*

lect." The mind must have a conception of how to achieve the ultimate goal. It must have "the paths which the impulse must follow."[7]

This process is repeated, for Dewey, on a higher level, in the deliberation between conflicting desires. Once a desire is established, that is, once a reasonable object is conceived, then the agent must decide whether that desire harmonizes with even larger goals, for example, with his faith. He must also choose between incompatible desires. Rising through a spiraling accession of sophisticated desires, the individual pursues self-realization in the most enlightened Christian sense, eventually discerning what is universally desirable and drawing the rest of society into his conception of self. Ethical ideas, in this scheme, function merely as the projections of possible selves to be realized; making ethical judgments or choosing between desires amounts to choosing between possible selves, or possible states of activity: "The conflict of desires is the conflict of self with self."[8]

The personal development of ethical judgment parallels the personal development of rational choice: both flow from chaotic, indifferentiated impulses toward an ordered, rationalized will. This position did not substantially change from 1886 to 1904, when Angell incorporated Dewey's argument (combined with those of William James and others) in the final chapters of his functionalist psychology textbook. The common thread between the childish impulse and the mature character of an adult is the will, which the pragmatists insisted emerges organically out of physiological impulses and reactions of the organism. The rationalizing agency of individual self-development and species evolution is more than just implicit in the primitive impulse; it is an evolved version, organized and reconstructed within the constant circuit of psychological coordination.

In Dewey's 1886 *Psychology,* self-realization culminated in membership in a Christian community led by a church, cooperatively seeking God's earthly Kingdom. By the early 1890s, as Dewey became increasingly estranged from the church, the goals he attributed to self-realization changed as well. Self-realization alone, "the realized will, the developed or satisfied self," now sufficed as the moral end

---

[7] The means, however, are not simply tools but ends in themselves, "proximate" ends, "the end analyzed into its constituent factors"; Dewey, *Psychology* (1886), *Early Works* 2:312, 317–18.
[8] Ibid., 315.

of all human activity and was found "in satisfaction of desires according to law," that is, with "adjustment" to the natural and social environment. Dewey's belief in the immanence of the spiritual and the masterful synthesis of Christian ethics and faith with science allowed him to drop any reference to a spiritual absolute standing at the end of history. Human conduct, individual and social, has a direction—self-development, a continually expanding scope of activity that enriches the agent materially and spiritually. Thus a good man for Dewey is not one who observes moral rules and maintains ethical order or one who strive toward utopia or knowledge of God, but one who is entirely engaged in self-realization. He "is his whole self in each of his acts," acting not simply according to habit and routine but self-conscious and aware of the environmental conditions of conduct. The bad man, in contrast, is "a partial...self in his conduct."[9]

One notices that Dewey described not simply the process of ethical judgment, but that of a certain kind of ethical judgment which he believed naturally and historically emerged from the initial human impulses. The drive for intelligent self-realization implies, he argued, social awareness. Psychological ethics, by virtue of the adaptiveness of mutual aid, entails social ethics.[10] To be aware of the circumstances and consequences of conduct and to coordinate the ends of activity with the means of achieving them is to be aware of one's "function," an "active relation established between the power of doing, on the one side, and something to be done on the other." This relation involves an interaction between individual and social environment. A true adherence to function means identifying personal and social development, in accepting social goals as one's own. "True adjustment must consist in *willing* the maintenance and development of moral surroundings as *one's own end*." True moral self-development entails the development of society, for the self functions in a social environment and self-identity depends on social function. One can be "self-active" only by reforming society, and this is possible only with the

[9] Dewey, *Outlines of a Critical Theory of Ethics* (1891), and *The Study of Ethics: A Syllabus* (1894), *Early Works* 3:300–301, 318, 4:245; James R. Angell, "The Relations of Structural and Functional Psychology to Philosophy," *Philosophical Review* 12 (May 1903): 262.

[10] Dewey, *Psychology*, 241, 243, 295.

faith that "moral self-satisfaction...means social satisfaction" and that the community in which one functions is indeed reformable.[11]

Political Psychology, Radical and Conservative

Their model of ethical human conduct (with some important variations) allowed the Chicago philosophers to move fluidly between philosophical, psychological, and reform discourses. Different political styles merged in the pragmatist scheme with philosophical positions, stages of evolution, and moments of the "act." Their language expressed their ambivalent postures relative to populism, socialism, and other radical political movements as well as their own radically humanist and collectivist criticism of industrial relations.

By reinterpreting Lotze's distinction between logic and object as a division of labor, Dewey linked psychological terms and issues to the larger questions of industrial development and social conflict. Reconstruction of individual action to achieve higher intellectual and ethical stages involved a social reconstruction that extended from individual behavior to social institutions and government policy to the disciplines of philosophy and psychology. Within this interlocking skein of evolving "action," words like "function" could mean biological function *and* social function, occupation, or role. "Coordination," then, did not just refer to the coordinated action of individuals but also to "cooperation," the coordination of social functions and occupations and the resolution of ethical and social differences in the community. These last were the class differences that plagued late nineteenth-century America, which Dewey and his colleagues preferred to interpret as atavistic conflicts between occupational groups or social functions.[12]

Thus, the overall structure and language of the reflex-circuit psychology provided a framework within which psychology and politics could be interpreted as linked coordinations of conflicting yet resolvable functions. In psychological terms, the most important of these

---

[11] Dewey, *Critical Theory of Ethics*, 303, 313, 320–23. See also John Dewey and James H. Tufts, *Ethics* (New York, 1908), chap. 3 (written by Tufts).

[12] On the equation of cooperation with physiological coordination, see James R. Angell, *Psychology* (Chicago, 1904), 14.

were sensation and reason (or, alternatively, habit). Their counterparts in politics were radicalism and conservatism:

> More especially, I suggest that the tendency for all the points at issue to precipitate in the opposition of sensationalism and rationalism is due to the fact that sensation and reason stand for the two forces contending for mastery in social life: the radical and the conservative. The reason that the contest does not end, the reason for the necessity of the combination of the two in the resultant statement, is that both factors are necessary in action: one stands for stimulus, for initiative, the other for control, for direction.

Thus the problem of knowledge reflects both human psychology and human history: "The distinctions which the philosophers raise, the oppositions which they erect, the weary treadmill which they pursue between sensation and thought, subject and object, mind and matter, are not invented *ad hoc,* but are simply the concise reports and condensed formulae of points of view and of practical conflicts having their source in the very nature of modern life."[13]

What many of his contemporaries interpreted as irreconcilable class conflict or unredeemable worldly depravity Dewey cast as the fruitful confrontation between radical and conservative social and psychological forces. The differences between the two, he argued, could ultimately be reconciled by rational acts of social and individual uplift which were also a natural part of well-coordinated behavior.

This was at heart a temporal process. Radicalism, Dewey argued, is not simply an ideology but a place in time, a future-oriented consciousness which without mediation by the past and the present is no better than a rash anticipation of the world as it might be. It is both vision of the future and stimulus to act. Conservatism, in contrast, represents the past: it is the voice of experience or established knowledge, but at the same time it is the tendency to stick to old, outworn habits and traditions. The present is where past and future meet, and it is the only time they can be synthesized into intelligent action. And synthesized they must be: without the interaction of the personal past and future, habit and impulse, neither consciousness nor perception would emerge, in the child or the species. The historical past and

[13] Dewey, *The Significance of the Problem of Knowledge* (1897), *Early Works* 5:5–6.

future, conservative and radical, also need each other. Neither can by itself solve social problems and contribute to human progress. Without future vision and the stimulus to act provided by radicalism, conservatism repeats old habits not suited to new contexts and problems. Radicalism without the wisdom of past experience is wanton and disorganized; it is the undeveloped impulse on a historical scale. Visionary but impractical, radicalism pays no attention to means and follows only "the random and confused excitation of the hour." "The strength of each school," Dewey intoned, "is the weakness of its opponent."[14]

This is why social conflict is essentially psychological: it occurs between the agency of the moment and the problematic situation, or between the impulse stimulated by an obstacle and the old habits that no longer suffice. Conservatives defend habits and fixed ideas; radicals are either impulsive and thoughtless or speculative and impractical. Each side represents a moment in the reflex-circuit. And each side behaves only as a partial human being, or group of partial human beings. Thus, just as a personality must be integrated in order to` function, opposing social groups must come together in order for society to act constructively, that is, to progress. As members of society, individuals constitute groups that perpetuate the "class view" and impede rational, nonviolent, progressive social reform. The social reformer, acting as psychologist, social worker, and educator, must interpret opposing sides to each other, simultaneously reconciling social antagonists and completing the incomplete personalities of individuals involved.[15]

Other department members cast the political and ethical dilemmas of the age in similar terms. Mead railed against what he called the "programist" socialism that guided European reform movements. "Socialism, in one form or another, lies back of the thought directing and inspiring reform," wrote Mead. But, he went on, "socialistic utopias have been recognized as impotent to lead to better conditions, and opportunists have succeeded [sic] to the programists." Programists project utopian visions of society without due regard to the means of attaining their goals, much as the impulsive child reaches

---

[14] Dewey, "Reconstruction" (June 1894), Early Works 4:102, and Problem of Knowledge, 18; Angell, Psychology, 58–59, 127, 177–78.

[15] Dewey, Problem of Knowledge, 6, and "Psychology and Social Practice" (1900), Middle Works 1:148.

for a stimulus without cognizance of the "object." Rather, Mead declared, we must have socialists like the Fabians, opportunists who recognize practicalities without abandoning their vision of achievable reforms, who project reform as a "working hypothesis" rather than a utopia, and who are capable of developing manageable social experiments. "The highest criterion that we can present is that the hypothesis shall *work* in the complex of forces into which we introduce it. We can never set up a detailed statement of the conditions that are to be ultimately attained. What we have is a method and a control in application, not an ideal to work toward."[16]

Mead interpreted utopian political terms much as Dewey had earlier interpreted religious concepts—as idealizations of the future which needed to be replaced by working hypotheses. If impulsive radicalism projects utopian visions of the future, out of touch with present realities, then working hypotheses approach reform in a more realistic manner, more reasoned and moderate, mediating between opposing points of view by testing solutions and perspectives. Like "coordination," the term "working hypothesis" could be found in psychological as well as reform discourse: "Every concept is in a sense a working hypothesis," Angell suggested in his 1904 textbook, implying that this functional manner of resolving psychological conflict and moving from childhood to maturity served as the type of all human intelligent action.[17]

Rendering historical conflicts in this psychological fashion was, not surprisingly, self-serving. If the conflict between radical and conservative, between classes, between various social and cultural groups involves psychological functions on a historical scale, then the psychologist played the key role in resolving social conflict and ushering in the new Kingdom. Psychology, Dewey argued in his 1899 presidential address before the American Psychological Association, "is the only alternative to an arbitrary and class view of society, to an aristocratic view in the sense of restricting the realization of the full worth of life to a section of society." Psychology was, for Dewey, the master social science, the method by which one could analyze and control behavior and find peaceful solutions to conflicts that had

[16] Mead, "The Working Hypothesis in Social Reform," *American Journal of Sociology* 5 (1899): 367, 369, and review of Gustave Le Bon, *The Psychology of Socialism, American Journal of Sociology* 5 (1899): 404–12.

[17] Angell, *Psychology*, 221.

always been decided by authority and force.[18] The history of philosophy written during this period by department members (mainly Tufts) justified psychology's central political role and characterized pragmatist functionalism as a historical culmination of the history of ideas and of the progress of culture.

The pragmatist philosophy and history of religion also fit nicely into reformist self-justification. Tufts and Edward Scribner Ames, a Chicago graduate and minister who joined the department in 1900, treated religion as an evolving cultural institution that responded to time-bound social needs. Their approach descended from the Progressive Orthodoxy's (and Dewey's) idealist historicism, which treated religion and theology as expressions of the spirit of an era, and from the anthropology of William Graham Sumner, who applied comparative method and biological models to the study of cultural institutions. It also echoed the arguments of social Christians such as Washington Gladden and George Herron, with whom the department shared an interest in turning the attention of middle-class Christians away from piety and prayer toward democratic and social scientific means of social change. As had their social Christian predecessors, Tufts and Ames closely linked the growth of democracy to the evolution of theistic faith: during eras ruled by authoritarian monarchies, people conceived of God in monarchical form, as an absolute sovereign and patriarch. In democratic societies of "intense social consciousness" and activism, however, this image of God was inappropriate and thus replaced by the concept of an immmanent God, for which the modernity of democratic politics was, in Ames's mind, prima facie evidence. Tufts called on ministers to "enlarge their conceptions of God" to accommodate new economic and technological contexts—ultimately, to adopt new ethical conceptions from science, education, and economics which bore little resemblance to earlier religious ethics, for example, personal worth and social justice.[19]

Religion's most important adjustment to the present would be its governance by the principles of scientific inquiry. For Ames this meant interpreting religion in terms of the functionalist psychology. Reli-

---

[18] Dewey, "Psychology and Social Practice," 148–49.

[19] Edward S. Ames, "Theology from the Standpoint of Functional Psychology," *American Journal of Theology* 10 (April 1906): 226–28; Tufts, "The Adjustment of the Church to the Psychological Conditions of the Present," *American Journal of Theology* 12 (April 1908): 181.

gious belief, he wrote, is an idea or set of ideas no different from any other ideas: as signs of past and future experiences that delay gratification and organize human relations they function in human action to facilitate survival (individual and social) in a potentially hostile environment. Thus, religious concepts are also working hypotheses, tested out in practice and adjusted to new situations.[20] By turning attention toward the working hypothesis, religion descended from transcendent spiritual truths to the spiritual truths immanent in society, and the gospel became a social gospel.[21]

Social Experimentation

Because the Chicago philosophers preferred the working hypothesis to the hortatory "program," certain reform institutions specially qualified as democratic, reconstructive, and reasonable. Robert Woods's early description of settlements as "experimental" captured his generation's expectations and hopes that new reform institutions would circumvent impulsive and irrational politics. Settlement activists practiced the sort of Christian sociology that Herron and Gladden insisted must replace "idealist" Christianity and would provide experimental models as well as carefully collected data for solving social and religious problems. This social scientific culture of reform would appeal, activists hoped, to discontented and sometimes insurrectionary working-class activists. Properly organized trade unions, focused on collective bargaining and comprising skilled, well-established workers, would follow a similarly reasoned and experimental strategy of solving the problems of industry.[22]

Settlement activity did include early sociological enterprises such as the Hull House survey of local housing. But following working hypotheses amounted largely to trying to mediate, as had earlier Christian labor activists, between opposing social (and psychological) forces. A settlement's function, wrote Jane Addams, was to "interpret

---

[20] Ames, "Theology," 225; Tufts, "Adjustment of the Church," 186.

[21] Tufts, "Adjustment of the Church," 186–88; Mead, "Working Hypothesis," 367–71, and "The Social Settlement: Its Basis and Function," *University of Chicago Record* 12 (1907–8): 108–10.

[22] Robert A. Woods, "The University Settlement Idea," in *Philanthropy and Social Progress* (New York, 1893), 57–97; Dewey and Tufts, *Ethics*, 499; George Herron, *The Christian Society* (Chicago, 1894), chap. 1.

opposing forces to each other." Hull House was "soberly opened on the theory that the dependence of classes on each other is reciprocal."[23] Addams optimistically believed that every social conflict could be rationally arbitrated in a way satisfactory to all parties, and that the results of arbitration would contribute to social progress and individual uplift. Violence and open confrontation, she repeatedly argued, were precipitated only by unreasonable and irresponsible people.

Settlement labor sympathies were qualified by the belief that classes could ultimately be reconciled—that the purpose of trade unions and cultural reform was to mediate class conflict rather than to promote working-class objectives and ideals. Despite contacts with such labor radicals as Eugene Debs, settlement workers in general aligned themselves with more conservative labor leaders; they usually counseled conciliation during strikes and were often accused of being prone to arbitration. Believing that common ground could always be reached, Graham Taylor's primary commitment to the labor movement came in the form of his repeated efforts to arbitrate industrial conflicts, such as the building trades strike of 1900 and the Teamsters strike of 1905. Writing in 1896 of the Pullman strike, Addams criticized manufacturers for letting profit motives override benevolence and social values. Nevertheless, workers should strike for reconciliation with manufacturers rather than to attack management authority: "The emancipation of working people will have to be inclusive of the employer from the first or it will encounter many failures, cruelties and reactions." Addams deplored recent labor violence and attacked revolutionary socialism and anarchism in religious terms as "doctrines of emancipation" preached to workers "for the sake of the fleshpots, rather than for the human affection and social justice which it involves."[24]

Like Dewey, Addams considered class conflict a conflict of time—between irrational radicals overzealously trying to reach an idealized future and reactionary defenders of an unjust past. There were two classes in Chicago during the 1890s, wrote Addams, the businesspeople who were "annoyed at the very thought of social control" and the radicals "who claimed nothing could be done to really moralize the industrial situation until society should be reorganized." It

[23] Jane Addams, *Twenty Years at Hull-House* (New York, 1910), 91.

[24] Allen Davis, *Spearheads for Reform* (New York, 1967), 3; Jane Addams, "A Modern Lear," *Survey* 29 (November 1912): 133, 137.

was Addams's hope that by decade's end these "abstract minds" would "yield to the inevitable or at least grow less ardent in their propaganda, while the concrete minds, dealing constantly with daily affairs, in the end demonstrate the reality of their abstract notions."[25] The solution to social problems, according to Addams, would be found only in the present.

When challenging anarchists' advocacy of political violence, Addams sounded like Dewey: no final end justified irrational or unintellegent means. But the belief in everpresent rational solutions also recalls the romantic faith that God is immanent in worldly affairs, a faith Addams embraced independently of Chicago pragmatism. Orthodox Calvinists had no trouble justifying present ills in terms of God's mystery: if the present seemed to have no intelligible purpose, they accepted it as God's will. Liberalism, however, converted the present into evidence of God's designs: history reveals God to humanity. For liberals, historical events had meaningful direction: they rendered God more intelligible rather than more mysterious.[26]

Mead, for example, likened the liberal faith to the confidence one has in the findings of natural science, based on the "faith in [the universe's] general rational character, that is perhaps best stated in the success of working hypotheses." By working hypotheses Mead meant both laboratory experimentation and the efforts of social reform guided by evolutionary social science, "the application of intelligence to the control of social conditions." Faith in social reform resembles faith in natural science in assuming the essentially rational character of the universe, in this case the social universe. Social reformers believe, rightly, argued Mead, "in the essentially social character of the human impulse and endeavor." We cannot know the form any future society will take but we "assume that human society is governed by laws that involve its solidarity, and we seek to find these out that they may be used."[27]

Savages, Children, and the Blessing of Work

The term "working hypothesis" suggests a kind of reform more akin to laboratory experimentation than to politics. The careful weighing

[25] Addams, *Twenty Years at Hull-House*, 184, 193.
[26] Bruce Kuklick, *Churchmen and Philosophers* (New Haven, 1985), chap. 17.
[27] Mead, "Working Hypothesis," 370.

of options and perspectives, the skilled manipulation of objects and circumstances, involve the kind of behavior one would expect of a technican subject only to those rules imposed by her well-defined goals—or, of a skilled artisan, who under the best of circumstances would run his shop with a sort of experimental and innovative yankee ingenuity.

During the decade after the Pullman strike, department members continued to link the producer ethic of the craft atelier to functionalist psychology, especially in the anthropological ethics of Tufts and Dewey. They esteemed a kind of character and conduct one might have found in the skilled craft occupations Chicago's factories were rapidly making obsolete. Tufts gave this theory its historical dimension, conjoining the evolution of ethics, the maturation of character, and the history of skilled industrial occupations, including what Marxists called the "social" division of labor.

This refined evolutionary ethics, elaborated in articles after 1900 and in Dewey and Tufts's *Ethics,* "genetically" studied evolving forms of conduct and custom. It began with the functionalist notion that one's practice and practical experience determine what one believes or idealizes to oneself, either as impulsive "idea" or as reasonable working hypothesis. To the extent that they believed individuals follow the rough outline of human evolution, Dewey and his colleagues subscribed to a recapitulation theory similar to those popularized by G. S. Hall and J.M. Baldwin: the individual develops morally, roughly, through the stages of society's ethical development to date. In social terms, the child is primitive, the adult is civilized. Ontogeny recapitulates phylogeny.

For Tufts and Dewey, the principles of evolution governed both personal moral development and the history of ethics. Like Herbert Spencer they conceived of moral evolution as moving from undifferentiated and impractical impulse to hierarchically ordered and rationally coordinated functions. Social customs evolve by virtue of the adaptive nature of psychological self-realization. "Unconscious solidarity is the status at the outset," wrote Tufts in 1906; "conscious individuality and conscious social interests are the final outcome."[28] They did not, however, attribute individual or social development to

---

[28] Tufts, "On Moral Evolution," in *Studies in Philosophy and Psychology,* ed. James H. Tufts (Boston, 1906), 4.

a scripted timetable or to the mechanisms of embryological development. The moral life, wrote Dewey and Tufts in 1908, is "a life, a moving process, something still in the making," not a "changeless structure."[29] Dewey repeatedly criticized the rigid culture epoch theory the Herbartians applied to Child Study and education on the grounds that allowance for the expression of individual differences of pace and sequence must be made. In the course of personal development, the individual interacts with the environment, transforming it as well as himself. The context of industrial society distorted and even precluded full expression of early "savage" stages of ontogenetic development.

Individual development follows social development, albeit inexactly, because, even though the environment of the child is socialized and she need not struggle for survival as a savage (without the amenities of civilization) struggled, she still faces similar problems and conflicts that demand a similar rationalization of impulse as occurred in the evolution of "civilized" culture. These problems and the adjustment to them are functional in a simultaneously psychological, biological, and sociological sense: gratification must be delayed for the full and most efficient satisfaction of need. Delay takes the form of cooperation, idealization, planning, experimentation, organization, and so on.

So Dewey and Tufts attributed the development of the "savage" mind to the same environmental and genetic forces that educational reformers perceived in the development of children. Writing as if he saw little difference between the schoolroom and the antediluvian forest, Dewey argued that "occupations determine the fundamental modes of activity, and hence control the formation and use of habits." This "affords the scheme or pattern of the structural organization of mental traits." Mentality and custom, Dewey maintained, are the product of the culture of social production. This is the case with savages, people who hunt for subsistence, acquiring highly specialized skills, but whose engagement in a volatile, unstable occupation requires quickness and accuracy rather than the kind of impersonal persistence demanded in industrial culture. Dewey criticized the reductionist anthropology that depicted the savage as psychologically inadequate. Still, he wrote of a "hunting psychosis" affecting all as-

[29] Dewey and Tufts, *Ethics*, 4.

pects of culture in which the mind is "dependent upon a present or immediate stimulus" for motivation and is unable to think abstractly. In the evolution of culture this was for Dewey and his colleagues the initial phase, "the structural form upon which present intelligence and emotion are built." New "mental patterns" emerge with new occupations, building on the "ground pattern" provided by hunting practices.[30]

Applying anthropology learned from Sumner at Yale and from W. I. Thomas, friend and colleague at Chicago, Tufts refined Dewey's argument. He reviewed the evolution of morality as a reconciliation of the impulsive tendencies of the individual and the primitive group (driven by instinct, by group fealty, by mass pscyhology) with the rationalizing social order, formed as the community evolved joint strategies for survival based on increasingly sophisticated forms of mutual aid, group solidarity, and law. In primitive society, Tufts argued, morality was imposed on the individual by the customs of the primitive social group (for example, the clan or family) to which he owed fealty. Thus character was first developed through social pressure and absolute law.[31] These were the product of the species' evolution, emerging out of the group solidarity needed to subsist successfully by hunting and gathering. This clan or kinship organization, although intensely cooperative and social, was as often irrational as not, governed by rules of honor, blood feuds, and taboos. A rational ethical system, based on positive law and universal ethical standards, evolved out of primitive culture through the development of industry and economy.

Moral "progress" from medieval clan and caste (or class) to individualism ultimately took root first in agriculture and then in the craft shop and marketplace. The rise of agriculture demanded a different social organization and a different "psychosis." Planting, harvesting, and storing food required delay of gratification and a more hierarchical and less impulsive social organization centered around the family. Instead of hunting, farmers engaged in "self-directed work" for less immediate ends, which "organizes character."[32] As civilization

---

[30] Dewey, "Interpretation of the Savage Mind" (1902), *Middle Works* 2:39–42.
[31] Tufts, "On Moral Evolution," 18.
[32] Ibid., 16, 18.

advanced, the initial impulsiveness of human character was rationalized by the demands of the historical situation.

With the rise of commerce and capitalism, the process of rationalization deepened. Exchange and business broke down class and supplanted taboos with contracts. The social division of labor further organized and rationalized society, with two consequences. First, the development of skilled crafts allowed individuals to be more civilized than in the hunting clan or primitive (subsistence) agricultural family, providing character-building work, leading to cooperation, and "realizing" the ideals of society in objects. The self as creator, argued Tufts, was the real self.[33] Second, the division of labor reorganized society around individual achievement, whether in business or in the artisanal shop. A new individualism emerged, the basis for a rational ethics based on freely accepted universal values rather than the automatically accepted (or enforced) mores of clans, kinship groups, and autocrats.

At first individualism was wanton and acquisitive, no longer restrained by clan custom and family fealty—thus the foundations of unrestrained capitalism. But the individualism "calls forth" or demands, functionally, a higher form of social order based on reason rather than custom—thus modern law, especially that governing contracts. The problem of the late nineteenth century is to extend reason and social justice through law and intelligence (that is, social science) and to reconstruct social values and institutions and thereby create a reconstructed individual.

Despite Tufts's evident distrust of much of the trade unionism practiced in such cities as Chicago, the social psychology of craft work was central to his vision of moral development, on historical and psychological scales. Concentration on the demands of artisanship forced the delay of gratification, socialized the impulses of the primitive (or the child), coordinated the emerging social functions in a division of labor, and continuously reconstructed objects and institutions to meet the needs of a changing society. This process of forming a responsible individual used only responsible means. Though

---

[33] Ibid., 16, 34. Like the term "working hypothesis," this argument echoed through the work of the department. For Angell, craft was prominent in the maturation of the instinct for "constructiveness"; see Angell, *Psychology,* 309.

reconstruction would break habits, it would not flirt with utopia, which expressed the impulsive visions of residual class and caste ideals found in trade unions and the pseudo-aristocracies of wealth.[34]

Social conflict and social activism lent their own imperatives and language to the Chicago school's philosophical endeavors. The Chicago philosophers, however, did not see that they wove their social, psychological, and ethical "science" out of the threads of turn-of-the-century politics and custom. Dewey and his colleagues redefined social and psychological conflict and change into terms compatible with their sentimental notion of salvation as an orderly and intelligible process of social improvement. Just as they and their contemporaries had called for a reconstruction of theology and religion, the Chicago pragmatists called for a reconstruction of philosophy and psychology. The parallel was more than a coincidence, for society's ability to address its problems without a transcendental faith rested on its ability to find a science of human action. Conversely, a true functionalist psychology depended on a well-lubricated practice of social reconstruction, the kind that precluded religious and political utopianism.

But their expectation that orderly social change would emerge with the evolving intelligence of human occupations reflects a faith in the availability of reasonable conduct in situations that may not have had the possibility of reasonable solution. Intelligence became far more problematic and difficult to discern in situations that demanded more than simple problem solving or testing of working hypotheses. Such was the case for the emerging social and political conflicts of industrial Chicago, increasingly dominated by the rhetoric of irreconcilable class interest.

[34] Dewey and Tufts, *Ethics*, chap. 3 (written by Tufts).

CHAPTER NINE

Between Head and Hand

During the Socialist party campaign of 1905, Eugene Debs urged on workers a new self-perception: It was time, Debs announced, for them to consider themselves more than just "hands" hired by a company. "Think of a hand with a soul in it," he implored, urging his listeners to gain new self-respect by uniting head and hand: "A thousand heads have grown for every thousand pairs of hands, a thousand hearts throb in testimony of the unity of heads and hands, and a thousand souls, though crushed and mangled, burn in protest and are pledged to redeem a thousand men."[1] Here Debs promoted as radically democratic a version of producer republicanism as one could find in the tangled political discourses of the early twentieth century. The unity of head and hand, the infusion of intelligence and spirit into the drudgery of industrial work life, promised a democratic renewal in which those who made America would become the self-active agents of their own social destiny.

In condemning the disintegration of rewarding work and the separation of manual from mental functions in society, Debs used words almost indistinguishable from Deweyan social pedagogy. But where Debs leaned increasingly toward a class-conscious (if still producerist)

---

[1] As quoted in Nick Salvatore, *Eugene Debs: Citizen and Socialist* (Urbana, 1985), 228. A similar speech, attacking capitalism's reduction of humanity to a "working hand," appeared in the Chicago *Daily Socialist*, November 21, 1906, 5.

critique of American capitalism, the middle-class (and some working-class) republicanism of the Chicago reform movement remained entangled in the ambiguities of the producerist discourse. For their part, the Chicago pragmatists at times espoused a radically democratic philosophy of self-activity quite similar to Debs's, embedding it in a functionalist psychology that reintegrated the manual with the mental. By proposing the social and psychological coordination of radical and conservative, the Chicago philosophers at least allowed a voice to the voiceless, to the factory workers silenced by drudgery, and to the radical "impulses" expressed in working-class demands. In the 1890s, at a time when those political voices were stifled or ignored, Chicago instrumentalism "radically" challenged the industrial order.

At the same time, the limits the Chicago pragmatists put on social reconstruction belied the democratic principles they simultaneously espoused. In large part this contradiction reflected the inconsistencies built into the philosophy. The Chicago philosophers advocated self-expression but believed it should follow a gradually progressive evolution from less to more rational social organization. If radical impulse played an increasingly important role, it did so within the confines of conservative habit and constructive working hypotheses. For the Chicago pragmatists as for Debs, anyone could be "intelligent;" no qualitative difference divided the laboring poor from the philosophizing elite. But, as many reformers of that generation saw it, social history had partitioned the psychological functions so effectively that one could no longer automatically expect to find a native intelligence side by side with radicalism and impulsive discontent. When a working-class leader such as Debs could exhort intelligence from the laboring poor themselves, intelligence had a different social role than when it had to be inculcated through schooling and properly educated leadership.

The Chicago philosophers, addressing the problems of the factory system mainly in academic books and articles written between the mid-1890s and the outbreak of the Great War, never rivaled Debs as masters of political oratory. Still, by offering their functionalist "via media" as one of the many reform discourses competing for audiences in Chicago, department members inevitably entered a wider arena of reform activism and confrontation.[2] Until the 1910s the

---

[2] On the emergence of the "via media" in international social theory, see James Klop-

Chicago philosophers largely confined their involvement in social reconstruction to the limited school reforms they accomplished under the auspices of the university and the settlement, and through Dewey's prestige as an educator and pedagogical philosopher. After 1908, the focus of political activism in the department shifted from the settlement house and the school to Chicago's City Club, founded in 1903 by reform-minded professionals and businesspeople. Their involvement in City Club activities led Mead and Tufts into broader avenues of labor reform, particularly the movement for labor arbitration. This expansion of reform activities widened the social applications of instrumentalist ideas and exerted an influence back on the philosophy.

Chicago Philosophy and the Crisis in Education

How we view instrumentalism and instrumentalist pedagogy during this period depends on how we interpret the course of school reform before World War I. After the late 1960s, revisionist historians regarded progressive educational reform as the imposition of middle-class values and new forms of bureaucratic social control on the nation's underclass. The revisionists contributed a grimmer realism to our understanding of reform movements, but historians have argued more recently that they overestimated the hegemony of the middle-class reformers and business interests in reorganizing and controlling the nation's school systems. The prominent role of trade unions and radical working-class movements in promoting public school reform suggests instead that educational institutions became contested terrain between social classes, each with a competing vision of how industrial society and American democracy should develop. Although, as one post-revisionist argues, competing reform factions "symbolically elevated" schools as "the new arena for class struggle," educational reform still did not break neatly along class lines. The intellectual history of Chicago's extended educational conflicts, which figured so prominently in Dewey's and Mead's writing, presents just such a complicated picture of competing philosophies and complex

penberg, *Uncertain Victory: Social Democracy and Progressivism in European and American Thought, 1870–1920* (New York, 1986).

political ideologies that crossed class boundaries and divided class identities.[3]

Chicago's educational crisis had its origins in the city's massive expansion after the 1870s. The influx of immigrants and the growth of industry put constant pressure on the school system and created circumstances in which building school facilities simply to absorb the number of students took priority over providing good education. The situation worsened as the city annexed new territory in 1889. Despite the frenzied construction, conditions in the schools were often abominable: classrooms in dilapidated buildings poorly accommodated a rapidly fluctuating immigrant student population. Inadequate sanitation plagued students and teachers alike, threatening to spread a typhoid epidemic through the school district in fall 1902. This situation prevailed despite the fact that school administrators slighted instruction budgets in favor of physical plant, thus additionally inflicting poor wages and heavy workloads on the city's teachers.

Meanwhile, Chicago was the last major American city to centralize administration of its school system, and with its enormous expansion the city found itself with an administrative bureaucracy that did not function as efficiently as the city fathers would have liked. A system of district committees governed the hiring of teachers and the daily administration of the system's affairs. Whereas the committees showed a certain responsiveness to the demands of particular localities, civic leaders pressured to centralize authority in a more compact

---

[3] The history of education in the Progressive Era went through two previous stages. In the labor education thesis, progressive historians such as John Commons attributed school reform to pressure put on authorities by an insurgent working class. The Commons school was succeeded by pluralists, who were succeeded by the revisionists in the late 1960s. More recently, educational historians have come full circle to a position resembling the labor education thesis; see Julia Wrigley, *Class Politics and Public Schools: Chicago, 1900–1950* (New Brunswick, 1982), chap. 1. For representative examples from this historiography, see Lawrence Cremin, *The Transformation of the School: Progressivism in American Education, 1876–1957* (New York, 1961), 3–176; Merle Curti, *The Social Ideas of American Educators* (New York, 1935), chaps. 9–11, 15; Clarence Karier, "Liberalism and the Quest for Orderly Change," *History of Education Quarterly* 12 (1972): 57–80; J. O. C. Phillips, "John Dewey and Social Control Reconsidered," *History of Education* 12 (1983): 25–37. The quotation is from Marjorie Murphy, *Blackboard Unions* (Ithaca, 1990), 17–19, as is the notion of Chicago schools as "contested terrain." The expression as applied to workplaces in general comes from Richard Edwards, *Contested Terrain: The Transformation of the Workplace in the Twentieth Century* (New York, 1979). See also Murphy, "From Artisan to Semi-Professional: White Collar Unionism among Chicago Public School Teachers, 1870–1930," Ph.D. diss., University of California, Davis, 1981, 90–91.

board and in the office of the school superintendent. Centralization also served to undermine what little power community contact gave teachers over their classrooms, the students, and the craft of teaching.

The two forces of economic hardship and centralization combined in the mid-1890s to create enormous discontent among the city's teachers, particularly in the elementary schools. Chicago teachers were excluded from civil service reform in 1895, which would have standardized wages and hiring practices and created pensions and job security. With the support of progressive governor J. Peter Altgeld, the teachers managed to squeeze a pension out of the state legislature in 1895, but it was a precarious arrangement that the lawmakers dissolved within a few years. The Chicago Teachers' Federation (CTF) formed in the aftermath of the pension drive in 1897 to protect that small gain and to push the Chicago Board of Education for salary increases and tenure. The board promised a raise immediately, but the money never materialized: the board pleaded poverty but earmarked most surplus revenues for the building fund, from which political favors and patronage could be generated. The teachers' union built its reputation with teachers and reformers on its efforts to find revenue that would cover the promised raises. In an elaborate and popular campaign, the teachers challenged city tax assessments of major corporations and utility companies, and, winning, they brought in close to $600,000 in additional revenue for the city, $250,000 of which went to the board of education. The board, however, refused to turn the windfall into higher salaries. The union won the increases in court only in 1904.[4]

From the union's point of view, the teachers' hardships were the product of business control in education. School budget shortfalls resulted directly from the public subsidization of utility profits through inadequate taxation, from corruption, and from a set of ninety-nine year leases on school land that benefited city enterprises at the expense of public education. Local capitalists who sent their children to private schools had no interest in providing adequate education to the city's working class. The appearance of a report on school reorganization, commissioned in 1898 by mayor Carter Harrison, Jr., reinforced the teachers' perceptions: the report called for the board of education to

---

[4] Murphy, "From Artisan to Semi-Professional," 15–21, and *Blackboard Unions*, chaps. 1–2; Wrigley, *Class Politics*, 32–35.

use business principles in running the schools and introduced legislation for school reorganization along managerial lines. Authored by University of Chicago president William Rainey Harper, by whose name it was known for the next twenty years, the report attacked the feminization of teaching and called among other things for male teachers to be paid on a higher salary schedule than women.[5]

Preparing the groundwork for future efforts by the city's business elite, Harper's report called for centralization of authority in the office of the superintendent and recommended that the school board continue to be appointed by the mayor. It also called for new hiring practices that would remove teacher election from local control and force teachers, many of them daughters of the laboring poor, to obtain a college education. For the teachers union and for many reformers (particularly women offended by its sexually discriminatory recommendations), Harper's plan and the legislation it generated were grave threats to democratic institutions.[6]

The Harper report was just the beginning, however, of a struggle for control of the school system and the classroom, waged between teachers, represented by the CTF, and managerial reformers such as Harper. From 1898 to 1909 the superintendent's office was occupied by men who, fancying themselves educational experts, tried to accumulate power over the conduct of education in Chicago. This group of superintendents pursued two strategies, one managerial, the other pedagogical. First they attempted to establish a centralized structure of authority that broke down the informal work relationships in the schools, between teachers and students, between teachers and district superintendents, and between teachers and the community. As Marjorie Murphy has argued, the earlier practices and relationships resembled the craft ethos of an artisan community. The program of the efficiency-minded reformers involved replacing independent craftsmanship with the managerial structure and regimented labor of a factory.[7]

When centralization proved only partially effective, managerial re-

[5] Harper dismissed the teachers' $50 a year raise with the observation that they were already making as much as his wife's maid; Margaret Haley, *Battleground: The Autobiography of Margaret Haley*, ed. Robert Reid (Urbana, 1982), 36; Murphy, "From Artisan to Semi-Professional, 40–41; Wrigley, *Class Politics*, 92–94.
[6] Murphy, *Blackboard Unions*, 26–29.
[7] Murphy, "From Artisan to Semi-Professional."

formers turned to university education programs as a means of professionalizing teaching within a controlled meritocratic system. A series of legislative proposals and administrative fiats became the center of the fight between the superintendent (supported by the board of education) and teachers trying to protect their job prerogatives. In 1900 the new superintendent, Edwin G. Cooley, introduced a merit system of evaluation that was purportedly designed to eliminate job patronage but effectively gave him complete and arbitrary authority over teachers' employment. Cooley also introduced a bill into the state legislature in 1903 for instituting many of the provisions of the Harper report. The bill failed to overcome CTF and related labor opposition. Cooley repeatedly tried to implement a new promotional system, which had as its aim the elimination of "incompetent" teachers through the use of standardized exams over a ten-year schedule. As the teachers pointed out, this merit system (which they called the "secret marking" system) operated either in an arbitrary fashion or to eliminate outspoken rather than poor teachers.[8]

Until 1917 the CTF and school administration waged a constant battle over similar attempts to centralize authority and erode teachers' power and independence in the classroom and their union. During his reign Cooley reduced the number of district superintendents, who held substantial power under the old system, from fourteen to six. He placed more power over operations and curriculum in the hands of assistant superintendents, who had little contact with and feedback from teachers and students, and gave almost autocratic final authority to the superintendent. The final victory of the centralizers came in 1917 when the Illinois Supreme Court upheld the "Loeb rule," an edict of the then conservative board of education outlawing membership in the union, against which school administrators and conservative boards had directed most of their ire.[9]

The teachers responded to centralization efforts with indignation and political passion, sending republican and class-conscious rhetoric against the factory system. The work of the CTF, prominent union publicist Margaret Haley insisted, was a "struggle to prevent the last institution of democracy, the public school, from becoming a prey to

---

[8] Wrigley, *Class Politics*, 83–104. Margaret Haley wrote regularly on the secret marking system in the *Union Labor Advocate* in 1903 and 1904.

[9] Haley, *Battleground*, 169–70, 179.

the dominant spirit of greed, commercialism, autocracy & all attendant evils." Supporters of teacher unionization dubbed the Loeb rule
the "Dred Scott decision of education," tantamount to the enslavement of teachers and the suspension of democratic rights in the schoolhouse.[10] Haley and CTF leader Catherine Goggin skillfully aligned
the CTF with the rest of organized labor and its heritage of class
confrontation, despite public sentiment against teacher unionization.
Yet, although the CTF joined the Chicago Federation of Labor (CFL)
in 1902, Haley simultaneously defended the teachers' professional
status, making quality of education the central issue and tying it
artfully to teacher autonomy and control in the classroom.[11]

Fellow Travelers

Members of the Chicago philosophy department made common cause
with Chicago's labor leaders and unionized teachers in their struggle
for a better educational system, one that would conform to their
conception of a democratic society. Together with like-minded followers of Colonel Francis Parker, members of the department and
their students became the main academic supporters of the CTF program. Professional philosophers and unionized teachers were able to
work together partly because they united against a common enemy,
the city's business elite and those academics and professionals who
supported business-oriented reformism. The pragmatists and Chicago
labor, especially the CTF, also held in common elements of a producer
ethic that envisioned the promise of American democracy in the preservation of productive forms of work that either predated or transcended the factory regimen. They applied this ethic to the classroom
by arguing for a kind of learning that united intellectual ability with
manual activity, basing democratic education on the psychological
reconciliation of head and hand.

The Chicago pragmatists thus gained a larger audience through the
contentious educational politics of the prewar period. Labor leaders
who pushed for improvements in Chicago's schools used "middle

---

[10] Margaret Haley to Jane Addams, May 4, 1906, Box 281, Anita McCormick Blaine
Papers, Wisconsin Historical Society (copy in Box 39, CTF Papers, Chicago Historical
Society Archives); Haley, *Battleground*, 173.
[11] Murphy, *Blackboard Unions*, 34–45.

class" pedagogy, largely from Dewey's pedagogy department and from Parker's Cook County Normal School, to justify their demands. Haley long acknowledged her debt to Dewey and the Parkerites, reserving her highest praise for Dewey student Ella Flagg Young, whose election to the presidency of the NEA Haley masterminded in 1910.[12] Teachers and supporters linked educational democracy to industrial democracy, and both were linked to the psychological reconstruction Dewey and others outlined in the 1890s: education would never be democratic, declared Haley, as long as the public accepted the "ideal of the industrial factory system, which makes the man at the top the only possessor of gray matter, and the thousands below the mere tools to carry out the directions of that gray matter." Centralization such as Cooley promoted was part of a tendency "to make the American teacher the fingers to carry out the plans of the gray matter resident only in the one head at the top."[13]

The Chicago philosophy department joined the educational battle early on. When Cooley tried to institute a new system to eliminate patronage from the appointment and promotion of teachers, Dewey and Mead along with City Club members fought it almost as bitterly as did the CTF. The Cooley centralization plan, Dewey declared in 1903, "would substitute for a partial democracy [the current system of accountability to district superintendents] an autocracy, a one-man power." Beginning an adversarial relationship with Cooley that would last for more than a decade, Mead attacked the plan as a "complete failure" and "utterly indefensible" as a way of increasing educational efficiency. The secret marking system Cooley introduced to evaluate teachers only incurred suspicion on the part of those being evaluated and neither eliminated personal and patronage factors in promotion nor accurately assessed teaching talents. It was no surprise, Mead contended, that the teachers should form a union and join the city labor federation, in light of the unsatisfactory policies of the school administration.[14] Reformers and teachers got satisfaction, briefly, un-

---

[12] Haley stated her encomiums for Young in Deweyan language: "She was an organism that took up thought with the most amazing speed. There never seemed to be a space of time between her grasp of a thought and her execution of the idea in action"; Haley, *Battleground*, 24, 86, 141, 141n.

[13] *Chicago Teachers' Federation Bulletin*, September 25, 1903, 4 (hereafter, *CTF Bulletin*).

[14] Dewey's made his remarks in an address to Boston's Twentieth Century Club on January 10, 1903. A partial transcript of his speech titled "More Freedom" appeared in

der the liberal school board of progressive Democratic mayor Edward F. Dunne. That board, which included Jane Addams, a Parker student (Dr. Cornelia de Bey), labor leaders John Sonsteby and John C. Harding, and City Club members Raymond Robins, Louis Post, and Emil Hirsch (among others), repealed Cooley's promotional system on Post's recommendation. Centralization was reintroduced with Dunne's defeat in 1907 and the board's replacement by the new Republican administration.[15]

Teachers and radical reformers offered a counterproposal to Cooley's, inspired by former district superintendent Young's dissertation on "isolation" in the schools. Young wrote her essay under Dewey's direction after resigning her position in 1899 to protest the equally centralizing policies of Cooley's predecessor, "Bulletin" Ben Andrews, a protégé of Harper. The inefficiency of teachers, Young argued, was not due to choosing poorly qualified candidates but to the lack of teacher participation in decisions governing the classroom. An "interaction between the workers [teachers] and their work," wrote Young, was necessary to prevent already certified teachers from losing their ability. Young expanded on Dewey's Herbartian theme of 1896. In the classroom the lack of interest on the part of student *and* teacher turned education into drudgery, into "the grinding of prescribed grists," the "turning of the crank of a revolving mechanism."[16]

Young insisted that one could achieve an educational democracy

---

School Journal 66 (January 24, 1903): 93. Haley endorsed Dewey's speech enthusiastically in the *CTF Bulletin*, February 20, 1903, 4. Mead followed for the most part a report by board member Louis Post, who also belonged to the City Club and eventually became an assistant secretary of labor in the Wilson administration. Mead's remarks are from a transcript of a February 2, 1907, address reprinted as "The Educational Situation in the Chicago Public Schools," *City Club Bulletin* 1 (May 8, 1907). Cooley, a founding club member, asked for equal time; see the minutes of City Club Board of Directors, May 5, 1907, Box I, Folder 3, City Club Papers.

[15] Haley, *Battleground*, 103, 106; Murphy, "From Artisan to Semi-Professional," 126–29. On the expulsion of labor representatives from the Dunne board, see the minutes of the CFL, printed in *Union Labor Advocate*, July 1907, 10–12, and September 1907, 7–14.

[16] On Andrews, whose nickname derived from his love of officious memos, see Wrigley, *Class Politics*, 100; Ella Flagg Young, *Isolation in the Schools* (Chicago, 1901), 23, 26. The exact pedagogical alignments here are confusing. During the 1890s the Herbartian emphasis on interest constituted an alternative to the more conservative idealism of such educators as William Torrey Harris. But the Herbartians also subscribed to a mechanistic associationalism that Dewey and Mead found entirely unacceptable—particularly Herbartian linguistics and philology, which Mead attacked in the 1910s.

only by psychologically cultivating interest and developing childish impulses. Following Dewey's reflex-arc critique, Young attacked rigid conceptions of the relation between habit, impulse and adjustment to changing experience. William James, J. M. Baldwin, and others did not clearly recognize that habits, such as the "good" ones educators want to inculcate in school children, originate in creative impulses: "The initiative and the habit, ... are two aspects of the same unity." Thus, habits must not be broken by authority, as conservative educators insisted, but reformed by "utiliz[ing] inherited and acquired tendencies and powers." Similarly, when teachers become isolated from authority, that is, when they cannot take initiative in education, they lose interest. No amount of centralization will make teachers more responsive, and as their work becomes drudgery so does the students' schooling. Any attempt to change this schoolhouse "factory system," Young predicted, would result in staunch resistance from conservative authorities. "The tyranny of an intellectual superiority," she warned, "is immeasurably severer than that of social class superiority. Coöperation in the realm of the mind is of much slower growth than coöperation in the world of labor. The trained intellect isolated from the less formally trained fears the approach of an intellectual democracy."[17]

As a remedy to isolation in the schools and declining teacher efficiency, Young proposed the institution of teachers' councils, which would include principals but not administrators. The purpose of the councils would be democratic self-government of the schools, primarily in gearing curriculum to the special needs of individual classes and students. The councils would also give teachers a voice in administrative decisions and provide administrators feedback on their policies.[18] In the early years of the school controversy, reformers, teachers, and labor leaders enthusiastically united around the demand for teachers' councils as a means to build educational democracy, often using identical language. Haley called Young's thesis "a declaration of independence in the war for academic freedom": the councils allowed workers democratic control over working conditions. Dewey agreed: giving teachers a voice in the formulation of curric-

[17] Young, *Isolation*, 55, 75.
[18] Young, "Isolation in the School," *CTF Bulletin*, July 3, 1903, 4.

ulum, the choice of textbooks, and the methods of teaching would "make the school democracy more complete."[19]

Teacher participation would nurture educational democracy additionally by helping free the self-activity of the child from the authority of a centralized educational autocracy. Democracy for teachers meant democracy and better schooling for students: "As long as the teacher, who is after all the only real educator in the school system, has no definite and authoritative position in shaping the course of study, that is likely to remain an external thing to be externally applied to the child." The teachers viewed this struggle as simply one part of their struggle for autonomy and control over the classroom. "Only through the freedom of the teachers could the children remain free," wrote Haley. As she archly noted, conservative pedagogues such as commissioner of education William Torrey Harris had "for many years preached to us the value of self-activity. It is the characteristic method of modern teaching." But "it is not surprising," she concluded, reappropriating the idealist discourse on self-activity, "that teachers should devise an application of it for their own development by entering as an effective force into the civic and economic life of the community."[20]

Radical reformers insisted that teachers in control of their own classrooms would naturally use democratic methods of instruction, along the lines prescribed by Dewey, Young, Parker and others. In particular, for Haley and Young as well as Dewey and Mead, the democratic character of instruction depended on the degree to which it united the intellectual pursuits of a traditional education with the more impulsive manual or motor practices toward which the child (particularly working class children, as Dewey and Mead saw it) was naturally inclined. This synthesis involved recognizing the principal tenet of Deweyan psychology, that the child's intellect develops in a continuous and immanent fashion out of its motor, emotional, and

[19] Haley, *Battleground*, 89. Haley cited Dewey in this definition of democracy; "More Freedom," 93; see also Mead, "The Educational Situation in the Chicago Public Schools," *City Club Bulletin* 1 (May 8, 1907): 131–38. The Dunne school board was planning to adopt a new system of teachers' advisory councils when Mayor Busse disbanded it. Labor prominently cited Dewey and Mead on this issue; see *Union Labor Advocate,* September 1907, 10.

[20] Dewey, "The Educational Situation," *Middle Works* 1:272; Haley, *Battleground*, 40, and "On the Value of an Educational Department," editorial in *CTF Bulletin,* October 3, 1902, 4.

volitional impulses. Much as Dewey, Mead, and Tufts feared the consequences of Kantian formalism in ethics and psychology, so too did educational reformers fear, as Parker protégé W. W. Speer put it, that "formalism will usurp the place of feeling in the heart of the teacher and the life of the child."[21] Thus Haley promoted not only better education for working-class children (that is, in the public schools) but also manual training and nature study, finding common cause with the progressive educationalists with whom she studied in Normal School. For Haley, the cultivation of interest and the restoration of a meaningful connection with the objects of labor (in the school and in industry) were the only antidotes to the factory system.[22]

On curricular matters also the teachers' union and the pragmatists had little disagreement, and again they shared a common enemy. Centralizers attacked experimental curricula that had been introduced over the years into the Chicago school system by individual teachers, principals, and district superintendents. These practical experiments were largely inspired by the same pedagogy that influenced the Chicago philosophers (manual education, Herbartianism, and the Froebellian kindergarten movement), by Dewey's and Mead's work at Chicago, and by the work of Parker. Haley regularly endorsed Dewey's statements, published speeches by Dewey, Mead, and others on psychology, and lectures by Young at the Chicago Art Institute on Deweyan theories of sensory-motor development (which stressed the primacy of motor functions in the child's growth and learning). She and others tended to link these notions, of a conflict between brain and brawn, to the conflict of social classes, using the Deweyan emphasis on motor development to stress the need for better material conditions for the laboring class.[23]

---

[21] W. W. Speer, "Freedom, the Condition of Individual Development," *CTF Bulletin*, July 3, 1903, 6. Speer, one of the district superintendents demoted by Cooley, enjoyed great popularity among labor activists; see *Union Labor Advocate*, April 1902, 3–4; Haley, *Battleground*, 23.

[22] Haley, *Battleground*, 19–20.

[23] For years Haley edited the *CTF Bulletin* and a substantial section of the *Union Labor Advocate*, a joint publication of the CFL, the Cigarmakers union, and the Union Label League. Besides Haley's own use of Parker's theories and the Chicago pedagogy, one could regularly find the words of Dewey, Mead, Young, Addams, and several Parker protégés in both publications. See, for instance, *Union Labor Advocate*, April 1904, 15–16. Anita McCormick Blaine sponsored courses by Young and others at the Chicago Art Institute as alternatives to costly university classes required for pay raises after 1905; Murphy, *Blackboard Unions*, 30.

Teachers, trade unionists, and radical pedagogical reformers came together in the first years of the new century to defend innovative curriculum introduced into the Chicago system, mainly by students and followers of Parker. Between 1901 and 1903 conservative newspaper editors and school administrators attacked the new schooling as fads and frills, demanding the discontinuation of manual training classes, rhythmic movement classes, and drawing, math, and reading instruction that dispensed with textbooks. In 1901 the CFL sent a committee to inspect several schools known for their use of the new pedagogy. The committee, whose report was unanimously endorsed by the whole labor body, emphatically tied the educational experiments they witnessed to the future of American democracy: "The time of the lock-step method of education is past" they declared. Innovation was the vitality of the public school, "the most democratic institution we have," providing equal opportunity to learn for poor and rich and empowering the working class in its struggle against capital: "As long as the masses can be deprived of the opportunity to obtain a proper education, just so long will they remain a sacrifice to greed and oppression." Opposition to the new curriculum, they argued, grew out of the class interests of businesspeople, book publishers, and tax dodgers. Administrators allowed state-of-the art instruction for middle-class private school students but not for working-class public school students.[24]

Throughout the report and elsewhere, the CFL committee used the new pedagogy: rhythmic movement and visualization techniques "shall aid in ennobling life for our children." Motor training brought "educational practice into harmony with the known laws of mental development," linking intellectual powers to interests, attention, impulses, and motor capabilities, such that "the eye and the hands are made to serve the brain." The city's labor leaders endorsed the new educational forms, such as manual education and motor training, particularly the value of motor training for the development of "greater mental and executive power," the "power of attention," "self-control", and "a desire to work."[25]

[24] Minutes of the CFL in *Union Labor Advocate*, April 1902, 3; George J. Thompson, Charles L. Fieldstack, and James H. Payne (Legislative Committee of the CFL), *A Report on Public School Fads* (Chicago, [1901]), 7 (copy available at Chicago Historical Society).
[25] Thompson et al., *Report*, 3–4; *Union Labor Advocate*, April 1902, 3. On Young's lecture series, see also "Lectures in Educational Psychology by Ella Flagg Young" and "An

For about a decade, then, Chicago philosophers allied with the most militant advocates of labor's educational cause, even self-professed radicals such as Haley, who earned a reputation for disrupting the comfortable offices of politicians and conservative reformers. That unity would be troubled, however, by school reform and labor issues soon to enter the public arena.

Application of Psychology," *CTF Bulletin,* October 31, 1902, 3–4. Dewey, "An Educational Creed," *CTF Bulletin,* November 6, 1903, 4; Haley, *Battleground,* 37, 87; on conservative pedagogical opposition to fads, see Curti, *Social Ideas,* 334, 338.

CHAPTER TEN

Splitting up the Schools

Barely a year after William James christened Chicago pragmatism a "new system of philosophy," Dewey left Chicago. Relations between the philosophy department and the university administration had been civil, though strained at times by president William Rainey Harper's imperiousness and unreliable support for the University Laboratory School. Despite these difficulties and the university's open hostility to radical politics, Dewey thrived at Chicago until spring 1904. In April, trying to manage internal professional conflicts over reorganization of the School of Education, Harper gracelessly informed Alice Dewey that her position as Laboratory School principle would end with the close of the school year. Affronted by Harper's treatment, Alice and John Dewey both resigned, citing grievances over "the history of years."[1]

Dewey's departure left a vacuum in the philosophy department. His role as inspiration and teacher to other department members would be sorely missed, but far more important was his unique ability to draw together the strands of Chicago philosophy into a project

---

[1] Dewey's departure is discussed in George Dykhuizen, *The Life and Mind of John Dewey* (Carbondale, 1973), 107–15; see also Robert B. Westbrook, *John Dewey and American Democracy* (Ithaca, 1991), 112–13; John Dewey to William Rainey Harper, May 10, 1904, Presidential Papers, Regenstein Library, University of Chicago. On funding of the Laboratory School, see Dewey to W. R. Harper, March 6 and 8, 1899, Presidential Papers, Chicago.

with a direction—to add, as he himself declared earlier of Franklin Ford, his "appreciation of the whole situation."

But this was, as James observed, a true school of philosophy, and though without its schoolmaster the department capably expanded on Dewey's experimentalist reconstruction of modern philosophy. In his studies of the social self, Mead enriched Dewey's concepts of action and meaning, finding new applications of pragmatist theory to social psychology, anthropology, and developmental psychology. Tufts continued Dewey's abortive and rather sketchy explorations of the history of philosophy with exhaustive geneologies of ethics and theology. Edward S. Ames applied Deweyan historicism and functionalism to the philosophy of religion. Although the least historicist of the department members, James R. Angell was the most wedded to the experimental findings of the psychology laboratory. His 1904 textbook on functionalist psychology rivaled James's *Principles* as a standard university text until the 1920s.

City Club Activism

After Dewey's departure, pragmatist politics continued involvement with Chicago's educational situation. The key department player in the next wave of educational confrontation was Mead, who made his most significant contributions to educational reform through his work as a member of Chicago's City Club, a municipal reform organization around which Mead's and Tufts's civic activism revolved until the war.

Walter Fisher, then secretary of the Municipal Voters League, organized the City Club in the summer and fall of 1903. By December he had enlisted 175 of the city's leading progressive businessmen and professionals to join at an annual fee of $20, and they set up headquarters, including a library and three dining rooms, over Vogelsang's, a downtown German restaurant. Soon the club moved to larger quarters on South Clark Street, not far from the city's vice district. At the outset, membership was at the invitation of the board and could be vetoed by three members. This restrictiveness was customary and important for the club's identity, for the organizers wanted only those men "who desire to co-operate in the investigation and improvement of municipal conditions and public affairs" by "nonpartisan" means.

Women were not permitted to join (the Women's City Club formed in 1911). The first membership list included newspaper magnates Victor Lawson and Medill McCormick. Settlement activists Graham Taylor and George E. Hooker were also inaugural members, as were Christian labor activist Raymond Robins and university professors Charles Merriam, Charles Zueblin, and Edmund J. James. From the University of Chicago philosophy department Dewey, Tufts, and Ames joined. Mead would join within two years. By 1912 he sat on the board of directors, and he served as president from 1918 to 1920.[2]

Like other municipal clubs, the City Club drew its members primarily from the Protestant business and professional elite. Its ranks included, however, some of the city's most prominent Jews and Catholics. And its membership was not intentionally limited by wealth or position (as was, for instance, the Commercial Club) except through the preferences of board members and through the dues, which were prohibitive for most Chicagoans. Moreover, the club services were minimal and the leadership struggled to keep the costs down to encourage younger and less affluent members to join, men who could not afford the dues at the city's more social civic clubs. The City Club "will not be a flunkey club," declared club president Henry Favill in 1912. Its primary concern was social reform and discussion of social issues. Its self-styled "militancy" limited its membership far below the ranks of primarily social city clubs; Boston's and Los Angeles' far outstripped the Chicago club in size and financial receipts.[3]

Growing out of the Municipal Voters League efforts to challenge domination of city politics by Chicago's city bosses (the "Grey Wolves"), the club took on the problems of the city as problems of corruption. As in much Protestant urban reform of the period, this stance opposed the club to the complex web of ethnocultural and political interests that ran the city's wards, which many reformers in the club movement simplistically characterized as a cabal of "interests." Chicago's City Club, however, maintained a peculiar balance

[2] Membership lists are in the Chicago Historical Society stacks and in Box 20, City Club Papers; "Preface" to Board Minutes, Box I, Folder 1, City Club Papers; City Club statement of purpose, 1903, Box 20, Folders 1 and 4, City Club Papers; *City Club Bulletin* 5 (May 5, 1912): 144. Chicago's was the second such club, preceded by New York's, founded in 1896. Only the Milwaukee City Club admitted women. Chicago City Club, *Yearbook*, 1915/16, 3–4; bound copy available in New York Public Library. City Club of Chicago, *City Clubs in America* (Chicago, 1922), 9–11, 19, 30–32.
[3] *City Club Bulletin* 5 (May 27, 1912): 180–83; *City Clubs of America*, 7–9, 17–18.

between the status politics of the Protestant elite and a more sincere commitment to social justice. It succeeded partly by "refrain[ing] from taking sides" and simply avoiding controversy. Its founders planned for it to be a nonpartisan advisory body to local political and civic leaders and to social activists. The civic committees were thus charged "to co-operate with the public authorities toward constructive results" and to achieve "active and effective touch with many important public interests."[4]

But, the club's charter aside, its members, as individuals and even as club representatives, did inevitably take controversial positions, often against each other, on issues ranging from education to the city charter and, especially, elections. The city's leading conservative socialist was an active member, as were Bull Moosers, progressive and moderate Republicans, liberal Democrats, and single taxers. Some members actively sought to create a local political movement that would be analogous to British Fabianism and eventually flirted with the founding of a local labor party after the war.[5]

The club's first major issue, traction, was shrouded in just this kind of political confusion. The control of the city's streetcar franchises, which periodically came up for renewal, was in the hands of several extremely powerful and corrupt businessmen with strong ties to the city's ward bosses. On the surface the traction dispute exemplified the kind of clean reform politics that targeted corruption over the inequities of class and poverty. But before the City Club addressed the streetcar dispute, the teachers' union had already made it and other forms of political deal making class issues in which the corruption of the city leadership clearly represented the sway of business leaders (some of them club men) over the laboring poor. Other equally complex issues, such as municipal charter reform, referendum and recall, immigration, election fraud, and public health, drew the club into class, ethnic, gender, and political conflict beyond the bounds of the original charter. These issues multiplied rapidly, and by 1906 club

[4] City Club Board of Directors reports, January 1, 1906–March 21, 1907, City Club Papers; Report of City Club Special Committees, vol. 3, pt. 1, April 17, 1908–March 31, 1909, City Club Papers.

[5] The attraction to British Fabianism began early in the City Club's history; see, for instance, Stanton Coit, "Recent English Labor Legislation," *City Club Bulletin* 1 (October 1907): 221–31, and "The Present Political Outlook in England," *City Club Bulletin* 2 (October 1909): 36–42.

committees were formed to deal with specific areas of social investigation and reform. Tufts sat on the housing committee, which he
chaired from 1910 on, Ames sat on the public health committee, and
Mead joined the education committee, which he chaired from 1908
until 1914.[6]

During Mead's tenure on the education committee, it addressed
most aspects of the dispute between the CTF and the Cooley administration. As a committee member, Mead was partly responsible for
a compromise bill on teacher promotion over which Margaret Haley
split with Jane Addams. Mead also investigated the city's public library system, reporting on extensive statistical comparisons with libraries in other cities. He concluded that the Chicago system was
overly centralized, inefficient, and biased against providing services
to the poorer neighborhoods.[7]

While Mead was chairman the education committee made its most
significant contribution on the issue of industrial education. Between
1908 and 1910 industrial education was the primary focus of Mead's
reform activities and continued to occupy him until the passage of
the Smith-Hughs Act in 1917 brought industrial education under the
auspices of the federal government. Industrial education pursued the
same goals as the earlier manual training reforms: maintaining a
student's direct interest in classroom work, breaking the exclusive
hold of "intellectualistic" instruction, and giving the student exposure
to a wider social and educational experience. As opposed, however,
to manual training, which eschewed all vocationalism and based educational practice on theories of sensory-motor coordination, industrial education incorporated vocational interests into school
curriculum. Training children in basic industrial, craft, and home
economy skills would help sustain their interest in more intellectual
facets of classroom instruction, especially if history and literature were
tied, as they were in Dewey's socially centered school, to occupational
training. It would also provide basic skills for children expected to
drop out for industrial work or marriage.

Industrial education brought manual training into a new era, com-
promising the purist antivocationalism found in much of the earlier
movement and responding to overwhelming demographic conditions

---

[6] Annual Reports, Box X, Folder 5, City Club Papers.
[7] *City Club Bulletin* 2 (April 21, 1909): 381–88.

in the schools of Chicago and other major cities after 1900. Mead's study of vocational training, published in 1912 by the City Club and often cited by local educational reformers, showed that 49 percent of students entering grade school did not complete the eighth grade. Since at least one third (seventy thousand) of Chicago elementary school students were "retarded" (that is, held back), the state compulsory education statute, which set the minimum dropout age at fourteen, was inadequate. Many fourteen-year-olds left the system in the fourth, fifth, or sixth grades. Reformers had long linked manual and vocational training to child labor laws and compulsory education statutes, which they feared would force a horde of potential juvenile delinquents onto the city streets. Unlike the G. Stanley Halls, however, who took retardation to be a neurological and hereditary problem, Mead recognized that the dropout rate, as well as "overage" (the term he preferred, since retardation had already come to mean mental incapacity), were caused primarily by lack of interest on the part of students and parents and, to a much lesser extent, by financial pressures on students' families.[8]

Whereas many educationalists aligned with Chicago's commercial interests favored a vocational education program simply to train skilled and semiskilled workers for the city's industries, reformers such as Mead had moral and political problems foremost in mind. Many supporters of industrial education still wanted to keep the schools as "common" as possible, hoping to preserve democratic education by providing a lure to keep working-class students in school. Advocates of "pure" nonvocational manual training learned to accept and even endorse industrial education, for they realized that the school system could not educate working-class children, neither for their own good nor for the social good, if those students did not stay in school well into adolescence. Former purists feared that the deskilling of work in the factory system would so degrade urban workers that they would lose their sense of civic responsibility as well as their skills. If students leave before the eighth grade, Mead argued, they will not receive the "minimum education for American citizenship," and, because the longer one stays in school the more one retains, they will not remember what little they have learned.

[8] George Herbert Mead, *A Report on Vocational Training in Chicago* (Chicago, 1912), 1–6.

The organic link Mead and others drew between citizenship and the acquisition of skills enjoyed a central place in this reform discourse. Robert Woods of Boston's South End House reported to the City Club education committee that the occupations of dropouts were generally unskilled and temporary. "Many lose entirely the opportunity to acquire skill and the vast majority have gone back in intelligence before they can begin apprenticeship in the skillfull occupations."[9] Mead expressed concern that dropouts working at unskilled jobs acquired no useful training and were often unemployed. "Their idleness during at least half the time," he warned, "their frequent passing from one job to another, their lack of any responsibility, necessarily leads to moral, mental, and frequently physical degeneration."[10] To substantiate this fear, he had a researcher interview adolescent employees at a major manufacturing firm to determine what amount of moral education they had retained since leaving school.

Similar interests guided labor activists through the thicket of educational debate. Labor leaders had long resisted the introduction of vocational education, suspecting that it would be controlled by local businesspeople, who would use it to undercut union apprenticeship programs and provide skilled and semiskilled nonunion labor to the nation's industries. Their fears were well founded: the major national organization pushing vocational education, the National Society for the Promotion of Industrial Education, sought industrial education at the public expense for exactly that purpose.[11] Labor initially rejected any vocationalism in the schools, but after 1910 the American Federation of Labor (AFL) conditionally accepted that vocational education need not threaten the labor movement. The AFL insisted that industrial education not be separated administratively from the rest of the curriculum and that equal control be given to organized labor and to industry. The labor federation also insisted that all the necessary academic subjects be part of the industrial education cur-

[9] As reported in the minutes of the City Club Education Committee, November 23, 1908, Box 10, Folder 3, City Club Papers; Mead, *Report,* 2.

[10] Mead, *Report,* 9–10.

[11] Sol Cohen, "The Industrial Education Movement in America, 1906–1917," *American Quarterly* 20 (1968): 95–110; Paul W. McBride, "The Co-op Industrial Education Experiment, 1900–1917," *History of Education Quarterly* 14 (1974): 209–21; Minutes of November 23, 1908, City Club Committee on Education, Box 10, Folder 3, City Club Papers.

riculum and that it include instruction in "the philosophy of collective bargaining" as well as in protective labor legislation.[12]

In Chicago, differences over vocational education came to a head in 1912 as three competing bills came up before the Illinois legislature, which, because of peculiarities in the Chicago city charter, had ultimate jurisdiction over Chicago schools. Business leaders had tried to introduce industrial education bills as early as 1901 but had not been able to overcome the stiff opposition from organized labor and progressive reformers.[13] In 1910, Chicago's exclusive Commercial Club hired recently resigned school superintendent Edwin G. Cooley to investigate vocational education in Europe, particularly Germany, where a highly developed system served that country's rapidly expanding and competitive machine and chemical industries. Dazzled by the economic miracle begun in Germany under Bismarck, Cooley attributed German success partly to the capacity of the German school system to turn out skilled workers. Like the National Association of Manufacturers, he considered a comparable vocational education system necessary if American industry was to compete successfully on the world market.[14]

In 1912, Cooley published a report on his investigation and introduced a bill in the state legislature that would have established something vaguely like the German system: compulsory education until the age of 14, at which point children would either continue in the academic track or go to work while taking vocational courses. The statewide system of vocational education would be administered separately from the standard academic curriculum. The state labor movement, which like the national AFL was by this time amenable to some kind of industrial education, reacted violently against Cooley's bill. The president of the Illinois State Federation of Labor (ISFL) called

---

[12] George J. Thompson, Charles L. Fieldstack, and James H. Payne, *A Report on Public School Fads* (Chicago, [1901]), 3; Margaret Dreier Robins, Address to National Women's Trade Union League in St. Louis, June 2, 1913, pamphlet (Chicago, 1913), copy in Box 4, Folder 19, Tufts Papers, Chicago; see *Union Labor Advocate*, April 1910, 31, for a report on the Toronto convention in which the AFL changed its position; see also Dewey, "Education vs. Trade-Training—Dr. Dewey's Reply," *New Republic* 2 (May 15, 1915): 42–43.
[13] Margaret Haley, *Battleground: The Autobiography of Margaret Haley*, ed. Robert Reid (Urbana, 1982), 60.
[14] Edwin G. Cooley, *Vocational Education in Europe* (Chicago, 1912), Introduction; see also Julia Wrigley, *Class Politics and Public Schools: Chicago, 1900–1950* (New Brunswick, 1982), 69.

a 1915 version "positively the most vicious thing that was introduced" into the legislature that year because of the dual administration it proposed. Labor leaders believed that the dual system would put working-class students "under the complete control of corporations."[15] Similar attacks were heard on a local level.

The bill met stiff opposition from other sources as well, primarily educational reformers like Mead who considered industrial education supplemental to common schooling. When the Commercial Club hired Cooley, Mead's committee had already been engaged in its study of industrial education in the city of Chicago. In November 1908, a subcommittee was established, chaired by Mead, to investigate the problem "from the standpoint of the three factors that are peculiarly involved, the school-system itself, the manufacturers and the laborers, especially . . . organized labor."[16] The subcommittee obtained money from Anita McCormick Blaine, Cyrus McCormick's daughter and Hull House benefactor, to hire three University of Chicago education school graduate students to conduct the study. They published their findings in 1912 and introduced an alternative bill to Cooley's that same year. The state bankers' association introduced a third bill, also markedly different from Cooley's legislation and in substantial agreement with the Mead bill.[17]

The City Club bill styled itself as a compromise between the Commercial Club legislation and the labor position, but Mead's committee, on all substantial issues except the teaching of collective bargaining in technical schools, agreed with organized labor. The presence of the CFL's John Sonsteby and John C. Harding on the committee may have been significant in forming that agreement. The central issue for all parties was separate administration of vocational education. By appearances a petty difference, the "splitting" question involved a complex set of ideological and political questions. Labor opposed separate administration not only because it feared domination by corporations but also because it was committed to the kind of edu-

---

[15] ISFL's president, John Walker, quoted in Wrigley, *Class Politics*, 82.

[16] Ironically, the discussion that led to the study included Cooley, who had returned from an earlier European research trip; Minutes of City Club Education Committee, November 23, 1908, City Club Papers; Letter to George E. Hooker, City Club Annual Report for 1910, Box X, Folder 5, City Club Papers.

[17] Mead, *Report*, v; *City Club Bulletin*, 12 (December 4, 1912): 373.

cation that integrated industrial and academic schooling. As Haley observed years later,

> all of [the business bills] were predicated upon the idea of separating cultural education from industrial. The cultural idea and aim of education would be wholly absent from the industrial training which they provided. There is an undying feud between the industrial advocates of industrial education and the educational advocates of industrial education. To the educator, industrial training stands for the development of children through activities and sufficient manual training, not as preparation for manual effort but as development of the child, of his brain and his hand. The industrial advocates . . . wanted industrial schools to supplement and aid industry and to prepare the children for it.[18]

Labor leaders did not view industrial education in exactly the same moralizing terms as many middle-class reformers did, but trade unionists did want to keep working-class children in school and provide them an education comparable to one that came with wealth. As Haley wryly pointed out, "if the rich had industrial training for their children, you may be certain that it would be the kind that would supplement academic work."[19] For labor, too, a common schooling trained students to be citizens, but in the sense of being empowered to participate fully in public life. Chicago labor leaders did not want an education in social conformity or in intelligent but responsible resignation to intolerable circumstances.

As indicated above, Mead opposed the dual system because it would deprive workers of academic training, which for the purposes of moral reform included training for citizenship. Mead, however, in sympathy with the aims of organized labor, carried this reasoning further than most of his fellow reformers, arguing that the lack of academic schooling, by diminishing the worker's intelligence, undercut working class power in the political arena and in the workplace. Mead was aware that the urban working class stood the worst to gain by any lack of liberal arts schooling. Courses in law, sociology, government, and history, he argued, not only expose working-class children to the dominant cultural values but allow them, when they become workers,

[18] Haley, *Battleground,* 160.
[19] Ibid., 161.

to better understand and to improve the conditions of employment in their society.[20]

The main reason, however, that Mead opposed the dual system was that it subverted the positive role education could play in the reconstruction of industrial society. In a 1908 article that laid some of the pedagogical groundwork for the ensuing struggle over vocational education, Mead traced the historical relation between common school education and the development of industrial skills through apprenticeship traditions. The educational tradition in America, he argued, had consistently separated instruction in academic knowledge (the three R's) from the aquisition of productive craft skills (that is, skills other than those needed in the professions or business). What craftspeople learned in school had no connection to what they learned in their apprenticeships. "Bookish" schooling held little interest for them, and so they acquired little knowledge of the history, social conditions, or even the technology of their own crafts. In failing to integrate intellectual and manual instruction, educators missed an ideal opportunity to enrich and broaden common school and trade education. They should have let liberal arts and apprenticeship "reinforce and interpret each other" as a "relation of theory and practice." Apprenticeship could have provided practical problems to which students would apply their theoretical knowledge, thereby supplying vocational interest to the classroom and intellectual depth to the learning of a craft.[21]

For all its drawbacks, the earlier system was better, in Mead's estimation, than the schooling given manually employed children of his day. The advent of mechanized factory production had changed education in the broadest sense, demanding primarily unskilled labor and destroying (often intentionally on the part of factory owners) the livelihood, power, and apprenticeship traditions of the increasingly obsolete craft worker. The apprenticeship tradition could not adjust

---

[20] Mead, "Industrial Education, the Working-Man, and the School," *Elementary School Teacher* 9 (1908): 382. Mead presented a similar argument before the city's chapter of the Women's Trade Union League, reported in the *Union Labor Advocate*, March 1908. A quotation from Mead's speech prominently appeared on that issue's front cover. Mead's words emerged from a common reform discourse; he shared the dais that day with Raymond Robins, to whose rousing rhetoric on the same theme the audience responded warmly, and Jane Addams presented a similar case in the *Advocate* four years earlier: Addams, "Educational Methods," *Union Labor Advocate*, April 1904, 15.

[21] Mead, "Industrial Education," 370.

to this transition and degenerated into the unions' primary means of limiting skills on the labor market. The connection between schooling and work became even weaker, so that working-class children had even less reason to be interested in school. Furthermore, the destruction of apprenticeship and the deskilling of factory labor eroded the practical intelligence of the working population. This, for Mead, had profound social and political repercussions. Our "early democratic institutions" rested on the "intelligence of the artisan," and without it we lost "practical...self-reliant men, as well as good workmen who did not have to blush for the work of their hands."[22]

The only way Mead saw to reverse this trend was to find a functional analogue to the old apprenticeship system that would be better adapted to the conditions of factory production. That new apprenticeship could be created only in a fully integrated school system that tied the learning of theory to vocational practice. To the fullest extent possible, workers would be taught skills that were adaptable to a wide variety of modern industrial jobs, avoiding the problem of teaching crafts soon rendered obsolete by automation and the intensive division of labor. They would be given full knowledge of the whole industrial process and the intellectual tools to evaluate industrial practice and make intelligent decisions. However utopian this program may have been (it essentially entailed certifying factory operatives as engineers), Mead did not place many limits on what would be taught to factory employees, and he had in mind a fuller democratic control of the workplace. In large part he wanted to improve industrial efficiency by enhancing employee feedback, but it is important to note that efficiency for Mead was contingent on the ability of workers to make decisions about what would go on in the factory and not on the exclusive decision-making power of a management expert. From New York, Dewey agreed. The "supreme regard" of vocational education, he contended in a debate that appeared on the pages of the fledgling *New Republic*, must be "the development of such intelligent initiative, ingenuity and executive capacity as shall make workers, as far as may be, the masters of their own industrial fate."[23]

---

[22] Ibid., 371.
[23] Ibid., 375–77; for a very different interpretation, see Steven J. Diner, *A City and Its Universities: Public Policy in Chicago, 1892–1919* (Chapel Hill, 1980), 77–97; Dewey, "Splitting up the School System," *New Republic* 2 (April 1915): 283–84, and "Education

Splitting the school system would compound the destruction of craft traditions by allowing even more intensive deskilling of crafts. This would occur directly through the degradation of craft training in the separated vocational system. It would also occur because workers without a richer cultural and social education would be at a disadvantage in the factory and less able to affect the choice of new technologies. The dual system would also exacerbate class tension and thus contribute to the erosion of democracy. In part, Mead's belief that the unskilled are less socially responsible than skilled artisans simply reasserted the traditional republican prejudice that with craftsmanship one acquires civic-mindedness. But, for Mead, as for his colleague Tufts who wrote extensively on the issue, this artisinal theory of civic virtue had a deeper psychological justification. Both Mead and Tufts argued that skill, as a practical intelligence, organically integrated the worker (and the professional) into the social order. In giving workers an intrinsically interesting social function, skill equally gave them a stake in society. At the same time, an artisanal occupation (or an integrated industrial education) morally uplifted, requiring one to view the ends of one's occupation in terms of the practical means by which those ends could be reached. This evaluation of ends by means was the crux of instrumentalist ethics and politics, distinguishing irresponsible "programist" radicals from responsible "opportunists." For Mead "the moral judgement is only possible where conflicting ends or purposes can be stated in terms of the common means of attaining them."[24]

Politics and psychology intersected in Mead's evaluation of the vocational education situation. Deskilling without compensatory education would have (and, Mead believed, was having) a dramatic psychological effect on the social stability of a country predicated on "manly" productive labor and class harmony. Cooley's dual system,

---

vs. Trade Training," 42–43; David Snedden, "Vocational Education," *New Republic* 3 (May 1915): 40–42.

[24] The last quotation comes from an unsigned and untitled typewritten copy of a speech with Mead's holograph corrections which can be found in Box III, Folder 29, Mead Papers. Tufts wrote on the role of craft in moral evolution at roughly the same time Mead engaged the industrial education issue. Although no documents exist to verify that they shared ideas on the subject, it is difficult to avoid that conclusion. Certainly both were influenced by Dewey, who probably originated the argument, drawing it from similar arguments made by his contemporaries. See Dewey, *Lectures on Ethics, 1900–1901*, ed. Donald F. Koch (Carbondale, 1991), 288.

Mead contended, would exacerbate existing class tensions and create new ones by destroying the interaction between the children of different classes in the common school. Not only would vocational education suffer by the loss of academic studies, but the liberal arts would suffer by loss of the most dynamic part of educational practice. The public school system under Cooley's plan "must inevitably become even more than its critics deem it to be today, a dispenser of a leisure class, formal, and 'academic' education."[25] Mead conceived of educational progress as issuing from the hands-on experiences of manual education, nature studies, home economics, and the practical demands of vocationally oriented instruction. When vocational and manual subjects were withdrawn from the common school, that dynamism would be lost. As Dewey insisted in the *New Republic*, in a unified school system "pupils are kept in constant personal association with youth not going into manual pursuits," and "the older type of school work is receiving constant stimulation and permeation." The teachers of theoretical subjects would be brought "into living touch with problems and needs of modern life which in the isolated state they might readily ignore." Writing that "industrial society [was] knocking at the doors of the schoolhouse seeking admittance," Mead went so far as to advocate teaching all public school children a trade, so that "immediate contact with life" would "lift the child out of story-telling into actual interpretation" of social and industrial life.[26]

Mead's and Dewey's reasoning reflected the instrumentalist conception of psychological growth. Growth, they maintained, was a rationalization of the conflict between newly encountered practical problems and existing habits, and it occurred through the mediums of an idealizing intellect and an impulsively emotional sensory-motor continuum. The argument also showed the political import instrumentalist psychology had for its proponents. Sensory-motor coordination, the psychological principle behind Chicago functionalism, directly referred to the social and political context of Chicago, sometimes even crudely in the form of a direct correspondence between social and psychological functions. As Mead occasionally put it, the vocational education controversy was a dispute over the "methods

---

[25] Mead, "Report of the Public Education Committee," *City Club Bulletin* 5 (December 4, 1912): 376.
[26] Dewey, "Splitting up the School System," 284; Mead, "Industrial Education and Trade Schools," *Elementary School Teacher* 8 (1907–8): 403.

of training hand, eye and brain."[27] It penetrated to the basics of human psychology and reflected the incomplete manner in which that psychology had been formed throughout the histories of American education and industry.

Divisions

However often academic philosophers joined labor activists in the struggle for democratic schooling, it would be a mistake to assume that they shared in an unambiguously radical reform discourse. A preference for conciliation distinguished the Chicago pragmatists from radical labor reformers and socialists such as Eugene Debs, who stood resolutely against the growth of corporate enterprise and increasingly used the rhetoric of class conflict eschewed by the Chicago philosophers. The pragmatists hoped to facilitate a dialogue and mediate conflict; the mere recognition of radical impulses seemed to suffice. Once that process could be started, once old habits could be broken and reconstructed, social self-realization would be possible. Consequently, the pragmatists' reform goals had less to do with the redistribution of power between existing social groups than with opening lines of communication and understanding. Their rhetoric reflected both a sincere commitment to democratic self-activity and the contrary desire to mediate and direct the outcome of social confrontation.

Nor did the Chicago philosophers always agree with labor in the area of educational reform, and although there was an interaction between academics and progressive labor leaders it was not always harmonious. Haley and the CFL saw the provision of better education as a matter of teaching the have-nots what the haves learn in school. The class content of education figured increasingly into their reform efforts. For Dewey, Mead, Tufts, and Young, however, educational progress primarily served the reconstruction of civic virtue, the shared values of a republic. Thus, Dewey and Mead emphasized the service of teachers' councils to democratic education rather than their empowerment of a class of people, whether the teachers themselves or their specifically working-class students. The same applied to the im-

---

[27] Mead, untitled and unsigned speech, see note 24.

provement of teachers' conditions, which Dewey and Mead often subordinated to the pursuit of better education in the *public* (rather than the working-class) interest. Thus, they supported Addams in her search for a compromise between the CTF and Cooley on the promotional question in 1906, stressing the need for continuous retraining and some form of evaluation. Haley considered this position a betrayal, though she attacked only Addams, who introduced it to the school board. This was no small matter, either. The moderate position advocated by Addams helped undermine solidarity in the women's labor movement, straining relations between trade unionists and their middle-class settlement house allies.[28]

None of the department members ever explicitly and unequivocally endorsed the CTF. At one point Mead, in fact, did the opposite, supporting teachers' councils because without them "there will always exist the situation out of which irresponsible bodies like the Teachers Federation will arise." True democracy, whether industrial or educational, certainly included a kind of workers' control founded on the principles of representative government, as Dewey put it. Mead, however, despite his strong support for "responsible" unionism, also saw worker participation as a form of self-control that would transcend confrontational trade unions, particularly in public institutions such as the school.[29] For Mead the public interest prevailed over the particular interests, as he saw them, of the teachers' union, which expressed the impulsive reaction of the teachers to poor conditions and autocratic authority. In general, Dewey and Mead sought improvements for children in improvements for teachers, and to this extent they supported teachers' unionization. The CTF tended to do the opposite, although its priorities were more evenly balanced.

[28] Dewey, "The Educational Situation," *Middle Works* 1:265, 275. The "situation," Dewey wrote, of both the "fads and frills" controversy and the promotional question, is "a question of the cooperative adjustment of necessary factors in a common situation." Mead, "The Educational Situation in the Chicago Public Schools," *City Club Bulletin* 1 (May 8, 1907): 131–38; Haley, *Battleground,* 105, 113. In a desperate attempt to cool down a deteriorating situation, Mead and Addams tried to persuade Dewey to return to Chicago in 1906 as superintendent in the hope that the philosopher could mediate between the two progressive factions. Mead to Helen Mead, July, 1, 1906, Mead Papers. On strains in the Women's Trade Union League, see Elizabeth Anne Payne, *Reform, Labor, and Feminism: Margaret Dreier Robins and the Women's Trade Union League* (Urbana, 1988), chap. 2.
[29] Dewey, "Democracy in Education" (1903), *Middle Works* 3:229–30; Mead, "Educational Situation," 135.

Within a few years it became clearer that it was the city's intransigence, not the unions, that prevented educational peace. This did not change Mead's views, but in 1916 he was less inclined to attack the CTF as he did in 1907, when the Dunne board was in power and Addams struggled vainly to conciliate Cooley and the CTF. In 1915, the board of education passed the notorious Loeb rule, named for the stridently antiunion board president, Jacob Loeb, and strongly endorsed by the city's business leaders. The edict, essentially a yellow-dog contract that excluded union members from employment as teachers, affected the entire teaching staff but specially targeted Haley and the CTF, who challenged it in the courts. Mead was annoyed that "smashing Margaret Haley" took precedence over true reforms for the board and "the gentlemen of the Manufacturers' Association and the Newspapers." The Illinois State Supreme Court, however, upheld the Loeb rule in 1917, allowing the board and its backers to easily break the CTF and severely hinder the new American Federation of Teachers, to which the CTF affiliated in 1916.[30]

Like others, Mead considered the Loeb rule one of several deleterious by-products of a politically appointed board and pushed for the adoption of the city council's reform bill, which would have made the board of education elective. The council bill, however, vested a great deal of authority in the office of the superintendent, in the name of efficiency and the separation of the board's legislative power from the superintendent's executive power. Neither the CTF nor teachers' councils figured largely in the new reforms, Mead's pursuit of democracy in the schools having given way to his interest in educational efficiency. The school system needs experts, Mead argued, especially to fill the specialized role of superintendent, people who can direct the operation of the increasingly complex Chicago system, arranging day-to-day operations and, above all, supervising and evaluating employees. Even though Mead warned that, if one were to maintain democratic institutions, one must still keep the experts responsible to elective bodies, his mind was more on efficiency than accountability: "It is possible . . . for a democracy to pick out experts and give them

---

[30] Mead to Irene Tufts Mead, January 28, 1917, Mead Papers. On the Loeb rule, see Majorie Murphy, *Blackboard Unions: The AFT and the NEA, 1900–1980* (Ithaca, 1990), 80–83.

full responsibility. For we will be able to see if they produce the results, which we demand."[31]

By 1917, then, Mead characterized democracy in the schools primarily as accountability to the public. No longer did the direct exercise of democratic control on the part of the school system's employees or its students have a prominent place on the pragmatists' reform agenda.

[31] Mead, "Fitting the Educational System into the Fabric of Government," *City Club Bulletin* 10 (March 27, 1917): 108.

CHAPTER ELEVEN

Between Management and Labor

As educational disputes occupied Mead, his colleagues, and their allies in the reform movement, several waves of industrial conflict passed through Chicago. After the Pullman strike, the trade union movement lost its foothold in the city's key industries, most notably in the stockyards, which employed the highest percentage of Chicago's wage earners and where in 1900 union sympathizers had to meet secretly to avoid dismissal. By 1903 labor had reversed its fortunes, with over half the workforce (around 245,000) in the CFL, the city's central trade union coalition. The labor movement recruited increasingly from the ranks of the unskilled, in the packinghouses and other mass production industries; among the new unionists, many women and recent immigrants could be counted.[1]

The labor upsurge of 1900 to 1903 met stubborn resistance from employers. Several bitter strikes tore through the city in that first decade of the new century, bringing sympathetic workers and communities into street confrontations with strike breakers, company guards, and the police which often dissolved into rioting and violence.[2]

[1] James Barrett, *Work and Community in the Jungle: Chicago's Packinghouse Workers, 1894–1922* (Urbana, 1987), 131–32, 142; David Montgomery, *The Fall of the House of Labor: The Workplace, the State, and American Labor Activism, 1865–1925* (Cambridge, 1987), 269.

[2] For example, the 1902 and 1905 Teamsters strikes; see Steven L. Piott, "The Chicago Teamsters' Strike of 1902: A Community Confronts the Beef Trust," *Labor History* 26

The economic downturn of 1903 prompted corporate leaders to launch an open shop drive to break the trade union movement on a national scale, with Chicago providing an important field of battle. Similar to the crises of 1877, 1886, and 1894, events in 1904 marked an important turning point in the city's labor relations. By fall, labor had conducted over ninety work stoppages, involving nearly 77,000 workers, but many of these conflicts were initiated by management. Labor, at a disadvantage, lost badly.[3] Still, Chicago's industrialists achieved only a momentary triumph. In 1910 yet another labor upsurge began with a confrontation over modern industrial practices, this time in the city's huge garment industry. Closely following similar strikes the year before in New York and Philadelphia, the 1910 garment strike drew a large segment of Chicago's reform community into the center of class conflict. Mead, already experienced in reform politics through his City Club activities, leapt to the front of the reformers' unsuccessful efforts to manage the crisis.

The strike began on September 22 in a west side sweatshop run by Hart, Schaffner and Marx (HSM), the city's largest, most modernized clothier. Hannah Shapiro, a young pocket sewer, led a spontaneous walkout over a piece-rate reduction, a frequent occurrence in an industry that was both brutally rationalized and infuriatingly erratic. An "advanced" company, HSM still operated in a seasonal and volatile market that encouraged managerial ruthlessness and sweating, the common practice of contracting out parts of the garment's production to tiny, squalid shops in the surrounding communities. And, although it surpassed its competitors in the size of its workforce, the volume of its output, and the modernization of its equipment and management techniques, HSM subdivided work into minute tasks, employing a large number of unskilled and semiskilled workers at dehumanizing jobs under dreadful conditions.[4]

(Spring 1985): 250–67; and Jane Addams, *Twenty Years at Hull-House* (Chicago, 1929), 224–25; also, on the 1904 packinghouse strike, Barrett, *Work and Community*, chap. 5.

[3] David Montgomery, *Workers Control in America* (Cambridge, 1977), 57–63; Steve Fraser, *Labor Will Rule: Sidney Hillman and the Rise of American Labor* (New York, 1991), 44; Barrett, *Work and Community*, 181–82.

[4] Hart, Schaffner and Marx led the industry in bringing contract work back "inside," but it still operated forty-eight sweatshops across the west side; see Fraser, *Labor Will Rule*, 27–29, 43; N. Sue Weiler, "Walkout: The Chicago Men's Garment Workers' Strike, 1910–1911," *Chicago History* 8 (Winter 1979–80): 238–40. Conditions in sweatshops are too notorious to describe in detail here; see Florence Kelley's description of the sweat-

Shapiro's defiant job action initially earned her the ridicule of HSM's skilled cutters, but she was soon joined by an army of unskilled and semiskilled operatives, mainly immigrants, mostly women disgusted by the indignities and hardships of assembly line and sweated labor. Within three weeks, HSM workers had closed down the giant company's far-flung operations in an apparently spontaneous expression of discontent. Within a month, the entire garment industry was out in sympathy with HSM workers as well as for similar grievances. Owners denounced the strike, insisting that the complaints were unfounded, but the strikers quickly found strong public support among progressive reformers with ties to garment worker communities, who had long been critical of mass production methods. Settlement house advocates of female protective labor legislation joined socialists mobilizing for the class struggle in a well-organized and well-funded coalition run by the Women's Trade Union League (WTUL) and the CFL. Many supporters feared the worst as winter approached and a settlement did not; violence seemed probable. Yet even moderate reformers looked beyond the fear of social disorder, supporting the strike as an opportunity to address the basic problems of emerging mass production: the intense subdivision of labor, deskilling, the exercise of arbitrary authority over unskilled operatives with few resources, and the need for a rational method of settling disputes in industries unmediated by familiar (and acceptable) ethics of craft and community.

On Sunday, October 30, as the strike entered its second month, a citizens' committee formed, composed primarily of moderate settlement house activists, City Club members, and wives of City Club members.[5] Mead chaired a subcommittee of five charged with inves-

---

shops in the neighborhood around Hull House: "The Sweating System," in *Hull-House Maps and Papers* (Boston, 1895), 27–45. On conditions in the textile industry leading to the strike, see Womens' Trade Union League of Chicago (WTUL), *Official Report of the Strike Committee*, pamphlet in the National Womens' Trade Union League Papers (NWTUL), Reel 4, Schlesinger Library, Harvard University.

[5] The WTUL strike committee formed the day before; WTUL, *Official Report*, 3. The citizens' committee met at the house of Mrs. Joseph T. Bowen, whose husband was an inaugural City Club member. Of the twenty-five participants in the committee, twelve were either City Club members or married to one. Settlement house participants included Jane Addams, Sophronisba Breckinridge, Grace Abbott, and Alice Hamilton of Hull House, Graham Taylor of Chicago Commons, Harriet Van der Vaart and Anna Nicholes of Neighborhood House (Nicholes also belonged to WTUL and edited the women's section of the *Union Labor Advocate*). See *Report of the Sub-committee to the Citizens Committee,*

tigating the strike. That week they interviewed workers from over three dozen workplaces, reporting their findings on the following Saturday. The subcommittee found that draconian rules prevailing in the city's garment factories and sweatshops had precipitated the walkout: managers imposed fines for loss of equipment, excessive use of washroom soap, and other trivial encroachments on company profits. Union membership was immediate grounds for dismissal, not subject to appeal, and manufacturers commonly blacklisted troublesome employees. Excessive supervision and the exercise of arbitrary and abusive authority by foremen plagued the daily work life of the seamstresses and cutters. And erratic hiring practices geared to the rise and fall of the market made survival tenuous. Few workers listed wages as a significant grievance, citing instead authoritarian management, yet the employers Mead's committee interviewed insisted that wages were the only issue, that the strike began over a misunderstanding, and that a small number of union members were keeping 90 percent of the workers out with threats of violence. Finding the employers' claims unfounded, Mead's subcommittee strongly supported the strikers and advocated the establishment of a union.[6]

The subcommittee report may have helped galvanize the support of a large and significant group of moderate reformers among the city's professionals and businesspeople. Throughout the city, in and outside the labor movement, sympathizers supplied material and spiritual aid to the striking workers, organizing commissary stores, collecting money for coal and food, supplying milk to children of strikers, and helping doctors treat wounded picketers. Members of the WTUL frequented the picket lines, risking arrest and violence, which escalated as the strike dragged on. During this time Mead took an active and prominent part in trying to resolve the conflict, though he avoided showing the kind of solidarity Margaret Dreier Robins, Ellen Gates Starr, and the more militant members of the WTUL displayed on the

Nov. 5, 1910, Box 9, Folder 22, Mead Papers (also in NWTUL Papers, Reel 4); Fraser, *Labor Will Rule*, 59; WTUL, *Official Report*, 24; Robert A. Woods and Albert J. Kennedy, eds., *Handbook of Settlements* (1911; rpt. New York, 1970), 65–66. Tensions among labor's allies in the middle-class reform community dated back to Margaret Dreier Robins's participation in an Industrial Workers of the World parade in 1905 and to conflicts the following year over educational reform between Robins and Jane Addams; see Elizabeth Anne Payne, *Reform, Labor, and Feminism* (Urbana, 1988), 60–72.

[6] *Report of the Sub-committee;* the report was signed by Breckinridge, Mead, and Nicholes.

picket line. Instead, as befit his professorial station, Mead tried to pressure the owners by appealing to public opinion, proposing that the City Club committee on labor conditions publicize as examples recent agreements in New York (the basis for the famous Protocols of Peace) and Philadelphia. Both of these provisions granted recognition to the union, though not the closed shop the Chicago strikers demanded. Otherwise, Mead recommended that the City Club bring in Louis Brandeis, the architect of the New York settlement, to study and adjudicate the strike, and that the club investigate the garment industry, presumably with an eye toward further public exposure. A public meeting of all parties involved to be organized and run by Mead was postponed because of an impending agreement at HSM.[7]

Mead's activities may have had some effect on the one positive settlement, between HSM and its employees. The strikers rejected HSM's first offer, providing for arbitration of workplace disputes but not recognition of the union, the week after the Mead subcommittee released its report. The second HSM offer, mediated by a city council committee headed by City Club member Charles Merriam, was drawn up by Northwestern University economist Earl Dean Howard, a former student of Tufts. Howard acted at the insistence of HSM partner and enlightened philanthropist Joseph Schaffner, a personal friend, after private guards killed a picketer in December. Both Schaffner and Howard were badly frightened by the situation, which Jane Addams described to Howard as "a spontaneous revolutionary movement."[8] The strikers rejected HSM's second offer as well, despite endorsement by the WTUL and militant labor leaders such as the CFL's John

---

[7] Public support for the strike was run by a joint conference board under the auspices of the CFL and WTUL. Whereas Helen Mead sat on the WTUL committee and contributed the substantial sum of $110 to the WTUL/CFL strike fund, members of the separate citizens' committee conspicuously absented themselves from the daily work of strike support. The timing of the committee's formation (the day after the WTUL formed its strike committee) and the presence of the WTUL's Katherine Coman (a key organizer of the solidarity campaign) at the first Citizens' committee meeting suggests that George Mead's group was formed on WTUL initiative and sequestered from more partisan activity to maintain the aura of impartiality. Nevertheless, the committees seem to have followed some political and ideological alignments, with moderates more favorable to arbitration participating in Mead's committee. WTUL, *Official Report*, 3, 12–21, 52; Chicago *Daily Socialist*, October 31, 1910, 1; Weiler, "Walkout," 247; Minutes of the City Club Labor Committee, November, 16, 17, and 22, 1910, Box 12, City Club Papers.

[8] Addams quoted in Matthew Josephson, *Sidney Hillman: Statesman of American Labor* (Garden City, 1952), 54; Weiler, "Walkout," 247; Fraser, *Labor Will Rule*, 52–53, 55.

Fitzpatrick. Resolution of the strike did not come until after the death of a second striker (at the hands of police) before the gates of Schaffner's plant. The final agreement granted full amnesty and, by setting up an arbitration board to resolve employee grievances, implicitly recognized some collective bargaining rights. It took effect on January 14, 1911, despite strong residual resistance from militant syndicalists in the strike meetings.[9]

As Chicago's largest clothing manufacturer, HSM accounted for almost one-quarter of employment in the needle trades. As significant as the agreement was, however, the rest of the industry did not follow Schaffner's lead and refused to recognize the legitimacy of the strike or collective bargaining. Incensed that the remaining employers continued to resist the strike, Mead dashed off a resolution for his subcommittee protesting that the employers' "obstinate refusal" to acknowledge the strikers' demands was "the merest subterfuge." He called for arbitration. Mead hoped his action would bring the "just condemnation of the community" down on the heads of the stonewalling captains of the clothing industry. It hardly influenced the employers though, who broke the strike in a few weeks with the cooperation of the United Garment Workers, a conservative craft union soon abandoned by industry employees. It was, as the WTUL angrily declared, a "hunger bargain."[10]

Labor Night

Together with his work on industrial education, the garment strike boosted Mead into a leading role in the city's reform movement. As

[9] It is possible if not likely that the City Club activity had effect through the agency of Merriam, James Mullenbach, and other members. The final HSM agreement loosely followed the pattern set in New York and Philadelphia. And the name of Schaffner's associate, Harry Hart, appears on the City Club rosters in spring 1911, suggesting that the club at least impressed *him*. Eventually HSM agreed to a "preferential shop" that forced owners to give hiring preference to union members. Josephson, *Sidney Hillman*, 47–48; Weiler, "Walkout," 248; Payne, *Reform, Labor, and Feminism*, 91. Employees accepted the agreement largely under the persuasive guidance of Sidney Hillman, who rose to leadership of the organized garment workers during the strike and was strongly influenced by members of the progressive community; Fraser, *Labor Will Rule*, 63–65. The agreements were published in *City Club Bulletin* 3 (1910): 401–5 (also available in NWTUL papers, Reel 4).

[10] A holograph text of the resolution can be found in Box 9, Folder 22, Mead Papers, cosigned by Sophronisba Breckinridge and Anna Nicholes but apparently composed by Mead; WTUL, *Official Report*, 35–36.

before, he concentrated most of his activity in the City Club, where in the 1910s he and Tufts rose to prominence.

By the time of the strike, the club's broad activities had attracted many new members, growing from 287 in 1904 to 931 in 1911. As its rooms on South Clark Street stretched beyond capacity, the club's leaders ambitiously built new headquarters nearby on Plymouth Court, expecting to attract members to cover the cost of the project. The board apparently calculated correctly: membership rose to 2,373 in March 1913, though the club's own analysis indicated that its reform agenda may have been compromised by an influx of businessmen and lawyers.[11]

The new building embodied the soaring expectations of the reform movement, as well as providing the material comforts of a middle-class social club. Its two-story dining-lecture hall, complete with balcony and private eating chambers, accommodated over two hundred for the weekly luncheon talks on social and political issues of the day. In the lounge and reading rooms, with leather chairs, large oak tables, and full fireplaces, members could relax, discuss events, and read from the club library. A grill served lunch and dinner, and a pool and game room occupied the basement. From its headquarters on the sixth floor, the club's bureau of efficiency provided the reform community presumably impartial investigations of city life. Architect and club member Irving K. Pond declared that "every line of the building illustrated some phase of the uplift movement."[12]

In January 1912, to inaugurate its new headquarters the City Club held a series of open houses to attract interest and present itself to the city. The theme for each night varied: political leaders spoke at "Government Night," ethnic leaders at "Nationalities Night," and so on. Mead sat on the committee that organized the series and acted as keynote speaker for "Labor Night," an event that reveals much about the complex relations between reformers like Mead and the city's multifaceted labor movement.

[11] Letter to members of the Board, March 23, 1904, Box 20, Folder 1, City Club Papers; "Report of Committee on Admissions," *City Club Bulletin* 5 (May 15, 1912): 143; Board of Directors reports for January 1, 1906 to March 31, 1907, *City Club Bulletin* 1 (1907–8). A report on membership in *City Club Bulletin* 9 (1916): 24, shows that, including lawyers, more than 50 percent of the membership were people in business. Social service occupations (generously construed) constituted at most 20 percent.

[12] *Union Labor Advocate*, January 13, 1912, 4. The quotation is of the *Advocate* paraphrasing Pond.

The organizers of Labor Night hoped to attract trade union members into the club, much as William Tucker and Newman Smyth had hoped to draw labor and capital into the church. Clearly sympathetic to unions, the club constructed its new building with union labor (at some expense and inconvenience) and organized strike support out of its rooms. Yet, for all its earlier work with organized labor, the club had to date been able to count only a handful of labor leaders on its membership roles, perhaps because trade unionists did not want to share a roster with industrial magnates like Hart, Schaffner, and the McCormicks. The City Club had roots in the Municipal Voters League (and through it the CCF), which organized labor had attacked just a few years earlier, specially targeting City Club organizer Walter Fisher.[13] Additionally, club members tended to distribute blame evenly when interpreting industrial conflicts, even in extreme cases like the Ludlow massacre, and labor activists probably found the nonpartisan stance and strenuous avoidance of class rhetoric uninspiring and suspicious.[14]

To open Labor Night, club president Henry Favill struck a pessimistic note, acknowledging that the club knew "its relations to organized labor are not what it hopes they may be." Other speakers, such as Robert Hoxie, longtime member and University of Chicago economist, expressed greater optimism, searching rather ethereally for a common ground between middle-class reformers and the city's working class. "Outside and above" classes he identified "an inclusive social whole, a sphere in which all classes commingle and in which a common social interest prevails." Hoxie offered the City Club as a common meeting place in which to explore the interests shared by capital and labor and to discuss the possibility of "cooperative action ... toward general civic betterment."[15]

In his keynote address Mead too voiced the hope that the club would serve as an institutional expression of the public will. "Instead of bringing together the common interests of all of us," Mead com-

[13] John Sontsteby of the conservative (and corrupt) United Garment Workers belonged to the City Club, as did several other CFL members (Emil Ritter of the CTF, Luke Grant of the Building Trades, and John C. Harding of the Typographers). They appear on the 1911 membership list and sat on the club's committees on education and labor. On CFL opposition to the Municipal Voters League, see *Union Labor Advocate,* March 1905, 18, and May 1905, 25.

[14] "The Colorado Strike," *City Club Bulletin* 7 (June 20, 1914): 242–44.

[15] "Labor Night," *City Club Bulletin* 5 (May 27, 1912): 214.

plained, political parties, the news media, and other cultural and social institutions "represent only single parts" and "erect barriers." Yet, though Mead envisioned the club mediating class tensions, he also hoped it would express a more enlightened popular sentiment, something beyond class unity for which class unity was only a necessary condition. Mead described this vision in populist tones: it was essential that "the great mass of the people" most affected by social injustices take a prominent role (through clubs such as his) in reform.[16]

Although Fitzpatrick, the militant president of the CFL, did not appear as expected, Labor Night organizers succeeded in attracting participants from the labor movement, including a large audience of union members. Their presence reflected the shifting and crisscrossing lines of solidarity and conflict within the alliance of Chicago's trade unionists and progressives. In reporting the event, the *Union Labor Advocate* praised the City Club for its "spirit of fair play" and for providing an "open forum" to labor. It also recognized that the club struggled to move reform politics into a stronger, more mutual alliance with labor: "If any of the union leaders had an idea that the affair was to be on the Civic Federation line, their doubts were soon dispelled, for it was apparent from the beginning of the program that it was not intended as a 'conciliation' dinner of labor representatives and capitalists."[17]

By contrast, John C. Frey, of the Cincinnati Iron Molders union, blamed the club's narrow reform interests and middle-class perspective for the lack of labor membership. Why are trade unions reluctant to work with other reformers? Frey asked. Because organizations "somewhat like the City Club" agitate for beautiful boulevards or

---

[16] Ibid., 215.

[17] *Union Labor Advocate*, January 20, 1912, 1. The *Advocate* had undergone some editorial changes, recently revising its slogan from "Devoted to the interests of all union labor and labels" to "Advocating the cause of organized labor along constructive lines." Its women's section, which had long reported the militant activism of the teachers, the WTUL, and female garment and stockyard workers, began running recipes, domestic columns, and advice for the lovelorn (for example, the February 3, 1912, issue). The 1911 McNamara bombing case in Los Angeles apparently turned many moderate union leaders against socialists and anarchists in the Chicago movement (erroneously associated with the bombing), a position made explicit when the *Advocate* ran an antisocialist crusade during Chicago's divisive newspaper strike that summer and during that fall's election campaigns. Soon the paper was defending the CCF against criticism by the left; see *Union Labor Advocate*, August 24–October 26, 1912. On the 1912 strike, see Philip Taft, "The Limits of Labor Unity: The Chicago Newspaper Strike of 1912," *Labor History* 19 (1978): 100–129.

more municipal art but oppose trade union initiatives on convict labor or child labor in the legislature.

> Let me say quite frankly to you that while your organization may be deeply interested in municipal art, in waterways, in civic expenditures and civic income, by far the majority of the citizens in Chicago are interested in other questions, vital questions. The average workingman and woman, the trade-unionist, is a good deal more interested in the type of a house that he must keep his family in, or in the question of burial cost, than he is in the question of municipal art. He is a great deal more interested in the kind of school his children are going to go to and the opportunity his children will have of going to that school, than he is in the question of a waterway to New Orleans or something of that sort.[18]

The City Club should address those issues first if it wanted working-class participation, insisted Frey.

The irony of Frey's remarks, an irony that also reveals the problematic relations reformers had to their city and its laboring citizens, is that the club, and particularly members such as Mead, seriously addressed the concerns of Frey's "average workingman and woman" in addition to increased expenditures on municipal art and beautiful boulevards. In response, one of the city's best-known moderate socialists and a club member, John C. Kennedy, unequivocally defended the club's reform record: "If [the club] were one of the so-called non-partisan organizations which are organized really to hold back the labor movement, I should not be here."[19]

Nor could labor activists argue that the club took trade union issues lightly. For Mead, who was by this time a leader in club affairs, labor's interests were not parochial, as many businesspeople (some of them apparently club members) claimed, but frequently represented the highest aspirations of the public. It was appropriate for the club to invite "representatives of the great mass of the community," because they worked for the common good.[20] Thus, Mead did not support unions as a necessary evil but viewed their emergence in the nineteenth century as a positive step in the evolution of society toward an in-

---

[18] "Labor Night," 216.

[19] Ibid., 218.

[20] Ernst Freund, a ubiquitous figure in Chicago's reform politics, declared to the audience that labor legislation was equally social legislation, representing the interests of the whole community; ibid., 221.

dustrial democracy. In the garment industry, for instance, uneven development created or allowed intolerable conditions that required democratic worker representation for their intelligent solution. Unions were thus necessary to aid "the working out of shop discipline and especially in order that minute grievances may find a natural expression."[21]

Although City Club reformers such as Mead came from different class backgrounds than did unionists, their commitment to organizing labor was no less sincere than their desire for social harmony, however misguided.[22] For his part in the remaking of American industrial relations, Mead expressed a genuine sense of solidarity with and sympathy for workers in mass production industries. It was the transformation of the American working class that disturbed Mead most profoundly: the degradation of crafts, the reduction of work to labor for pecuniary incentives, the elimination of play and art from their previously integral role in social production, the subordination of human relationships to the rules of the marketplace, the exploitation of children in mills and sweatshops. His perspective was neither unusual nor simple. Leaders of the solidarity movement in the 1910 strike (and again in its 1915 reprise) expressed a similarly complex understanding of the issues before them. The WTUL, without which the strike would probably have failed in December, pursued meliorative reforms yet was instrumental in the formation of new industrial unions in Chicago and elsewhere.[23] Robins and Starr preached a Christian Kingdom of fellowship, "self-control, fidelity and self-reliance" to a largely Jewish and Catholic immigrant female workforce, yet they also hoped to create the circumstances in which those women could achieve the highest levels of self-activity and self-realization.[24]

---

[21] *Report of the Sub-committee.* It did not occur to Mead, at least in this context, that sweatshops were an integral part of the fully evolved clothing industry, although by 1910 many people were aware of this fact.

[22] On the occupational composition of the Chicago reform movement, see David Hogan, *Class and Reform: School and Society in Chicago 1880–1930* (Philadelphia, 1985), 46–50.

[23] On Mary McDowell's work in the stockyards, see Barrett, *Work and Community,* 85–86, 143; Addams, *Twenty Years at Hull-House,* 212–14. On the WTUL in the 1910 strike, see Payne, *Reform, Labor, and Feminism,* 86–94, Fraser, *Labor Will Rule,* 57–62, and Weiler, "Walkout," 243–46. Payne argues that without the WTUL's Robins an agreement would have been improbable.

[24] WTUL, *Official Report,* 37; Ellen Gates Starr, "Art and Labor," in *Hull-House Maps and Papers,* 165–79, and "Art and Democracy," notes for speech, in Ellen Gates Starr

But Frey was not wrong, either, in attacking his hosts for class-biased reformism. Civic reformers such as Mead (and even moderate socialists such as Kennedy) in principle subordinated labor's particular interests to a set of values theoretically higher and more universal. There was plenty of room for self-serving interpretation of what those higher values were (for example, municipal art instead of better housing or vocational instead of liberal arts education). Many club members did prefer city beautification plans to substantial improvements in the standard of living, and few outside the Socialist party (which itself covered a wide political spectrum) seriously pursued the greater political and economic empowerment of workers.

Although Mead followed many reformers and labor leaders, militant and conservative alike, in identifying the growth of trade unionism with the development of industrial democracy, he did so in terms of the community of interest between capital and labor. His appeal to "the public" conformed to his (and others') belief that some social force stood above or emerged from the unfolding industrial conflict, a neutral and intelligent force capable of reconciling social groups that seemed otherwise destined for mutual destruction. Although this belief was conservative in a naively meliorative way, it was not opportunistic, as has been justly argued for those few reformers who actually accrued power and status through the institutionalization of mediatory agencies (for example, Howard, who became the labor director for HSM).

Nor did Mead simply act out a middle-class role in a liberal republican "moment," helping to rationalize changing industrial, social, and market relations. With hindsight one can see that out of the tumultuous wrangling over the labor problem emerged a new set of rationalizing and bureaucratic institutions, in the form of government regulation, arbitration agreements, and meliorative trade unions. Both the significance and the agencies of those changes, however, are extremely unclear: manufacturers had a stake (and an objective interest)

Papers, Box 21, Folder 273, Sophia Smith Collection, Smith College, Northhampton, Mass. As Barrett acutely observed, many of the customary forms of social and political organization in Chicago's ethnic communities (bars, social clubs) excluded women from the public life, including union activism, sustained within their walls. The settlement provided women a social equivalent to the saloon, though it presented its own discomforts to working-class women; Barrett, *Work and Community*, 85, Payne, *Reform, Labor, and Feminism*, 61–68.

in regulating production and labor relations, but in their own way so did the many workers who had long suffered the irrationalities of an unregulated marketplace, including a chaotic and difficult to organize labor market. Labor, with its own difficulties defining union and industrial democracy, found no simple answers in the socialist tradition. Older socialist labor leaders such as the Carpenters' P. J. McGuire, who had envisioned a cooperative commonwealth emerging from the labor movement, by 1894 vigorously pursued class conciliation in the AFL (against younger socialists such as Chicago's Thomas Morgan and Henry Demarest Lloyd). The AFL's Samuel Gompers turned a more polarized conception of class interest into his well-known advocacy of economistic, business unionism, which preferred particularistic gains to universalist ideals.[25]

When CFL progressives such as Haley and Fitzpatrick spoke of democracy in industry, they shared Mead's desire for fuller worker participation as well as his belief that labor, as the expression of a democratic impulse, would lead the rest of society in social change.[26] Mead parted company when labor took what he and his colleagues called the "class view," denying the existence of a common interest discernable by intelligent men and women searching for reasonable solutions to industrial disputes. For Haley, unions represented class interests, for instance, of the teachers in their fight for control of the schools, or of the clothing workers in their struggle against the rule of mass production. For Mead, unions brought intelligent working-class leadership, which under good conditions would control the radical impulses of "the men," as both he and Tufts were apt to call union members (fully one-third of Amalgamated Clothing Workers, founded in 1914, were women). Consequently, Mead and Tufts tended to associate with "responsible" trade unionists such as George Perkins of Chicago's cigar workers or Sidney Hillman of the clothing workers (though not by any means exclusively) and attacked radical syndicalism and anarchism.[27]

---

[25] Hogan, *Class and Reform,* Preface. On labor's historical agency in progressive reform, see Barrett, *Work and Community,* chap. 5, and Montgomery, *Fall of the House,* chap. 6. For a favorable assessment of McGuire, see Mark Erlich, "Peter J. McGuire's Trade Unionism: Socialism of a Trades Union Kind?" *Labor History* 24 (1983): 165–97.

[26] The Fitzpatrick forces won control of the CFL in 1905. For assessments of Fitzpatrick's progressive union politics, see Barbara Warne Newell, *Chicago and the Labor Movement in the 1930s* (Urbana, 1961), 9–26; Barrett, *Work and Community,* 191–93.

[27] Mead also strongly supported the British Labour party after the war, lamenting that

The Arbitration Board

In the aftermath of the 1910 garment strike, the labor agreement instituted at HSM became a model, with the Protocols of Peace in New York City, for the ongoing peaceful settlement of labor disputes. Besides recognizing the union's right to represent the workers, the Chicago agreement called for the establishment of a true board of arbitration, composed of one representative each from management and the union and a third, neutral member to be chosen by the other two to act as chair. The arrangement substituted mediation for strikes and confrontation and the rule of law for more brutal (and honest) tests of power. This was, however, one of the first instances of institutionalized industrial mediation in which labor and capital faced each other, at least nominally, as equals. It provided the basis for building the garment workers' union in Chicago, implicitly, then explicitly recognizing collective bargaining rights and union representation.

By successfully engineering the HSM agreement, moderate reformers helped realize their ideal of peaceful industrial conciliation. This moment in the history of labor reform constituted an important if limited acting out of the principles of mediation, cooperation, and reconstruction at the core of pragmatist social psychology.

All the Chicago philosophers who wrote on the subject advocated some form of arbitration in industrial disputes, though what they meant by that term was not clear. Before 1900, "arbitration" applied to simple informal conciliation between employers and employees as well as to more formal mechanisms of mediation between official representatives of management and labor. Until well after 1900 it applied to all manner of peaceful settlement in labor-management disputes, whether by the parties themselves or by outsiders.[28]

American labor had "not got far enough along" to accept the British labor platform. But this position still tread the precarious balance between calling for the institution of greater democratic rights for labor and advocating the organization of radical impulses immanent in working-class discontent. Mead to Henry Mead (son), March 3, 1918, and February 4, 1919, Mead Papers.

[28] Edwin Witte, *Historical Survey of Labor Arbitration* (Philadelphia, 1952), 3–6. In the United States arbitration was advocated by American unions as early as 1829 as a way to avoid strikes, but through the 1880s many advocates meant by the term what we now call collective bargaining, that is, the negotiated settlement of disputes between employers and recognized union representatives.

Something like the kind of arbitration called for by Mead and Tufts, what we would now call mediation, began to appear in the late 1870s with the passage of state arbitration laws and the establishment of boards of arbitration (or conciliation and arbitration) in several states. The most effective law was that of Massachusetts, but like most other arbitration legislation its irregular use and limited power rendered it of little significance except as a symbol for later reformers.[29] Some genuine cases of third-party mediation (called arbitration) occurred on an ad hoc basis—for example, in the 1871 Pennsylvania anthracite coal strike and in railroad labor disputes throughout the late nineteenth century—but these were sporadic and often unsuccessful. By 1900 labor leaders, though they favored the concept as a legal lever for union recognition, were disillusioned with arbitration laws, mainly because employers refused to recognize them.[30]

These obstacles did not stop the movement for arbitration, however, and interest grew in the aftermath of major strikes such as the Pullman strike in 1894. In November of that year the industrial committee of the newly established CCF held a congress on conciliation and arbitration, for which Addams acted as secretary. Business, labor, and civic leaders from around the country met to promote "orderly methods" for the resolution of industrial conflict. Almost all agreed that state intervention in the process would be undesirable and only one (a judge) advocated compulsory arbitration by the state. Each group, of course, had its own agenda, and the business representatives were somewhat desultory in their support of an institutionalized system of negotiation. For labor leaders, who supported collective bargaining and negotiation under the fuzzy rubric of "arbitration and conciliation," the main concern was union recognition. McGuire described how he implored builders' associations in several cities to ward off strikes by negotiating with employee committees, a tacit recognition of collective bargaining. Employers invariably refused to recognize the unions as representative of their employees.[31]

The behavior of Chicago manufacturers bore out McGuire's observations that employers had little interest in peaceful settlements

---

[29] Ibid., 8.

[30] R. W. Fleming, *The Labor Arbitration Process* (Urbana, 1965), 3; Witte, *Survey of Arbitration*, 10.

[31] CCF, *Congress on Industrial Conciliation and Arbitration* (Chicago, 1894), remarks by McGuire, 85–86; see also remarks by Samuel Gompers, 91.

that recognized collective bargaining rights. In 1896 the Hull House *Bulletin* complained that local garment manufacturers' refusal to submit the demands of a tailors' strike to arbitration hinged on their refusal to recognize the union. In the Hull House view, this was a matter that struck at the heart of democracy: it was "incredible" that "intelligent men" would "disavow the fundamental principle of representation, upon which our entire government is founded."[32] Except for the establishment of a state board of arbitration in 1895, a string of failures characterized the history of progressive efforts to institute the rule of law in the workplace: arbitration attempts in the 1900 building trades strike, the 1904 packinghouse strike, the 1905 Teamsters strike, and, except for HSM, the 1910 garment strike all ended with the union either broken or ignored. Strong opposition came on the workers' side as well, particularly among radical syndicalists in the Industrial Workers of the World and traditional anarchists, who adamantly opposed the HSM and subsequent arbitration agreements in the needle trade.[33]

For the most part Mead, Dewey, and Tufts limited their efforts to conciliate labor and capital to local settlement houses and to educational reform, which many considered a cornerstone of the conciliation process. It was through Hull House that Dewey first became involved more directly in industrial mediation, recommending and supporting a student to run a social welfare department at the local McCormick reaper plant. It was not until 1910, however, that any department member was involved in efforts to establish an arbitration process. And it was not until 1919 that any of them directly participated on an arbitration board. After a second major garment strike in 1915, reformers and union leaders gradually extended the HSM agreement to cover the rest of the garment industry, expanding as well the power of the industry's arbitration board to govern various aspects of the collective bargaining agreement. When that board's chair John E. Williams died in 1919, Howard, still acting as the company's representative, asked his former professor Tufts to take the post.[34]

---

[32] *Hull-House Bulletin*, April 1896, 4, available in Hull House Papers, University of Illinois, Chicago.

[33] Hogan, *Class and Reform*, 35–36; Fraser, *Labor Will Rule*, 70–72.

[34] Robert W. Ozanne, *A Century of Labor-Management Relations at McCormick and International Harvester* (Madison, 1967), 41; Tufts, "Clothing Arbitration," from unpub-

By 1919, Tufts had enjoyed a long and successful career in academics, serving as the University of Chicago dean, vice-president, and acting president, presiding over the American Philosophical Association in 1914 and over the Western Philosophical Association in 1906 and 1914.[35] He also achieved prominence in the progressive reform movement, through the City Club's housing committee and the Illinois Committee for Social Legislation, a coalition of state organizations for the promotion of progressive reform.

Tufts's reform work typified the moderate progressive approach to the problems of the new industrial city: his housing committee methodically investigated rental and private housing in Chicago and elsewhere in the state, closely tying injustices, housing deficiencies, and "demoralizing" conditions to the structural forces of the unregulated market. Inadequate transportation, excessive rents, low income, land and building speculation, loose zoning regulations, and the transience of neighborhoods all contributed to the deterioration of living conditions in the city's poor neighborhoods. For the committee's statewide study, Tufts tramped through slums and "Dogtowns" across Illinois, detailing conditions in ramshackle cottages, tenements, and "shanty boats" (skiff-shaped shacks clustered in the Mississippi River flood plain). The committee was less adventurous when considering solutions, however. Although it investigated the provision of public and cooperative housing in European cities ("idealistic housing achievements"), generally it favored bettering American housing by regulation of the private market.[36] Similarly, the Illinois Committee for Social Legislation studied the inadequacy of free markets for the provision of basic human services such as medical care yet preferred voluntary and regulatory solutions over socialization on a state or national level.[37]

---

lished autobiography, Box 3, Folder 25, Tufts Papers, Chicago; Witte, *Survey of Arbitration*, 25–26.

[35] "James Hayden Tufts," privately published memorial pamphlet, 1942, in Box II, Folder 18, Tufts Papers, Amherst.

[36] Minutes of the City Club Housing Committee, December 8, 1909, Box 11, Folder 3, City Club Papers; Tufts, "Housing in Illinois Cities," *Chicago Medical Recorder*, November 1909, Box 10, Folder 6, City Club Papers; Housing Exhibit Outline, Box 4, Folder 7, Tufts Papers, Chicago; "Report of the Housing Exhibit Committee," *City Club Bulletin* 6 (June 28, 1913): 200–201; annual reports and minutes of the housing committee are in Box 10, City Club Papers.

[37] Tufts, "Autobiography," Box 3, Folder 25, Tufts Papers, Chicago; "Social Legislation in Illinois," *City Club Bulletin* 1 (April 17, 1907): 21–23; founding statement of Illinois

When Tufts joined the garment industry arbitration board, he entered an apparently successful experiment in industrial democracy. Engineered by Williams, the board's first chairman, in collaboration with the Amalgamated Clothing Workers' Hillman, the garment industry accord became a model of durability in a field of short-lived arbitration protocols. Williams's success included persuading first HSM (in 1913), then the rest of the city's needle trade to confer a "preferential" shop in hiring which gave union members priority. The accords allowed for the general improvement of wages and working conditions and, most important, given the grievances of 1910, limited abuses of authority by management. A former coal miner and newspaper editor from Streator, Illinois, a downstate coal town, Williams represented the most idealistic and participatory phase in the movement for industrial democracy, which had not yet become completely dominated by the meliorative and manipulative practices of industrial managers. Adhering to a pluralistic conception of industrial relations, Williams believed as did many idealistic progressives of his generation that true social democracy could come about only with power sharing in industry, engineered in agreements like Chicago's.[38]

Williams steadfastly defended collective bargaining rights as a necessary condition for modern democracy, and he did his best to see the situation in mass production industry from labor's perspective. But he held as well a view of industrial negotiation that characterized many of the progressive visions of industrial democracy. After the successful negotiation of a wartime contract, he instructed an audience of garment workers on the "meaning of self-government in industry": workers, he insisted, are fit for self-government only if they demonstrate their "ability to select conscientious, devoted and competent leaders" and their willingness to observe the rule of law in the workplace. Moreover, true industrial democracy required that workers internalize industrial responsibility: "You get rid of the outside boss by having a better boss inside of you, one who keeps you up to your work and makes you choose to do it out of a sense of honor and duty." In this sense, the garment accords served not only to redis-

---

Committee for Social Legislation, Box 4, Folder 11, Tufts Papers, Chicago. Tufts served as chair and as the representative from the Illinois Committee for Labor Legislation, which likewise eschewed state provision of assistance to labor.

[38] Fraser, *Labor Will Rule*, 73–75; Milton Derber, *The American Ideal of Industrial Democracy, 1865–1965* (Urbana, 1970), 137–39.

tribute industrial power but also to educate the masses to their civic responsibility.[39] Similar moralistic conceptions echoed through the history of the arbitration movement, in which the characters of employers and employees were targeted for reform as often as were industrial relations and workplace rules. The "ideal," held one advocate in 1894, is to "go still farther back" behind boards of arbitration in order to "prevent the feelings and the actions which tend to cause a dispute." A more "Christian relation" must be achieved, and this would be possible only if the characters of employers and employees were "modified and educated."[40]

Immanent Solutions and the Rule of Reason

The degree to which Tufts shared Williams's understanding of industrial democracy is evident in his most important decision while board chairman: his 1919 judgment in favor of the union, granting across-the-board wage increases to keep pace with increases in the clothing markets of other cities. For his decision, the Amalgamated Clothing Workers hailed Tufts as a "pathfinder among industrial arbitrators." This praise did not just reflect the gratitude of union leaders, for newspapers across the country declared the agreement "one of the most important documents in the history of the industry," although critics also attacked it as a decision that would raise the price of clothing.[41]

Tufts's decision extended earlier judgments by Williams. It uniquely allowed wage increases despite the fact, readily acknowledged by the union, that wages had been keeping pace with the rising cost of living. Establishing new guidelines by which to judge the ethics of wage disputes, Tufts's argument hinged on the fact that Chicago clothiers, who sold on a national market, lagged behind in the wages they paid

[39] [John E. Williams], "War and Wages—an Arbitrator's Decision," Streator *Daily Independent-Times,* June 9, 1917, clipping in Box 19, Folder 4, City Club Papers. Williams signed the article "Fabius."

[40] CCF, *Congress on Industrial Conciliation and Arbitration,* 41 (remarks by Josephine Shaw Lowell), 47 (Bemis), 51 (Weeks), 48–49 (Addams).

[41] The first quote comes from a newspaper of the Amalgamated Clothing Workers, probably the *Advance.* "Prof. Tufts' Decision," editorial in [*Advance*], [n.d., n.p.]; New York *News Record,* December 24, 1919, [n.p.]. Copies of both articles are in the Tufts Papers, Morris Library, Southern Illinois University, Carbondale.

their workers while keeping abreast of price increases, many of which followed from war contracts. In other parts of the country, some of them not strictly governed by agreements like Chicago's, workers had used strikes to force management to raise wages. Consequently, under the rule of law (that is, without strikes) the Chicago industry was making a killing on the market and not distributing its profits to any of its employees.

Until that time (and thereafter, except in unusual cases such as this one) raises were considered adequate if they allowed employees to maintain their standard of living. Tufts instead implemented a form of gain sharing long advocated by one segment of the reform movement (embodied, unsuccessfully, in the Towne plan of the 1870s): he tied wage increases to what the market would bear and to the seasonal increases in productivity of industry. The latter basis for wage increases would become the foundation of labor management relations in major industries after World War II. Tufts dismissed the claim that consumer prices would increase as a result, observing that the companies had raised them already to match clothing prices from other cities.

For Tufts the decision was not merely an act of labor-management mediation but the kind of intellectual intervention that constituted the meeting place between philosophical ethics, social psychology, and politics. His more reflective observations reveal a great deal about how he and his colleagues regarded their social reformism and the meaning of industrial democracy. In an autobiography written years later, he introduced the account of his experiences in labor arbitration by recounting Plato's allegory of the cave. Those who rise from the cave to see the sun, Tufts maintained, must come back down inside to describe what they have seen, but they must also know human passion and frailty. Tufts's intent was to criticize "abstract ethics," which does not attend to the realities of life in the cave, or to the passions of social life. The passage, however, also discloses Tufts's essential and unintentional elitism, for however cognizant the social psychologist may be of the passions shared by the denizens of the darkness, his stature theoretically is greater than theirs because he has seen the light of reason. Moreover, as he praised the clothing protocols for substituting reason for force, Tufts more readily blamed labor than management for the irrationalities of violent industrial conflict. The HSM agreement was signed thanks to Schaffner's benevolence and Hillman's "responsibility." The rule of reason, Tufts intoned, is "the method of advancing civilization, a method which the whole labor movement might wisely adopt as the circumstances permit."[42]

Tufts argued that the agreement introduced a legal order hitherto unknown in labor relations and that its adherence to law was its most distinctive characteristic. This legalism Tufts attributed to the board's continuity (it sat for three-year terms) and to the fact that board members, because they represented interests other than their own, identified as much with the board as with their clients. This, argued Tufts, reflected the "same influences of group psychology" one finds in any courtroom, where the professional interests of the lawyers lead them to "manifest respect for a principle higher than any private interest."[43]

The rule of law, however, had deeper implications than the rule of professionals for Tufts. For the arbitrators' identification with the board raised the issue of the relation of social values to social reality, the persistent question for Chicago philosophy and the social science it spawned. On a board such as the Chicago clothing board, one was confronted with the question of whether one should simply mediate the interests of the parties involved, letting the balance of power determine the outcome, or intervene on behalf of those with less power (in this case, invariably, the union) in the name of a higher and more rational social justice. In labor disputes the standard pluralist conception held for Tufts, in which "the voluntary contract in the labor agreements reflects the limits of concessions which each is willing to make and the limits of the demands which each is prepared to insist upon in the existing circumstances."[44] This was the reality of social change, the interaction of forces, which in more psychological moments Tufts characterized in terms of habits and impulses.

But whatever the balance of power at the moment, the arbitrator, who presumably could "see farther from his position above the

---

[42] Tufts, "Clothing Arbitration." Such agreements seldom ended confrontations in the workplace, as was the case in the Chicago clothing industry, where work stoppages were a daily but necessary occurrence from the workers' (if not the union's) point of view; Fraser, *Labor Will Rule*, 70.

[43] Tufts, "Judicial Law-Making Exemplified in Industrial Arbitration," *Columbia Law Review* 21 (May 1921): 405–15.

[44] Ibid., 408.

battle," must decide between the "rule of reason" and the "will of the people," as expressed by the resolution of contending forces.[45] A decision must reflect what was immanent in the circumstances of the moment, what was desired by the parties that contended for power. But the arbitrator also had the more universal vantage point of reason, in his unique role as intellectual, an opportunity to "advance a philosophy of social order," what was desirable and not simply desired. Tufts by no means wanted to invoke a transcendental reason or the orthodox rule of law except in the provisional sense of what is produced by the balance of power. But he recognized the dilemma that cut to the heart of pragmatist ethics and social activism. Always insistent that the principles of social order must and do emerge out of the interaction of irrational historical and psychological forces, the Chicago philosophers nevertheless had a vision of rational social order that they hoped would obtain in the progress of immanent self-development.

Their position was less hypocritical than confused by the systematically ambiguous nature of instrumentalist theory. Committed to the immanence of values in the real, in the evolution of society, they championed the expression of political passions. This led them to support the democratic rights of Chicago's workers, and of Americans in general, through the development of militant trade unions, even those willing to strike when necessary. This support was of a piece with their cultural relativism, which recognized that each culture can reach only that level of ethical development which circumstances (mainly economic) allow. But the Chicago philosophers were no less committed to the belief that self-development had a direction, which intellectuals like themselves (especially social psychologists) could see better than those embroiled in the passions of the moment. The arbitrator's position was supposed to transcend those passions, and if his decisions were "merely a reflection of the actual balance of power he seems not fully to justify the confidence reposed in him by the parties." And though he should be guided by "the prevalent philosophy of present American life," Tufts saw some reason to appeal to a philosophy of "some supposedly better order."[46]

Both roles for the philosopher-arbitrator (and social psychologist)

---

[45] Ibid., 409.
[46] Ibid., 409–10.

had the potential either to be authoritarian or to encourage democratic participation. As the midwife of the pluralist balance of power, the arbitrator defended the right of workers to organize and express their discontent. Yet he also subjected that power to the will, legitimated as the repository of tradition and rationality, of the industrial managers. As the visionary who ascended from the cave of social disorder, the arbitrator could endorse popular movements on the grounds of some higher principle of social justice. Yet he also wielded his vision as knowledge superior to that of the cave dwellers, especially the irresponsible ones.

In practice Tufts preferred to play the role of midwife, adjudicating differences according to the rules set down in contracts over their three-year duration. Yet he did two things that subverted that role. First, he imposed a sense of social justice explicitly on the arbitration process, an imposition he felt was justified by the fact that employees were always at a disadvantage in their relations with capitalists. In a muddled effort to square with his departure from the role of midwife he argued that whatever sensibility the board used must not be "too widely at variance with our present social and economic order." "The Board," he wrote, defending his decision to grant higher wages in 1919, "believes that it must be governed largely, although not exclusively, by the prevailing principles and policies of the country as embodied in its institutions."[47]

Tufts's second subversion was entirely implicit and unintentional. Although eschewing the imposition of transcendent values on a situation that must be governed by the values immanent in social action, he interpreted the immanent values of the nation, the institutions in which those values were embodied, according to another set of values. On honest examination he would have had to call that other set of values "transcendent," as he meant the term. To some extent this was a matter of adopting rhetoric uncritically, but far more important was the psychological theory Tufts used as a baseline for all his political and ethical judgments. That psychology could not reconcile irrational social forces with the rationality he believed was immanent in history. Ultimately, all the Chicago philosophers, sharing this psy-

[47] Board of Arbitration for the Agreements between the Amalgamated Clothing Workers of America and Chicago Clothing Manufacturers, Decision of December 22, 1919, 8. The decision was written by Tufts. A copy is available in Tufts Papers, Carbondale (see note 41).

chology, shared its problems. Dewey and his colleagues could not prove that reason *was* the rose in the cross of the present, as Hegel argued. So, like Tufts, they fell back instead on power and coercion to impose a dubious rationality on history. For his part, Tufts insisted that justice emerged from the political, social, and economic conditions of the present. That alone presumed a certain conception of justice, of social order and of social change that did not necessarily come from the actual relations that obtained in society. The belief in the rule of reason in industrial relations was optimistic yet also presumptuous, for precisely the reason that Tufts felt it necessary to intercede on behalf of workers in the first place.

CHAPTER TWELVE

A *Cloud of Witnesses*

Tufts's contribution to the history of labor arbitration reflects the paradox at the heart of the Chicago pragmatists' social reform experience. They sought social legislation, political and economic organizations, and educational institutions that would encourage the democratic agency of the dispossessed. It was not enough, they argued, to simply redistribute wealth; reform must foster the self-activity and self-realization of common citizens, allowing the full development of their interests in a cooperative, constructive social environment. But Tufts and his colleagues believed as well that self-realization would follow a preferred course, that it would be a learning experience in which leadership responsibility, the rule of law, and the progressives' own faith in an immanent reason would be found. And they possessed an imperious certainty, with roots back into the nineteenth-century discourses of producer republicanism and liberal theology, that a community of interest between managerial heads and laboring hands would always prevail.

One can also read the traces of this tension between a theory of radical self-realization and a doctrine of moral immanence in their social theory and social psychology. The most interesting and most troubling example can be found in Mead's concept of the social self, at the heart of the social interactionism for which he is now famous.

Mead began writing about the social self around 1900. By that time Dewey had already been exploring its philosophical implications for over fifteen years. It is worth taking a moment to review a couple of the objectives of Dewey's earlier philosophical investigations, which he passed on to his younger colleague. First, in his effort to reconstruct the theistic idealism of his youth, Dewey proposed that the rational was immanent in experience. Rational consciousness and spirituality emerged out of the struggle for survival, transforming it into intelligent and ethical action, behavior with a higher rational goal. Thus, neurological reflex-arc responses contained a kernel of constructive intelligence, and an organic continuity existed between the elements of human action: the rational was immanent in the impulse.

Second, influenced by the social Christianity of the 1880s, Dewey hoped to show that the emerging rationality was cooperative rather than prudential, motivated by socially constructive reciprocity rather than individual gain. He tried to escape the individualistic and utilitarian implications of the most mechanistic and reductionist psychologies then following on the post-Darwinian controversy. Reconstruction, cooperation, and reciprocity are, argued Dewey, psychologically and therefore biologically natural to humans. Thus, the reflex-arc critique made an important political as well as philosophical point, which many hoped would lead to a stronger concept of reciprocity or cooperation, justifying a more humane social ethic and stressing Christian harmony in historical development rather than the tooth-and-nail struggle for survival.

Dewey, however, encountered serious philosophical obstacles in his effort to demonstrate a biologically based ethic of cooperation. An evolutionist like most of his contemporaries, he argued that an individual achieved social and ethical conduct because, in the broadest sense, one *had to* for the purposes of survival. It was not particularly convincing, however, to argue that social consciousness developed as an adaptation to individual need, and this obviously was not Dewey's intent. Yet he could not adequately distinguish his understanding of self-activity and self-realization from a utilitarian calculus or Darwinian prudence. Dewey did not demonstrate that the intelligence, by which an individual discovered the means to achieve the goals of ongoing action, necessarily (and psychologically) involved recognizing the significance and autonomy of others.[1]

---

[1] Thus Dewey opened his philosophy to the long prevailing interpretation of it as a form of utilitarian Darwinism; see, for example, Gail Kennedy, "The Pragmatic Naturalism of

Mead and the Problem of Sociability

During the 1890s, Mead, picking up where Dewey left off, tried to establish the natural origins of social cooperation in human evolution without relying on Darwinian or utilitarian notions of individual prudence. Like Dewey, Mead understood this project in the reform context: before we undertake "the application of intelligence to the control of social conditions," Mead argued, we must believe "in the essentially social character of human impulse and endeavor. We cannot make persons social by legislative enactment, but we can allow the essentially social nature of their actions to come to expression under conditions which favor this."[2]

By 1909, Mead had traced the foundation of his interactionist social psychology, and he refined his theory in a series of articles on the social nature of the self and of consciousness between 1909 and 1913. By 1914 a fairly complete outline of Mead's mature social psychology, such as is usually taken from his later lectures, *Mind, Self, and Society,* could be found in lectures given that year at the university.

It was with the later work of Wilhelm Wundt that Mead began a psychological argument for the social nature of humans. Wundt appealed to Mead for two reasons. First, Wundt argued that language begins with the gesture, initially an impulsive act, or near act, which becomes in a social context a sign of emotion and intention. Because language is an act rather than a reflection of ideas or transcendent meanings, its content, rather than being the subject matter of logic and philology, instead should be the subject matter of a functionalist psychology that studies voluntary acts. Mead found Wundt's study particularly appealing because the German philosopher interpreted communication and sociality in psychological terms. The community "mind" or *Volkseele,* inhered in the common language, which emerged from the psychological processes of social interaction.[3]

Chauncey Wright," in *Studies in the History of Ideas,* 3 vols., ed. Columbia University Philosophy Department (New York, 1935), 3:486, 503; also Philip Wiener, "Chauncey Wright's Defense of Darwin and the Neutrality of Science," *Journal of the History of Ideas* 6 (1945): 27; John Dewey, *The Study of Ethics: A Syllabus* (Ann Arbor, 1894), *Early Works* 4:338–39.

[2] George Herbert Mead, "The Working Hypothesis in Social Reform," *American Journal of Sociology* 5 (1899): 370.

[3] Mead, "The Relations of Psychology and Philology," *Psychological Bulletin* 1 (1904): 377.

Second, Wundt's theory of language seemed to confirm Dewey's belief in the continuity between reason and impulse. Wundt's notion that the primitive gesture led to fully developed language linked the individual's irrational, biological nature to the socially ordered world of communication, suggesting the continuity between impulsive, unreflective behavior and rational socialized conduct. Unlike traditional philologists, wrote Mead, Wundt "is able to refer the beginning of language to the primitive impulse to expression. The sound is at first but a gesture." Wundt, according to Mead, could move fluidly from the physical gestures to sound gestures to articulate language, demonstrating the origins of language in the primitive act (that is, in human and animal biology), "instead of being forced to build it up out of intellectual elements."[4]

Building on a critical interpretation of Wundt's theory, Mead speculated that social consciousness emerged as an interaction between individuals (or "forms," as Mead called them) through the interplay of gestures. The key to social organization, and to the origin of social attitudes, would then be in communication, the way in which "the conduct of one form is a stimulus to another." This stimulus is for the other to perform a certain act, which in turn becomes "a stimulus to [the] first to a certain reaction, and so on in ceaseless interaction." It is not the similarity of acts that constitutes or encourages social interaction but the meaning each act has, in terms of the act's consequences, for the other form. Thus "the probable beginning of human communication was in cooperation . . . where conduct differed and yet where the act of the one answered to and called out the act of the other." This seemed the solution to Dewey's dilemma. Communication (hence, humanness) did not begin in prudence or competition, or in imitation, but in constructive cooperation, suggesting that sociability likewise did not emerge as a prudent strategy for individual adaptation but was present with the appearance of language.[5]

Mead needed, however, to extend Wundt's theory to address fully the problems raised by Dewey. He believed that Wundt's theory of language still did not adequately explain the emergence of sociability or communication from individual gestures and impulses. Wundt, like

[4] Ibid., 380, 382.
[5] Mead, "Social Psychology as Counterpart to Physiological Psychology," *Psychological Bulletin* 6 (1909): 406.

most of his contemporaries in laboratory psychology, began with the individual as a unit of analysis, explaining sociability as something added to that individual identity.[6] Mead wanted to explain that individual identity, in fact all aspects of individual psychology, with sociability as a starting point: "Until the social sciences are able to state the social individual in terms of social processes, as the physical sciences define their objects in terms of physical change, they will not have risen to the point at which they can force their object upon an introspective psychology."[7] He wanted, not just a theory of communication, but a scientifically convincing genetic psychology of human cooperation. In other words, he hoped to convince his readers that people could not be human, in any sense of the term, unless they were social (that is, cooperative).

Mead found particular fault with Wundt's explanation of the meaning of gestures. Gestures are acts that signal something to another individual. What they signal, however, was a matter of some dispute. Wundt argued that gestures signal emotional states, and that those emotions constitute their meaning. In the broadest sense Mead agreed. But, according to the prevailing psychologies, emotions were reactions to stimuli. Wundt accepted this prevailing view, and it was on this count that Mead considered his explanation mechanistic, based on individualistic reflex psychology. Mead preferred Dewey's theory, which paralleled his critique of the reflex-arc, that the emotions are "truncated acts," acts that do not achieve their purpose because they are inhibited by either circumstances or the actor. Emotions signify the inhibition of the act and spur the actor to find a solution to the problem.[8] A gesture, by expressing an emotional state, then, expresses an intended or inhibited act. An animal gnashes its teeth when it wants to tear at the throat of another animal but has not yet done so, expressing the emotional state that reflects the unsatisfied desire, the uncompleted response to the combative situation.

The gesture, therefore, does not simply express an emotional state but also signifies to the other the possible consequences of the emo-

---

[6] Mead, "1914 Class Lectures in Social Psychology," in *The Individual and the Social Self* (Chicago, 1982), 37.

[7] Mead, "What Social Objects Must Psychology Presuppose?" *Journal of Philosophy* 7 (1910): 176.

[8] Mead, "1914 Class Lectures," 40; Dewey, "A Theory of Emotion" (1894–95), *Early Works* 4:152–88.

tional state, of the truncated act that constitutes the emotion—the "value of the act for the other individual." As the other responds "in terms of another syncopated act," a "field of social signification" is born within which communication and social interaction takes place. Gestures have meanings "when they reflect possible acts," that is, possible consequences for another individual who can see in that gesture a repressed, yet latent, act.[9]

To Wundt's theory of the gesture Mead grafted a conception of meaning adopted from Dewey and Josiah Royce—that the meaning of an object, for a sentient being, is the purpose that object will serve in some forseeable future or the role it will play in some action that culminates desire or need. Like Dewey and Royce, Mead argued that meaning involves the reference, through signs (that is, ideas, emotions, and attitudes), to future acts and experiences. But that meaning, he continued, can only be constituted as an intention conveyed to some "other," through gestures and language. According to Mead, therefore, meaning is actional (as Dewey argued), but it is also fundamentally social. In this way the play of gestures represents "the birth of the symbol, and the possibility of thought," a form of "sublimated conversation." Thus, he argued, "reflective consciousness implies a social situation which has been its precondition."[10]

Mead believed that he had added two things to Wundt's theory of the gesture. First, by referring the meaning of gestures entirely to social acts, he thought he had eliminated a main vestige of individualistic psychology that referred psychological events in the other direction, to internal states of mind (in this case internal emotions). Second, by externalizing and socializing emotional states, he laid the groundwork for socializing even more fundamental psychological concepts. In 1910, Mead expanded this second line of argument. In two articles he tried to demonstrate that consciousness of the self and of objects also has cooperative social origins.

Based on the principle that "meaning is consciousness of attitude," Mead argued that one cannot be *self*-conscious without being conscious of others, because the self is no more than an awareness of one's own attitude. It is only through the responses of others to one's

[9] Mead, "Social Psychology as a Counterpart," 407.
[10] Mead, "Social Consciousness and the Consciousness of Meaning," *Psychological Bulletin* 7 (1910): 399, and "Social Psychology as Counterpart," 407.

actions, especially to one's gestures, that one becomes conscious of one's own attitudes, including one's self-identity. Thus, "other selves in a social environment logically antedate the consciousness of self which introspection analyzes. They must be admitted as there, as given, in the same sense in which psychology accepts the given reality of physical organisms as a condition of individual consciousness." The self is not "an attitude which we assume ... toward our inner feelings" (that is, private introspection) but one directed "toward other individuals whose reality was implied even in the inhibitions and reorganizations which characterize this inner consciousness."[11]

Two years later Mead described two kinds of self that evolved from the primary interpersonal interaction. There is no true self in the philosophical meaning of the term, argued Mead. We do not identify ourselves first as knowers that precede the experience, physical or social, of the world. Rather, we are primarily object rather than subject, "me" rather than "I." Our self identity follows rather than precedes conversation, whether it is the actual conversation of language or the "inner conversation" that Mead argued constitutes thought. The self is a constant product of an imagination striving to see itself as others see it. The "I," the self of Decartes, of idealism, of Kant's transcendental apperception, is never accessible to us. It is forever immanent in our conversations, with others and ourselves, the sum total of our social experience.[12]

Sociality, however, penetrates consciousness and perception even more deeply. Not only can we not know ourselves without first being enmeshed in some form of symbolic social interaction, but our consciousness of things, of physical objects, postdates our entrance into the conversation of gestures. An object, for us, can be an object only if it retains some meaning in the course of our practical activity. Since Mead argued that consciousness of meaning emerges from the play of gestures, then it followed that consciousness of objects themselves

---

[11] Mead, "What Social Objects Must Psychology Presuppose?" 179. "We are conscious of our attitudes because they are responsible for the changes in the conduct of other individuals," wrote Mead; "Social Consciousness and the Consciousness of Meaning," 403; see also "1914 Class Lectures," 46. For a systematic discussion of the concepts "attitude" and "self" in the social psychology and sociology of Mead's colleagues in Chicago, see Norbert Wiley, "Early American Sociology and the *Polish Peasant*," *Sociological Theory* 4 (1986): 20–40.

[12] Mead, "The Mechanism of Social Consciousness," *Journal of Philosophy* 9 (1912): 405–6.

depends on social interaction. So he contended that, "whatever our theory may be as to the history of things, social consciousness must antedate physical consciousness" and that "experience in its original form became reflective in the recognition of selves, and only gradually was there differentiated a reflective experience of things which were purely physical."[13]

So, by 1910, Mead had demonstrated (to his own satisfaction) that consciousness is social and that the objects of our consciousness (including the self) are socially constructed. Sociability, he concluded, is not just grafted onto the experience of fully conscious, rational individuals already capable of prudent decisions (including the decision to recognize other people). Sociability developmentally precedes conscious rationality, individual self-identity, and even the objects between which individuals rationally or prudentially choose.

A Higher Individualism

It is no coincidence that Mead developed these theories while mediating conflicts between Chicago industrialists and their workers. His discourse on social psychology was inaccessible to most participants in Chicago's class struggle, but he addressed his writing to the problems raised in that conflict as much as to the inadequacy of earlier social psychologies.

As he struggled in the pages of learned journals to demonstrate the cooperative origins of all consciousness, Mead preached to Chicagoans the need for industrial cooperation and reciprocity between capital and labor. The key common term in his psychology and his reform was "cooperation," or reciprocity. He called for cooperation between classes and opposing social groups, which would be based on the reciprocity natural to human interaction and communication: "The recognition of the given character of other selves" (that is, the recognition of others as significant) comes "from psychology itself, and arises out of the psychological theory of the origin of language and its relation to meaning."[14]

Such a synthesis of psychology and social analysis was the hallmark

---

[13] Mead, "What Social Objects Must Psychology Presuppose?" 180.
[14] Ibid., 177.

of Chicago's activist social psychology. For the Chicago pragmatists the organic continuity of human action had suggested that the social conflict tearing Chicago apart, caused by the inadequate organization of modern industrial society in general, reflected a break in the coherence of human psychology. The factory system and the marketplace had divided the psychological functions between different classes, thereby creating opponents in the political arena as well. Industrial leaders controlled the intellectual functions of production, such as planning and evaluation. Their employees participated only as the hands, the final executors of social action.

Labor and capital acted out on a social and political scale the circuit of psychological coordination Dewey had proposed as an alternative to reflexology. Owners and managers pursued a conservative politics of a class unaffected by social ills, expressing a psychology of rational managerial planning. The responsibilities of management inclined them to habitually perpetuate hitherto successful forms of social conduct and organization, even to the detriment of the city's manual workers.[15] Social problems, however, emerged from the habitual practice of a society run by an intellectual and economic elite. The working class responded to these problems as a class that experienced the injustices and hardships of industrialism directly. Having been denied intellectual training and control, workers, especially the unskilled, tended toward politics that expressed the essentially impulsive nature of manual activity to the exclusion of political foresight. They haphazardly experimented with and projected, in radically utopian and revolutionary form, new social practices. This, according to department members, was the nature of the radicalism that flourished in the working-class districts of "red" Chicago and periodically inflamed (as the middle class saw it) social conflagrations such as the Haymarket incident or the Pullman strike. Yet this could be a functional evolutionary relation. Industrial management and political leadership conservatively protected social habits but conceded new, provisional practices under the demand of impulsive radicalism. New practices that dealt with a problem successfully would be implemented as new habits. As Dewey argued in 1897, the two sides psychologically and

---

[15] Mead, "Industrial Education, the Working Man, and the School," *Elementary-School Teacher* 9 (1908–9): 369–83, and, "1914 Class Lectures," 86–93; Dewey and James H. Tufts, *Ethics* (New York, 1908), chap. 12 (written by Tufts).

socially needed each other, and needed to resolve social conflict through reconciliation, because it was only through the interpenetration of impulse and habit that psychological and social development could occur.[16]

Mead considered it especially urgent "to establish a theory of social reform among inductive science" that would mediate between "conservatism" and "utopian" revolution.[17] Without changing Dewey's political or philosophical assumptions, Mead deepened the elder philosopher's psychological explanation of social conflict. Not only is social reciprocity psychologically necessary to social order, but without it even human consciousness would be impossible. The thought that makes us human, what Mead called the "inner conversation," depends on social cooperation and reciprocity, even if it is only implicit in the evolution of human capacities.

In applying this psychology to politics, Mead and his colleagues tried to balance impulse against reason, radical vision against conservative habit. The central feature of their social psychology was cooperation between social classes, each of which articulated a partially developed facet of human psychology. The department's goal was "social control," but by that they meant a form of cooperative self-control through reciprocal agreements, such as the arbitration agreement that governed Chicago's garment industry. Such agreements required that opposing classes take the roles of their opponents, recognizing the other's perspective in order to find a new social practice acceptable to all and beneficial to a reconstructed social order.

The simple imposition of rules was also psychologically unacceptable, as demonstrated by the department's opposition to psychologies that originated rule-governed, socialized behavior in imitation (such as J. Mark Baldwin's). Imitation suggested the imposition of community authority on the individual rather than the exercise of rational social control, by which Mead meant the kind of self-consciousness and self-control that comes from taking others' roles, the process of "constantly carrying about with us this self which is seen through the eyes of others" and subjecting that self-image to criticism.[18]

Similarly, Mead's colleague Edward Scribner Ames called for a

---

[16] Dewey, *The Significance of the Problem of Knowledge* (1897), *Early Works* 5:4–24.
[17] Mead, "Working Hypothesis," 367.
[18] Mead, "Social Psychology as Counterpart," 406, and "1914 Class Lectures," 72.

"higher individualism," a social consciousness neither based on imitation nor exhibiting a uniformity of behavior under control of authority. Rather, the higher individualism grew out of the functional integration of people occupying different roles in constant interactive communication. Skilled at moving from psychology to sermon and then to political invocation, Ames also applied Mead's notion of an "inner conversation" to the revolution in Christian ethics that Ames believed his generation led. The higher individualism develops out of a functionalist Christianity that stresses one's social role as a guide to ethical and political decisions. We live in a "cloud of witnesses," declared Ames in his 1912 sermons to Harvard students. Our self-identities are determined by our interaction with people of different social stations, different ethical and political viewpoints, different personal needs, and, through literature, different eras.[19]

The world according to Ames and Mead was a Greek drama of roles and choruses, interacting, readjusting, and responding. Social life and language, maintained Mead, involve the "continued readjustment of one individual to another." So do social reconstruction and individual growth, the "play back and forth between the selves," between impulsive tendencies, embodied in real individuals, or in the imaginary voices of one's inner conversation, the real or imaginary cloud of witnesses. Individual intellectual and moral development, in fact, is a form of social reconstruction, for, although "the organization of this inner social consciousness is a reflex of the organization of the outer world," the individual nonetheless strains to "reconstruct" the conflicting chorus of her consciousness. As the individual comes to terms with her conflicting social roles, she proposes a new order to the society as well.[20]

Mead's social conception of the self and his commitment to social reconstruction have led historians to link his theory with European social democracy. Like the European socialists, he insisted that the labor movement and its social democratic leaders most effectively contributed to reconstructing society. Social democratic labor, guided by theorists such as Ferdinand Lassalle, created a situation "in which people *had* to put themselves in the place of others." Labor *demanded*

---

[19] Edward S. Ames, *The Higher Individualism* (Boston, 1915), 9, 14–15, 67–71.

[20] Mead, "1914 Class Lectures," 43, 74–75, and "The Social Self," *Journal of Philosophy* 10 (1913): 377.

reciprocity, a voice in the chorus, and therefore, through the constructive expression of worker demands, "forced communities to think in social terms" and individuals to "put themselves into other people's places."[21]

Labor's demands encouraged constructive social reform in yet another manner peculiar to the role workers played in industrial society. A capitalist economy, Mead argued, distorts human social psychology by forcing everyone to enter practical, industrial relations through the exchange of money, as wages and profits, on the marketplace. Consequently, the industrialist, who does not actually work in the factory he owns, can no longer understand the actual social relations involved in manufacturing, nor can he grasp the "human products of the process," the hardships and injustices of industrialism. Rather than put himself in the place of others, the industrialist calculates the bottom line of his ledger book.

The industrialist's pecuniary narrow-mindedness, his inability to understand the factory system in social rather than merely economic terms, leads him to adopt a narrow and abstract philosophy of life, hedonism, the calculation of one's own pleasure and pain without regard to others and without a real understanding of the objects he finds pleasurable.[22] Although he may have a practical understanding of the economy and of money, he has little understanding of the practicalities of life in the concrete. This side of experience is reserved, in limited form, to the industrialist's workers, who produce society's goods. In such a situation a barrier is erected between people, deep within the social psychology of industrial life. Workers handle the concrete objects of social existence; elite castes and intellectuals understand the world in abstract terms. To the latter the calculation of the future comes easy. But the exigencies of the present, the direct contact with industrial life, are beyond their experience. So to become perceptually and psychologically whole, the rationality of the businessperson has to be united, through communication and reciprocal cooperation, with the manual practicality of the industrial worker. The functional integration of these two kinds of experience is at the heart of Mead's notion of industrial democracy. [23]

[21] Mead, "1914 Class Lectures," 98.
[22] Ibid., 96–97, 100.
[23] Mead, "Concerning Animal Perception," *Psychological Review* 14 (1907): 383–90, and "1914 Class Lectures," 100.

While championing the labor movement, however, Mead rejected the "class view" of European socialism. If the occupation of separate roles amounted to a significant or enduring conflict, something would be socially and psychologically wrong. Perceiving ourselves as members of a class or caste defies the natural development of social relations, undermining efforts to pursue radical social change or promote even a limited social interest. For Mead and his colleagues, class conflict was a vestige of primitive societies governed by military practices in which people identified themselves exclusively as members of a clan, caste, or nation.[24]

Going even further than this historical condemnation, Mead held that class consciousness disrupts our natural social and psychological growth. When an individual belongs to a caste, he is unable to take the role of someone from another caste, for that is precluded by the rules of caste membership: "Where there is a fixed, stratified society, a person does not present himself in the form of another." This inability to assume another's role prevents the caste member from reconciling conflicts in the caste system. One can no longer reform the social order, because "there is no social problem" to reform (that is, it is not recognized) and because one is not able to reconcile unassumed roles. Nor does one hear an inner conversation between opposing selves, because that ability requires assuming the roles of socially significant others. Thus, personal development is also limited. Someone who is unable to "enter into the place of the other" is, Mead insisted, "intellectually deficient": "Inability to put yourself in the place of another puts up a barrier, prevents grasping of the social situation at all. The process of clear and adequate thinking is the process of putting one's self completely in the place of the other. The process of thought is simply the abstraction of this social procedure." The object of constructive social conflict is "such a reconstruction of the situation that different and enlarged and more adequate personalities may emerge." The new social situation is truly reconstructed only if "all the personal interests are adequately recognized" and one has a "new world harmonizing the conflicting interests into which enters the new self." It is only under these conditions, in which in-

---

[24] Dewey and Tufts, *Ethics*, 500; Mead, "1914 Class Lectures," 87.

dividuals assume roles integrated in a harmonious social whole, that truly "democratic consciousness" occurs.[25]

In a normally developing social situation, opposing social roles simply represent conflicting but reconcilable social functions. This ability to achieve consensus in any conflict, Mead believed, exists on the most fundamental psychological level, at which humans form their conceptions of the world through the reconciliation of conflicting stimuli. An example from Dewey's 1896 essay illustrated Mead's point. A child confronted with a flame, Dewey had argued, reconstructs her understanding of the flame by playing with it. At first the flame attracts the child, as if it were a toy. The child fits the flame into a set of perceptions that do not distinguish flames from toys. More important, habitually *behaving* as though the flame were a toy, the child grabs the flame and is burned. Now, or after a few more attempts, the child has learned that the flame is a flame, that is, a bright, shiny, but dangerous and painful object. But, Dewey asked, what *exactly* has the child learned? Dewey analyzed the problem as a process of adjusting habitual behavior to new, problematic stimuli. The child can treat the flame as a toy until interacting with it as if it were a toy, at which point it makes painfully problematic the *habit* of playing with all bright objects. The child deals with that problem by coming up with a new set of ideas and habits that distinguish, *behaviorally*, between toys and flames.[26]

Mead looked at the problem from a slightly different angle, as a situation in which the child is trying to reconcile two opposing perceptions or conceptions (of the object as plaything and of the object as dangerous) and therefore two different *roles*. After initially being burned, the child now has two objects in the field of consciousness, the flame as bright shiny toylike object and the flame as dangerous. When the child comes up with a new habit of dealing with flames and similar objects, she is learning to perceive the object in a more complete way by finding an object that combines the earlier two: the flame looks like a toy but burns like a flame. In this way she reconciles contradictions faced in her experience. So far, Mead did not significantly expand Dewey's theory. But Mead, dissatisfied, asked, how does this happen? How can the child do this but not, say, a dog?

[25] Mead, "1914 Class Lectures," 68, 95, and "Social Self," 379.
[26] Dewey, "The Reflex-Arc Concept in Philosophy" (July 1896), *Early Works* 5:97–99.

Animals cannot perceive objects as humans do: "There is a conscious construction which men carry out that we do not find in the lower animals," contended Mead. "There is an ability to hold in consciousness the conflicting stimulations and tendencies to respond in a conflicting fashion." We can perceive objects clearly because we are able to see ourselves from more perspectives than one. Our conflicting versions of the object before us, our conflicting sets of raw data, our working hypotheses, really represent conflicting responses we might make to given stimuli. Our ability to see those responses comes from our ability to view ourselves in different roles, the role, for example, of child avoiding flames, or, alternatively, the role of child burning her fingers. Our process of reflection, of forming hypotheses (and habits), argued Mead, amounts to "our own responses to our own replies to these conflicting stimuli." Thought is a "field of discourse, a social field." But it is a process in which we reconcile all opposing tendencies, all roles. It is a process of achieving agreement between the conflicting voices.[27]

Our ability to reason and act rationally, then, depends on our natural ability to reconcile opposing voices within the cloud of witnesses that constitutes our consciousness. This self-construction, the creation of new roles out of old conflicting ones, is fundamentally human. It is also naturally cooperative, conciliatory, and social, in the manner Mead prescribed for opposing social groups.

[27] Mead, "1914 Class Lectures," 52–53, 77.

CHAPTER THIRTEEN

The Twilight of Cooperation

With reformers such as Jane Addams, and even radicals such as Eugene Debs or Margaret Haley, Mead shared the hope, born of earlier visions of a Kingdom of God growing in the fertile soil of American democracy, that industrial society could be reconstructed to enhance the human tendency to converse, commune, and share. By depicting the self as emerging in an inherently social conversation, Mead blessed the Chicago reform movement with a psychological model of human action that naturalized mutual aid, cooperation, and "organized intelligence." As counterposed to laissez-faire liberalism, this psychologically rooted civic republicanism (which Dewey insisted for many years was the true liberalism) allowed the pragmatists to distance themselves from that side of the American republican tradition centered in the marketplace rather than the beloved community.[1]

Mead's theory also supported, though less conclusively, fuller democratic participation in political rule and social management on all levels, including industrial organization. As Dewey argued against Henry Maine in 1888, the classical liberal presumption that the individual was asocial suggested that average people could not be trusted to choose political leaders who would serve the larger interests

---

[1] John Dewey, *Liberalism and Social Action* (1935; rpt. New York, 1963); on civic republicanism, see William M. Sullivan, *Reconstructing Public Philosophy* (Berkeley, 1982), 14–22, and Richard J. Bernstein, "One Step Forward, Two Steps Backward: Richard Rorty on Liberal Democracy and Philosophy," *Political Theory* 15 (November 1987): 549.

of the community. Later "democratic realists," opposing fully participatory democracy, cited such moral and political incapacities of
"the public" when they called for the sensible exercise of authority
to guide the unreasonable impulses of the crowd. In this sense, as
opponents of conservative and realist political theories, the Chicago
pragmatists in general and Mead in particular presented a radically
democratic self-realization theory, which trusted that as agents of
social reconstruction ordinary people would create a cooperative and
just "great community" rather than a chaos of selfish aggrandizement
and unredeemed competition, a war of all against all. As Richard
Bernstein and others have pointed out, Dewey's concept of democracy
cannot be understood apart from such a concept of community. "Regarded as an idea," Dewey wrote in 1927, democracy is "the idea of
community life itself." In a practical sense democracy meant to Dewey
the free and constructive exchange of ideas in a "practice" of everyday
life in which common values inhere. Similarly, Mead's insistence that
socialization is interactive rather than imitative or imposed reiterated
this link between creative self-activity, democracy, and reciprocal social relations.[2]

Thus, in philosophical principle *and* often in social and political
practice the pragmatists committed themselves to the enhancement
of democratic participation in modern industrial societies. They envisioned human action as at once historically determined and creative,
reflecting historical circumstances yet also transforming them, reconstructing the social self in an intricate ecology of human action.

The Chicago pragmatists, then, gave us a liberating model of human
self-activity and democratic communion, but they also confined and
undermined the very democratic agency they championed so enthusiastically. By no means authoritarian or corporatist, they were not
exactly "plebeian" or "radical communal" democrats either.[3] Ironically, they qualified and limited democracy as they justified it, by
naturalizing sociability and mutual aid and by assuming the imman-

[2] Richard J. Bernstein, *Philosophical Profiles: Essays in the Pragmatic Mode* (Oxford,
1986), 268–70, and "One Step Forward," 539–40; on Dewey's disputes with democratic
realists, see Robert B. Westbrook, *John Dewey and American Democracy* (Ithaca, 1991),
286–318; Dewey, *The Public and Its Problems* (1927; rpt. Chicago, 1954), 148.
[3] For an account of Deweyan theory as "plebeian humanism," see Cornel West, *The
American Evasion of Philosophy* (Madison, 1989), 205; on Dewey's "vision of radical
communal democracy," see Bernstein, "One Step Forward," 539.

ence of organized intelligence in history. This led them to deny rather obvious limitations in the "social situations" about which they otherwise knew quite alot. Although perhaps the most politically astute of the department members, Mead left little room in his social psychology for the kind of persistent and irreconcilable conflicts that plagued the inhabitants of cities such as Chicago. As a result, his expectations for cooperative reforms were unrealistic, psychologically as well as politically. As critics have pointed out, Mead often assumed what he was trying to explain: the cooperative rationality that distinguished humans from animals, and a rational individual subject with the capacity to recognize common meanings and symbolic communication. The circularity of Mead's argument led him to ignore questions that would trouble his view of political events and social relations. Why was it necessarily the case that the individual would be able to reconcile opposing voices in the inner conversation or in the outer cloud of witnesses, in her consciousness or in the social environment? Why not the persistence of psychological conflict, or psychosis, or social and political pathologies?[4]

Unfortunately for the pragmatists and for those Chicago reformers who sought out the evolutionary wellsprings of mutual aid and cooperation, the social disorder of modern America often could be more convincingly explained (at least in the short term) by theories that assumed a fundamentally irrational and coercive self rather than a rational conciliatory one. Mead's social psychology by contrast, explained only that limited set of social relations such as found in industrial arbitration agreements, in which parties agree beforehand that rational and amicable resolutions of conflict shall be reached. It was very difficult to generalize Mead's conception of human action beyond the bounds of such conversational civility: knowledge of the other's role is no guarantee of cooperation or ethical reciprocity in which the knower acts for that other's benefit. Such knowledge can be used to gain a selfish advantage, as in the new advertising techniques appearing at the time Mead wrote, which studied consumer desires and needs to manipulate buying. Behavioral theory increasingly served as a guide to consumer preferences and attitudes rather

---

[4] Jurgen Habermas, *The Theory of Communicative Action*, 2 vols. (Boston, 1987), 2:11–12, 23, 27, 43–46; Julian Henriques et al., *Changing the Subject* (London, 1984), 17–19, 23.

than as the science of social reconstruction envisioned by Dewey and his colleagues in the 1890s. Although much of the debased "psychology" used on Madison Avenue violated the basic principles of Deweyan voluntarism, its incorporation into market strategies underscores the naivete of the Deweyan philosophy.[5]

An explanatory failure more pertinent to Mead's own history involves the managers of Chicago industry with whom he and Tufts negotiated on behalf of the city's working class. Many industrialists, repudiating the hedonism of classical economics, tried more sophisticated, "corporate" personnel policies, enlisting the expertise of men and women educated or influenced by professors at the University of Chicago (for example, Earl Dean Howard). By the 1920s, a form of capitalist relations within the corporation developed which applied some of the notions of self-realization championed by Mead and his colleagues. The rise of welfare capitalism, which incorporated social psychology into workplace management, did not truly involve the kind of expanded self Mead had in mind but rather allowed factory managers to control workplace relations in the pursuit of higher profits.[6] This shift in industrial management strategy brought with it a shift in the meaning of cooperation. At the beginning of the century, industrial cooperation in part meant liberating the self-activity of workers, organizing their pursuit of self-realization into effective unions and political organizations. Throughout the Progressive Era, however, emerging social classes fought for control of the rhetoric of social cooperation and democratic self-activity. Under the banner of cooperation, the working class promoted workers' power in various workplaces. The city's industrial leaders, in contrast, used "cooperation" and similar words to demand greater responsibility from Chi-

---

[5] Roland Marchand, *Advertising the American Dream: Making Way for Modernity, 1920–1940* (Berkeley, 1986), 9–24, 72–77; T. J. Jackson Lears, "From Salvation to Self-Realization: Advertising and the Therapeutic Roots of the Consumer Culture, 1880–1930, in *The Culture of Consumption: Critical Essays in American History, 1880–1980,* ed. Richard Wrightman Fox and T. J. Jackson Lears (New York, 1983), 17–30; Stuart Ewen, *Captains of Consciousness: Advertising and the Social Roots of the Consumer Culture* (New York, 1976), 30–39, 81–84.

[6] Richard Edwards, *Contested Terrain* (New York, 1979); Dewey was indirectly involved in an early experiment in such welfare capitalism, one which management approached with little sincerity and which degenerated into a means of breaking a later strike; Robert W. Ozanne, *A Century of Labor-Management Relations at McCormick and International Harvester* (Madison, 1967), 41–43; James Weinstein, *The Corporate Ideal in the Liberal State* (Boston, 1968), chaps. 1.

cago's working class. Some time in the 1910s the progressive discourse on industrial democracy and social cooperation underwent a subtle change through which the managerial perspective prevailed. By 1920 only tightly controlled profit-sharing schemes, nonunion representation, and sophisticated personnel management had been implemented.[7]

One saw a similar contest over the terrain of Chicago school politics and over the terms used to describe the city's educational goals: Haley's notion of educational democracy conflicted in practice if not always in rhetoric with the proposals of more conservative progressives allied with commercial and business organizations. Like the teachers, school superintendent Edwin Cooley promoted his educational reforms as the means of achieving greater worker self-activity and cooperation in a modern industrial democracy. But for Cooley cooperation meant responsibility and submission to the larger and more centralized plans of the community, represented by Chicago's Commercial Club. Industrial education would create more efficient employees, morally uplifting them from the degradation of machine operation. Teachers had to cooperate with the school board, cease irresponsible demands such as that for teachers' councils, and recognize the rational forms of social and educational administration which civic leaders thought right and just. As is not surprising, an essential part of Cooley's, the Commerical Club's and the conservative school boards' program was to remove Haley's union, which they successfully achieved in 1917.[8] To understand the social dynamics underlying this chain of events, however, one had to take the class view of someone like Haley or John Fitzpatrick, a view repudiated by the Chicago philosophers.

War and the Intellectuals

As it did for many progressive intellectuals of their generation, the pursuit of industrial democracy and social cooperation drew the Chicago pragmatists into support of World War I. When Woodrow Wil-

[7] Milton Derber, *The American Ideal of Industrial Democracy, 1865–1965* (Urbana, 1970), chaps. 8–9.
[8] Edwin G. Cooley, *Vocational Education in Europe* (Chicago, 1912), 22–23, 57, 329–36.

son brought the country into the war in April 1917, the entire department readily contributed to a mobilization and propaganda machine that squelched criticism and rationalized the widespread
suspension of civil liberties. They did so believing, with limited justification, that federal war planning would usher in a new era of cooperation and industrial rationalization. This episode revealed the
paradox at the heart of the Chicago pragmatists' philosophy, the
tension between their assertion of democratic agency and their concept
of moral immanence.[9]

Mead's experience during the war years was especially instructive.
His conversion to the war effort did not come easily. Although supporters of Wilson in the 1916 election, Mead and his family backed
Germany over England in the first years of the conflict. The Meads
still had friends in Germany as well as in-laws from the first marriage
of Henry Castle (Helen Mead's brother), and they visited regularly
until the outbreak of the fighting. The Meads' son Henry and their
nephew Raymond Swing remained in Germany during the war to
report the German side of events. Swing's dispatches even earned him
a pro-German reputation among the many German-speaking members of the Hyde Park university community. This stance apparently
was not unusual among reformers and academics, many of whom
were German nationals or Germanophiles like Mead. At least one
City Club member, a close associate of Mead's, returned to Germany
to enlist in the kaiser's army.[10]

Mead viewed the war as a conflict between English liberalism and
German nationalism. His sympathies clearly lay with German politics
and *Kultur:* the Germans' patriotic morale derived from their social
organization and "efficiency in dealing with social problems." Unfortunately, Germany in large part also owed its social solidarity to
its "military organization." The British, in contrast, appealed to "un-
ashamed individualism" to gain morale in time of war, a exercise in
futility inasmuch as "a rampant individualism cannot control the
individual in the interest of the social whole." Insofar as Germany
fought by means of "social control," Mead viewed the kaiser's war

[9] Weinstein, *Corporate Ideal,* chap. 8.

[10] George Herbert Mead to Henry Mead, July 16 and October 3, 1914, Mead Papers.
The man was Victor von Borosini, former member of the club's labor committee. In 1916
he was interned in a British POW camp, which he announced to the club in a holiday card
with a barbed wire border design; "Club Notes," *City Club Bulletin* 9 (1916):23.

effort as a contribution to social progress. That it did so by authoritarian military means Mead could not accept.[11]

Until 1917, Mead doggedly argued for the United States to maintain
a neutral "internationalist" position, a foreign policy that he believed
embodied the same reciprocity as found in his social psychology.
Nations, Mead wrote in 1915, like individuals, acquire identities
"within international society" only as part of a system of reciprocal
relations. Ideally, conflicts occur as part of a process by which the
international order is reconstructed, in which the conversation of
national voices is amicably sorted out. Otherwise, fighting simply
perpetuates primitive militaristic habits or mob impulses, or both, as
was the case, Mead maintained, in 1914. The problem was a psychological one—of attitudes rather than institutions, of habits rather
than power—and could be solved only if such countries as the United
States stayed out of the war yet promoted the cooperative internationalist position.[12]

Support for Mead's position in the reform community at the university and elsewhere did not last long. The City Club, representing
informed opinion in Chicago's professional and business middle class,
at first tried to maintain its official impartiality. Through the first two
years of the war the club hosted pacifists and interventionists, representatives of the British side as well as supporters, like Mead, of
the Germans. If anything, pacifists, including socialists William English Walling and Charlotte Perkins Gilman, outnumbered militarists
in club forums through 1915. Impartiality melted away as American
liberals and socialists, including Walling, rallied behind the emerging
war effort in spring 1917. The club's war symposium that May, quite
unlike its earlier war series, presented an unrelenting litany of slogans
and rationalizations for American mobilization: Americans must fight
against the "German dark forces" trying to take over the world,
insisted Harry Pratt Judson, University of Chicago president. Judson
was bolstered by colleagues such as divinity school professor Shailer
Matthews, who saw the war as an "irrepressible conflict" between
autocracy and democracy. The lone voice against intervention, offered
at the club as an afterthought, came from Addams, one of the few
local progressives who continued to oppose the use of military force.

[11] Mead to H. Mead, April 28, 1916, Mead Papers.
[12] Mead, "The Psychological Bases of Internationalism," *Survey* 33 (1915): 603–7.

By winter 1917 the club had abandoned any semblence of political detachment, enthusiastically and officially cheering on the "colony" of club members "doing big things" for the war effort in Washington, boostering the sale of war bonds, and setting up a loyalty committee, "an intelligence corps in the Club" to persuade members to buy liberty bonds.[13]

By 1917 the notions of reciprocity and cooperation Mead used to criticize the war became the reasons he and his pragmatist colleagues cited for entering it. Having declared himself for Wilsonian internationalism, Mead found it difficult to dissociate himself from Wilson's evangelical military quest for world peace. Spring 1917 found Mead extremely distressed at the prospect of American involvement. He hoped that if Germany committed "overt acts" against American shipping the United States would only arm merchant ships to protect commerce.[14] Mead wanted the impossible, that the United States "continue her life in the international society" as an equal of other states, without being entangled in war. Like Wilson, whom he supported and admired, Mead wanted to dictate terms to the militarists yet not take part in that aspect of international life by which terms are usually set. Above all, Mead, still the Germanophile, did not want to enter on the side of England and France, which he believed had an agenda the United States could not accept.

Yet, even though they had long considered patriotism primitive and impulsive, Mead and his colleagues joined the ranks of the patriots. After long condemning the militaristic class view as unnatural to the resolution of social problems, the Chicago philosophers declared the war the midwife of a new cooperative order. "The great war," wrote Edward Scribner Ames in 1918, "has already written in blood and tears the end of the old and the beginning of the new." Tufts, who made the rounds of midwestern colleges for the government, teaching trigonometry to officers in training and patriotism to college students, declared that the war was a boon to industrial society, particularly

---

[13] "City Club War Series," *City Club Bulletin* 8 (1915): 101–4; "Socialists and the War," and "The War and the World's Hope," *City Club Bulletin* 9 (1916): 42–43, 172–73; "Symposium—'America at War'," and Jane Addams, "Patriotism and Pacifists in War Time," *City Club Bulletin* 10 (1917): 173–83, 184–90; "Club War Colony at Capital," advertisement for Club Day, and report on Club Day, *City Club Bulletin* 10 (1917): 298, 301, 311; "Annual Meeting Held," *City Club Bulletin* 11 (1918): 139.

[14] Mead to Irene Tufts Mead, February 2 and March 1, 1917, Mead Papers.

in relations between classes. With the regulatory policies of the War Industries Board and Felix Frankfurter's War Labor Policies Board in mind, Tufts argued that mobilization brought cooperation between labor and management in production and market planning and the peaceful resolution of conflict through the reciprocal recognition of each other's needs: "The war is teaching with dramatic swiftness what it might have needed decades of peace to bring home to us," he wrote. "We *are* thinking of the common welfare." The war, by fostering nationalism of precisely the kind Tufts condemned in most of his ethical writings, created cooperation at home. And, because the Allied powers would destroy the main bastion of militarism in Germany, a major impediment to cooperative internationalism would be forcibly removed. In New York, Dewey issued similar arguments in the *New Republic*, beginning in summer 1917, to the dismay of radical followers such as Randolph Bourne.[15]

Mead's only justification for his newly found militarism was the familiar Wilsonian rationale, that the United States entered the war on behalf of democracy, fighting for ideals rather than territory or power. The war seems unreal, he wrote his daughter-in-law two days after the American declaration, but there was no doubt in his mind "that the hour has struck at which America from the standpoint of her own history and the philosophy of her own institutions must become a part of the world society in responsibility, and that this involves a getting ready to fight as the other nations are fighting, but to end fighting, not settle the quarrels of the European states out of which this Armageddon arose."[16]

Thereafter, Mead threw himself wholeheartedly into the war effort, writing prowar articles for the Chicago *Herald* and propaganda for the National Security League. In the *Herald*, Mead appealed to American labor to join in "the energetic pushing of the war," arguing that defeating German militarism supported German labor and social democracy. Although the Reichstag socialists had, like Mead, supported German militarism in the name of social control and industrial de-

[15] James H. Tufts to Ralph J. Ricker, October 31, 1937, Box I, Folder 20, Tufts Papers, Amherst. Tufts, *The Ethics of Cooperation* (Boston, 1918), 41–44; Edward S. Ames, *The New Orthodoxy* (Chicago, 1918), 1. For Dewey's arguments, see, for instance, the series of articles reprinted in John Dewey, *Characters and Events*, ed. Joseph Ratner (New York, 1929), 551–71, 581–86; also Westbrook, *John Dewey*, 202–12.

[16] Mead to I. T. Mead, April 8, 1917, Mead Papers.

mocracy, by 1917 they had learned their lesson on the battlefield, and they now pursued a peace similar to that demanded by the Russians and Americans.[17]

Mead's piece for the National Security League's "Patriotism through Education" series dealt with the ethical problems of conscientious objection during war. Echoing Ames, he described the war as a "contest for a higher individualism" but worried over possible violations of individual rights in its pursuit. The persistent jailing of genuine conscientious objectors Mead considered an injustice, but the state, he argued, was justified in subjecting conscience to the stringent test of religious conviction. Like most of the prowar liberals and socialists, he countenanced the suspension of civil liberties during wartime's exceptional conditions. Issues that "are debatable and must be debated under a democracy" cannot be discussed during war if "they involve the war itself and its successful conduct." Cooperation brought out in war may lead to enforced conformity and political repression, Mead concluded, as long as that conformity is well defined in the law.[18]

Otherwise, Mead seemed oblivious to widespread opposition to the war on the part of labor and the left. In spring 1918, at the height of war hysteria and with Debs's sedition trial still in the courts, he wrote that it was clear that America entered the war for the sake of democracy, and that "workingmen and socialists have come to believe it." "So far," he continued, "there has been nothing here to mar our attitude or our spirit."[19] Ironically, Mead came to support a war effort that achieved social solidarity by precisely those means he condemned in German militarism (the state and propaganda) in the name of a future international society that, arguably, had no roots whatsoever in the actual international world order.

The war expectations of the Chicago pragmatists, like those of other progressive reformers, remained unfulfilled at war's end. Federally mandated regulation under the War Industries Board was suspended.

[17] Mead, "Germany's Crisis—Its Effect on Labor," Chicago *Herald* (n.d. [probably summer 1917]), clipping available in Box 9, Folder 34, Mead Papers.

[18] Mead, *The Conscientious Objector* (New York, 1918).

[19] Mead to H. Mead, May 8, 1918. In fall 1919, as attorney general A. Mitchell Palmer prepared to round up American radicals and trade unionists, Mead wished Palmer and Woodrow Wilson "the most striking success" in their management of current economic problems; Mead to I. T. Mead, September 2, 1919, Mead Papers.

In 1920 the government relinquished control of the railroads to their prewar corporate managers, the Plumb plan for rail nationalization having met defeat in Congress. Congress rejected as well the extension of labor codes after the war years. The experiment in industrial democracy that led radically democratic progressives like Dewey and Mead to support the "war for democracy" was ended.[20]

So too was the prospect for industrial peace. Having increased unions membership during the war, labor sought to continue wartime labor practices, consolidate economic gains, and extend collective bargaining to those industries in which the open shop still ruled. The year after the war, spurred by public dissatisfaction with profit-laden war industries, American wage earners went out on a series of work stoppages that culminated in a massive (and unsuccessful) steel strike in the fall. Labor made a concerted effort to realize its ideal of industrial democracy, exerting employee self-activity through autonomous, democratic industrial unions. The rule of law that characterized more conservative visions broke down. Chicago played a central role in that year of industrial confrontation: under the progressive leadership of the CFL's Fitzpatrick, who sponsored the organizing activities of a young William Z. Foster, a packinghouse organizing drive built during the war years seemed about to succeed. That fall the city was a center of steel organizing.[21]

Rather than clarify their vision of industrial democracy, however, the year's events seemed to cloud the Chicago pragmatists' understanding of social reconstruction. The most committed of his colleagues to radically democratic reform, Mead briefly flirted with Russian bolshevism, enamored of Lenin's internationalism.[22] He held out hope that a labor party similar to Britain's would emerge out of the regulated war economy: the British party's 1918 platform was the only political program "that makes an industry and commerce of exploitation impossible." But, Mead lamented, American labor had

---

[20] For a sympathetic appraisal of Dewey's support of the war effort, see Paul F. Bourke, "Philosophy and Social Criticism: John Dewey, 1910–1920," *History of Education Quarterly* 15 (1975): 3–16; see also Sidney Kaplan, "Social Engineers as Saviors: Effects of World War I on Some American Liberals," *Journal of the History of Ideas* 17 (1956): 346–50, 360–63.

[21] James Barret, *Work and Community in the Jungle* (Urbana, 1987), 191–202.

[22] Untitled, unsigned typescript with holograph corrections in Box 2, Folder 32, Addendum, Mead Papers. Mead to H. Mead, January 9, 1918; Mead to I. T. Mead, August 15, 1919, Mead Papers.

"not got far enough along to accept and stand for this admirable document."[23] He and Tufts still expected of labor leaders and their union members an unreasonable level of social and economic responsibility, especially given the actions of their managerial opponents. American labor remained irresponsible, Mead insisted, driven by uncontrollable demands and impulses, emanating primarily from its rank and file, who "have gone their own way irrespective of the counsels of the leaders." The only thing that recommended the CFL to him in 1919 was Fitzpatrick's formation of a local labor party. Mead welcomed Wilson's imposition on the railroads of government control in 1918 and condemned the rail brotherhood's threatened strike the following year as equivalent to war profiteering. In general, he believed, labor was "being difficult." Together with business it was taking advantage of the war economy to advance its limited interests.[24]

Mead's respect for the labor movement was not enhanced by the Chicago race riot in late July 1919, sparked by confrontations over racial segregation on Lake Michigan beaches and by the racially motivated drowning of a black teenager. The racial conflicts expressed chronic resentment in part of the city's white working class of more recently arrived black workers, many of whom were blatantly used by Chicago industrialists to break strikes. Such had been the case in local stockyards, on which much of the racial tension focused, although little of the rioting can be attributed to stockyard workers. Despite efforts by the packinghouse union to sustain racial solidarity, by August a key issue was whether blacks would cross picket lines to work in the slaughterhouses. The stockyard management manipulated the situation without remorse; nevertheless, Mead supported the antiunion Urban League, advocating that nonunion black workers return to work under police protection. The breakdown of race relations in the packinghouse industry collapsed the nearly successful union organizing drive.[25]

Meanwhile, the City Club offered Mead little solace or direction,

---

[23] Mead to H. Mead, March 3, 1918, Mead Papers.

[24] Mead to I. T. Mead, July 18, August 26 and 27, 1919, Mead Papers.

[25] For a narrative account of the riot, see William M. Tuttle, Jr., *Race Riot: Chicago in the Red Summer of 1919* (New York, 1970), 3–66. I am largely following the analysis of Barrett, *Work and Community*, 202–31. Mead to I. T. Mead, August 4, 1919, Mead Papers.

having undergone a transformation that would eventually contribute to its demise as a progressive civic organization. During the war years club membership declined precipitously, depleted by the draft and economic hardship. The club handled that problem and the resulting financial deficit with a membership drive, but the war had exhausted as well the activist energy on which the club had originally been founded. In an apparent effort to revive the old civic activism, Mead became club president in spring 1918. His other purpose, however, was to fend off a conservative bid to remove his friend and long-time associate George Hooker as civic secretary, a position Hooker had held since its inception in 1908 and from which he exercised a great deal of influence over the many civic committees that were the heart of the club's activism. A Hull House resident for his entire adult life, Hooker was well known as a radical critic of privilege and corruption in Chicago politics and industry. The conservatives, however, won. Hooker resigned in April 1919, citing long and growing differences with club directors. Mead finished out his term the following spring.[26]

By August 1919, Mead found himself disillusioned with reform efforts in Chicago. Reflecting on the city's politics while vacationing in New Mexico, he confided that he had "seen there nothing but things, and things which have always called out criticisms." These things, reforms and institutions "put there by human hands," "have always fallen short of their purposes." Mead contrasted Chicago's political terrain with the southwestern landscape of "enduring little trees and lofty pines, its ledges worn by such incalculable periods of times, times that never marked either the beginning of distasteful undertakings nor their bankrupt end, neither the bare ruined choirs where late the sweet birds sang, nor the shipwreck of ill adventured youths." The reform movement seemed trapped by its own circumstances, in communities "forced to use old, out-dated habits and

---

[26] Hooker's conflicts were with the administration preceding Mead's and with some of the current directors, who had been responsible for centralizing authority over the civic committees in the hands of the club administration in a move to reduce club partisanship. After resigning, Hooker was prominent in the abortive effort to establish a labor party that year. On the City Club during and after the war, see "Annual Meeting Held," *City Club Bulletin* 11 (1918): 139–40; "The City Club Election," and "President Mead's Message to Members," *City Club Bulletin* 12 (1919): 87, 101–4; "Great Growth in Membership," *City Club Bulletin* 13 (1920): 94. On Hooker, see Mead to I. T. Mead, October 22 and 25, 1917, Mead Papers; "Civic Secretary Resigns," *City Club Bulletin* 12 (1919): 99–100.

customs, and traditions suited to old unhappy far off things." Humanity, he wrote, was unable to fit vision of the future to the means of the present and remained "helplessly driven on to the accomplishment of ends that it cannot conceive and to which therefore it cannot fit the means." On returning to Chicago, Mead resumed the settlement house and City Club activities of earlier years, but his enthusiasm apparently had waned, replaced by a detached and increasingly irascible disposition toward local and national politics.[27]

An Ambiguous Legacy

It is easy to misread the Chicago pragmatists' enthusiasm for the war and their meliorist response to the turmoil of 1919 as evidence that they sacrificed democracy for technocracy. But, although department members and former member Dewey supported authoritarian mobilization measures for the sake of "organized intelligence," they were too committed to democratic participation, at least in principle, to be technocrats or corporate liberals. Above all, they did not think that the political and social problems of modern society could be solved simply by applying technical expertise, even though they considered technical knowledge of indispensible service to democratic government. This position did not change much over the years. Dewey's differences with democratic realists such as Walter Lippmann showed the extent to which his democratic theory continued to evolve after the war. But it is important to recognize that in writing his later defenses of democracy, *The Public and its Problems* (1927) and *Liberalism and Social Action* (1935), Dewey extrapolated on the long-standing Chicago pragmatist argument that a well-ordered society needed democratic self-activity and participation, a position he and Mead had defended earlier against the school reorganization schemes of true corporate liberals such as Cooley.

Instead of pursuing a stereotypically corporate liberal agenda, the Chicago pragmatists, including Dewey, did something more troubling.

[27] Mead to I. T. Mead, August 30, 1919, Mead Papers. Alice Hamilton, a close friend of the Meads, reported that by 1923 Mead had grown "less intimate and less interesting," with "so much more superficial an attitude toward things"; Alice Hamilton to Margaret Hamilton, March 30, 1923, in *Alice Hamilton: A Life in Letters*, ed. Barbara Sicherman (Cambridge, Mass., 1984), 269.

They supported American entrance into World War I guided by thoughtful political ideals that were, in large part, consistent with their democratic philosophy and their earlier reform activities. They genuinely, if naively, expected Wilson's "war for democracy" to yield industrial cooperation while avoiding the imperial aims of the European powers. They just as sincerely believed that the brutal history of industrial relations could be civilized through negotiation and arbitration. As we know, American foreign policy, especially in Latin America, dashed hopes of achieving internationalism without empire. Nor did the often temporary application of welfare reform and labor arbitration to a limited number of industries fulfill the pragmatist dream of a new America birthed by war mobilization. Moreover, the outcomes of most industrial conflicts before and after the war were not decided reciprocally as expected but by the imbalance of power in favor of dominant classes and groups (as Tufts admitted). The laboring poor and others could only exert limited influence over their own future, and management dominated industrial relations until the 1930s.

If there was an element of unreality in these expectations it was not missed by later critics, who savaged Deweyan politics for its undying faith in class conciliation, its naive expectation that industrial development would yield social progress, its assumption that an ill-informed public could make sound political judgments, and its fundamental belief that intelligent social reform could redeem industrial capitalism. These observations suited a generation disillusioned by the Great War, the Depression, and the rise of fascism, and hardened by the cruelties and class conflicts of the 1930s.[28]

Such criticism has its points. The Chicago philosophers often espoused principles and set standards of political conduct that did not match the available instruments of (and obstacles to) political power. They believed in community and solidarity, yet they had many misperceptions about the formation and deformation of actual communities. They called for radical reconstruction of society and

---

[28] Reinhold Niebuhr, *Moral Man and Immoral Society: A Study in Ethics and Politics* (New York, 1960); Howard Selsam, "Science and Ethics," in *Pragmatism and American Culture*, ed. Gail Kennedy (Boston, 1950), 84–85, 88; Walter Lippmann, *Public Opinion* (New York, 1938), 3–32; Lyle H. Lanier, "A Critique of the Philosophy of Progress," in *I'll Take My Stand: The South and the Agrarian Tradition* (Baton Rouge, 1977), 122–54.

economy, using the "method of democracy," as Dewey termed it, yet they said little about what that meant as a political strategy, in theory or practice. Their inconsistencies could be quite irritating and at times hypocritical. They harshly condemned "programists," utopians, radicals, and fanatics (the labels changed with the passage of time) for pursuing ends without adequate attention to means, demanding that no utopia guide the politics of the present, no "sermons given on the mount" and other radically "impulsive" visions of the future dictate terms to the habits of the past. And yet they naively assumed that the means for amicable negotiations were readily available for anyone with the intelligence to use them. The Chicago pragmatist notions of cooperation, organized intelligence, responsibility, and social control hardly conformed to an industrial order that destroyed rather than fostered democratic, cooperative self-activity. These were not "ends in view," as Dewey liked to call them; they were as distant from the real conditions of life as the goals of radical visionaries.[29]

Yet the pragmatist myopia was not the simple product of a lack of political realism, a rejection of class analysis, a naive faith in human civility, or a blind spot when it came to human frailties. It was inherited in large part from the history of American political rhetoric and the traditions of social and church reform. One of these traditions, producer republicanism, framed a picture of American culture in which class antagonism was always superceded by common interests. In the 1890s it still made some sense to hope that class conciliation could be built on a traditional belief in the civic virtue of a productive community. And the vision of a harmonious community of small producers, skilled artisans, and farmers provided a critical resource in the struggle to realize republican values in a changing industrial world. Increasingly, however, the class view prevailed. Nineteenth-century republicanism, with its visions of a cooperative commonwealth and the community of productive citizens, no longer made sense in a world transformed by mass production, industrial consolidation, population migration, imperial expansion, and the intrusion of the corporate cash economy into community life.

The Chicago philosophers meant to adjust this producer ethic to the new reality, to unite head and hand through education, industrial

---

[29] Richard J. Bernstein, *Philosophical Profiles*, 271; Dewey, *Liberalism and Social Action*, 77.

reform, and social reconstruction, but they retained far too much of the old expectations and values as well as many illusions about the character of the American past. Thus, by 1917 Mead and his colleagues found themselves adrift in a political universe polarized between conflicting social forces, each interpreting America's political heritage and political lexicon differently. Waging a "war for democracy" simply did not do justice to the competing visions of the national purpose. Similarly, demanding cooperation and reconciliation of the "social situation" proved an equally inadequate approach to the social tensions of the pre- and postwar years. The Chicago pragmatists would give labor a political voice, but they would also exact a form of responsibility inappropriate to the actual distribution of power and the terms of political contention in American society.

The Chicago pragmatists wrote in another tradition, emerging from nineteenth-century religious modernism, which intersected the republican heritage and shaped their understanding of democratic politics in the twentieth century. Their commitment to class conciliation rested on the same notions of immanent reasonableness and sociability in which they rooted their faith in a communitarian democracy. Their adherence to a philosophy of moral immanence led them to insist that scientific study could elucidate values, goals latent in a factual present—that is, more specifically, that they *could* indeed find, through the exploration of biologically based psychology, the seeds of social cooperation in the necessary conditions for human consciousness. It also suggested that social and political agencies could resolve differences by the systematic testing of reasonable working hypotheses. This philosophical stance disposed them to believe, as Dewey insisted against George Herron's 1890 call for moral sacrifice, that a rational social order based on cooperation and reciprocity lay immanent in the present, in the actual social and political relations of late nineteenth-century America.

One found this theory of moral immanence embedded in Deweyan psychology in 1886, and it stayed there in some form long after Dewey's neo-Hegelianism became "Chicago pragmatism." Not only did the Chicago philosophers persistently interpret politics in psychological terms, but they applied a model of action that imposed an implicitly conservative and illusory shape on political events, including the process of democratic participation. Late in his life Dewey continued to define "organized intelligence" and the "method of democracy" as he had in 1899, as a conflict between divided functions in the coordinated circuit of human action, the conflict between radical impulse and conservative habit. While communitarian in intent, Dewey's "method of democracy" of 1935 still closed "fanaticism" and "sentimentalism" out of the public space in which "intelligence as method" could be applied. If Dewey was hopelessly vague when it came to defining political intelligence, he was quite clear about who should be excluded: there was no room on his political agenda for the class view, by which he and his colleagues meant not only Marxist class analysis but any social and political theory that questioned the possiblity of reconciliation and cooperation between existing social groups, that disbelieved the Deweyan faith that competing claims could be "judged in the light of more inclusive interests than are represented by either of them separately." The class view failed to recognize the functional dynamic the pragmatists perceived behind all historical events: the conflict between "the old and the new," conservative habit and radical impulse that must be integrated by the "method of intelligence." It was this attitude that made the pragmatists and their allies in the reform movement self-righteous, as Reinhold Niebuhr quite correctly pointed out: they would never be willing to allow the disruption of a comfortable middle-class conversational approach to the problems of economic exploitation, distributive injustice, cultural confrontation, and brute power. It was also a denial of history.[30]

The endurance of this perspective in the pragmatist tradition should lead us to be cautious about uncritically borrowing Deweyan rhetoric to address our current dilemmas over the future of democracy. If some roots of radically democratic "prophetic pragmatism" can be traced to the Deweyan belief in participatory social reconstruction, so too can the roots of an equally American tradition that fears the excesses of democracy—that expects uncontrolled self-activity in public life to disrupt what is believed to be (or in some cases cynically claimed to be) a reasonable and constructive community. Those who did not meet standards of reasonableness embedded in the pragmatist conception of history had a lesser voice in the imagined chorus of democratic voices. This was hardly a plebeian radicalism, even if it

---

[30] Dewey, *The Public and Its Problems*, 149–55, and *Liberalism and Social Action*, 48–51, 76–81; Niebuhr, *Moral Man*, xiii–xv.

was open to the contribution of many previously excluded sectors of American society, notably the organized working class (when responsibly led). For all their optimism and hope, the Chicago pragmatists could not tolerate truly discordant voices in their reform conversations.[31]

Thus the Chicago pragmatists found themselves caught between a commitment to democratic participation and a theory of moral immanence that undermined true democratic agency. This dilemma led the Chicago philosophers to simultaneously embrace and deny utopian advocacy. The philosophical problem of immanence, of which Mead's political bitterness was an expression, bedevilled their politics. They premised political reform on the democratic impulse of the American public, on the participation of workers in contract negotiations, of teachers in setting school policy, of students in forming their curriculum. Yet they demanded political intelligence that hinged on the cooperation and generosity of people in power. Their notion of democracy could not accommodate popular sentiment that did not meet the standards of organized intelligence, as in the case of pacifists during the war or rank and file union members afterward. In the face of a disorderly public or an unintelligible situation like a war, the Chicago philosophers sought guidance from institutions and political leadership that stood above the fray yet embodied the qualities pragmatism valued—labor leaders sufficiently "responsible" or political "visionaries" like Woodrow Wilson, who preached something resembling Christian reciprocity (but meant something quite different). And consistently they turned to the state as the source of cooperative authority, despite the fact that the state and its subsidiary institutions (such as investigative commissions or the War Industries Board) were usually in the control of one party to a dispute and, as the behavior of Wilson's Justice Department in 1920 demonstrated, far from sensitive to the needs and desires of its critics. Dewey and his colleagues attacked the "utopians" for their visions of the future and their inattention to the means of achieving it. In actuality, it was the "method of intelligence" that did not lie within the grasp of the present. It needed some kind of vision as a guide to dialogue, a greater witness above the cloud of witnesses, a conversationalist outside the inner conversation.

[31] On "prophetic pragmatism," see West, *Evasion of Philosophy,* chap. 6.

It is here that we reach the contextual and conceptual limits of the pragmatist tradition. As a radical self-realization theory, pragmatist social psychology offered a democratic alternative to an emerging mass production society in which education and participatory organizations would heal social divisions and enrich otherwise degraded lives. It suggested that the agency of social change would be ordinary people encouraged to self-active reconstruction by a democratic reform movement. But as a theory of moral immanence, Chicago pragmatism also rooted social transformation in a dying tradition of civic virtue, community, and productive labor, thereby imposing a shape and direction on what should have been a process of self-transformation.

Index

Library of Congress Cataloging-in-Publication Data

Feffer, Andrew, 1954–
    The Chicago pragmatists and American progressivism / Andrew Feffer.
        p.   cm.
    Includes bibliographical references and index.
    ISBN 0-8014-2502-6 (alk. paper)
        1. United States—Intellectual life—1865–1918.   2. Chicago school of sociology.
3. Pragmatism.   4. Dewey, John, 1859–1952.   5. Progressivism (United States
politics)   6. United States—Social conditions—1865–1918.   I. Title.
E169.1.F32   1993
997.3'11041—dc20   92–54974